Ballad of the Whiskey Robber

Ballad of the Whiskey Robber

A True Story of Bank Heists, Ice Hockey,
Transylvanian Pelt Smuggling,
Moonlighting Detectives, and Broken Hearts

Julian Rubinstein

LITTLE, BROWN AND COMPANY
New York Boston

Little, Brown and Company
Time Warner Book Group
1271 Avenue of the Americas, New York, NY 10020
Visit our Web site at www.twbookmark.com

First Edition

Library of Congress Cataloging-in-Publication Data
Rubinstein, Julian.
  Ballad of the whiskey robber : a true story of bank heists, ice hockey,
Transylvanian pelt smuggling, moonlighting detectives, and broken hearts /
Julian Rubinstein. — 1st ed.
      p.   cm.
  Includes bibliographical references.
  ISBN 0-316-07167-6
  1. Ambrus, Attila.   2. Thieves — Hungary — Biography.   3. Bank
robberies — Hungary.   4. Post-communism — Hungary.   5. Folk
heroes.   I. Title.

HV6653.A47R8   2004
364.15'52'092 — dc22   2004003645

10 9 8 7 6 5 4 3 2 1

Q-FF

Design by Renato Stanisic

Maps by Jeffrey Ward

For Lisa

And in memory of my father,
David Rubinstein
1942–2003

Cast of Characters

UTE HOCKEY CLUB
Attila Ambrus, aka the Whiskey Robber: Goalie, church painter, gravedigger, animal-pelt smuggler, serial bank robber, folk hero

Gábor "Gabi" Orbán: Forward, coroner's assistant, bank robber

Jenő "Bubu" Salamon: Defenseman, trouble

George Pék: Forward, UTE player-coach, 24-hour mini-mart owner

Károly "Karcsi" Antal: Forward, videotape salesman, used-car dealer, toy-store stockboy, bank robber

George Orbán: Former national Hungarian hockey team goalie, UTE coach (1994–95), Gabi Orbán's father

János Egri: Former UTE player, sports broadcaster, game-show host (*Játek a Betűkkel!* [Scrabble])

Gustáv Bóta: UTE general manager, freelance everything

THE COPS

Lajos Varjú: Chief of the Budapest police robbery department

Tibor Vági, aka Mound of Asshead: Deputy chief of the Budapest police robbery department

Lajos Seres, aka The Dance Instructor: Detective and expert criminal profiler

József Keszthelyi: Detective and, eventually, chief of the Budapest police robbery department

Zsolt Bérdi: Chief of post-arrest investigations, Budapest police

Valter Fülöp: Post-arrest investigator, Budapest police

Sándor Pintér: Hungary's national police chief and, eventually, interior minister

THE LÁSZLÓS

László Juszt: Host of the hit television show *Kriminális*

László "Laczika" Veres: Attila's Transylvanian cousin and first accomplice

László Szabó: Attila's uncle and the man who raised Attila in eastern Transylvania with his wife, Margit

László Valenta, aka The 12 Percent: Top Budapest police official

László Klányi: Convicted fraud, Whiskey Robber informant

THE WOMEN

Judit Milos: English teacher, Attila's first girlfriend in Budapest, the first woman for whom he bought liposuction and second whom he asked to marry

Éva Fodor: Car wash owner, Attila's second girlfriend in Budapest and true love

Betty Gergely: Exotic dancer, Attila's third girlfriend in Budapest

Zsuzsa Hamer: Grocery-store clerk, second mother to Attila

THE OTHERS
George Magyar: Attila's lawyer, failed mayoral candidate

Márta Tocsik: Budapest lawyer, linchpin in the "Scandal of the Century"

Uncle Béla: Csángó Pelt King

Hansi: Austrian mountain lodge owner, pelt buyer

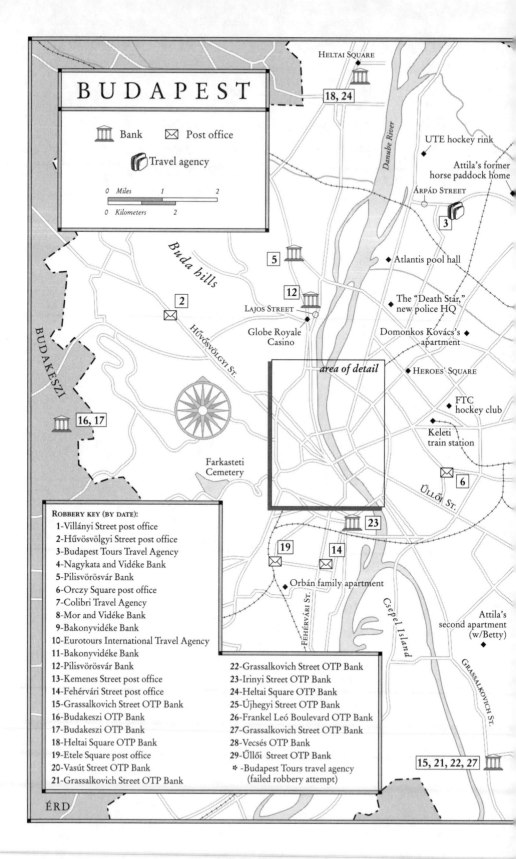

BUDAPEST

🏛 Bank   ⊠ Post office

🗇 Travel agency

0   Miles   1   2

0   Kilometers   2

HELTAI SQUARE

18, 24

Danube River

UTE hockey rink

Attila's former horse paddock home

ÁRPÁD STREET

3

Buda hills

5

2

12

LAJOS STREET

Atlantis pool hall

The "Death Star," new police HQ

Globe Royale Casino

Domonkos Kovács's apartment

HÚVÖSVÖLGYI ST.

BUDAKESZI

🏛 16, 17

area of detail

HEROES' SQUARE

FTC hockey club

Keleti train station

Farkasteti Cemetery

⊠ 6

ÜLLŐI ST.

🏛 23

19

14

Orbán family apartment

FEHÉRVÁRI ST.

Csepel Island

Attila's second apartment (w/Betty)

GRASSALKOVICH ST.

ÉRD

15, 21, 22, 27 🏛

ROBBERY KEY (BY DATE):

1-Villányi Street post office
2-Hűvösvölgyi Street post office
3-Budapest Tours Travel Agency
4-Nagykata and Vidéke Bank
5-Pilisvörösvár Bank
6-Orczy Square post office
7-Colibri Travel Agency
8-Mor and Vidéke Bank
9-Bakonyvidéke Bank
10-Eurotours International Travel Agency
11-Bakonyvidéke Bank
12-Pilisvörösvár Bank
13-Kemenes Street post office
14-Fehérvári Street post office
15-Grassalkovich Street OTP Bank
16-Budakeszi OTP Bank
17-Budakeszi OTP Bank
18-Heltai Square OTP Bank
19-Etele Square post office
20-Vasút Street OTP Bank
21-Grassalkovich Street OTP Bank

22-Grassalkovich Street OTP Bank
23-Irinyi Street OTP Bank
24-Heltai Square OTP Bank
25-Újhegyi Street OTP Bank
26-Frankel Leó Boulevard OTP Bank
27-Grassalkovich Street OTP Bank
28-Vecsés OTP Bank
29-Űllői Street OTP Bank
✷ -Budapest Tours travel agency (failed robbery attempt)

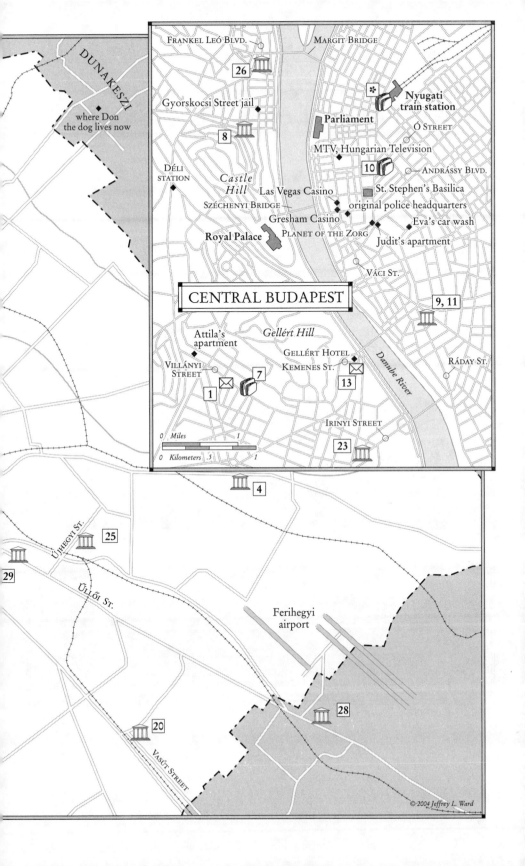

DUNAKESZI

where Don
the dog lives now

FRANKEL LEÓ BLVD.

MARGIT BRIDGE

26

Nyugati
train station

Gyorskocsi Street jail

Ó STREET

Parliament

8

MTV, Hungarian Television

ANDRÁSSY BLVD.

DÉLI
STATION

10

*Castle
Hill*

St. Stephen's Basilica

Las Vegas Casino

SZÉCHENYI BRIDGE

original police headquarters

Gresham Casino

Eva's car wash

Royal Palace

PLANET OF THE ZORG

Judit's apartment

VÁCI ST.

CENTRAL BUDAPEST

9, 11

Gellért Hill

Attila's
apartment

GELLÉRT HOTEL

RÁDAY ST.

VILLÁNYI
STREET

KEMENES ST.

7

13

1

Danube River

IRINYI STREET

0 | Miles   1

23

0 | Kilometers .5   1

4

ÚJHEGYI ST.

25

29

ÜLLŐI ST.

Ferihegyi
airport

20

28

VASÚT STREET

© 2004 Jeffrey L. Ward

CENTRAL EASTERN EUROPE

0 Miles   100   200

0 Kilometers   200

POLAND

CZECH
REPUBLIC

SLOVAKIA

UKRAINE

Carpathian Mountains

Vienna •   • Bratislava   • Sátoraljaújhely

AUSTRIA   Danube R.

MOLDOVA

• Szentendre   Gyergyószentmiklós
Érd • • Budapest   Kolozsvár (Cluj)   (Gheorgheni)   Chisinau

Lake
Balaton

HUNGARY

Csángóföld

Fitód

Székelyföld

• Curtici
• Arad   TRANSYLVANIA   Csíkszereda
                                   (Miercurea-Ciuc)

Zagreb •

• Timisoara

CROATIA   Bran • • Brasov   Galati •

Danube R.

• Belgrade   R O M A N I A

BOSNIA &
HERZEGOVINA   • Bucharest

Sarajevo •   SERBIA &
                MONTENEGRO

Danube R.

Adriatic Sea

KOSOVO   • Sofia

                BULGARIA   Black Sea

• Skopje

Tirane • MACEDONIA

ITALY   ALBANIA   TURKEY

GREECE

© 2004 Jeffrey L. Ward

Ballad of the Whiskey Robber

In the tavern
On the Lowlands
Vinegar is burning in the lamps
Nine highwaymen are the guests
Landlady, my sweetheart, have you got a sweet wine?

— a Hungarian folk song

Prologue

Budapest
Saturday, July 10, 1999

The sweet smell of a triple-crème *torta* hung in the air like a good idea. It was morning, summer, and by the time the narrow streets awakened to the Kalashnikov rattle of the newsstand gates, already humid and warm. Up and down the Danube riverbank, old men in sagging underwear and sleeveless shirts hobbled barefoot onto cracked cement balconies, gazing blankly at the sun streaks stalking the rank, still water. At the north end of chestnut-lined Andrássy Boulevard, wisps of steam puffed from the thousand-year-old springs beneath the Széchenyi bathhouse like an eternal Chernobyl.

From the faded royal Hapsburg palace on Castle Hill to the plump pool-green dome of St. Stephen's Cathedral downtown, the opportunities to imagine that nothing was amiss here in the Hungarian capital were indeed everywhere. That was about to change.

Károly Benkő startled from his guard post, a peg-legged chair at the end of a musty hall, and trundled down the jail's pale corridor. Starving and exhausted from a shift that had begun at 6:00 A.M. the previous day, the balding thirty-two-year-old jail guard called out the number of each cell he approached in a nasally semiconscious drone. "Three-oh-nine, three-ten . . ."

It was time for the morning walk.

Corporal Benkő, who had forgone university for a chance at such employment, was already a veteran of these hallowed, hated halls. He was the top man in charge of three others on duty that day and 298 prisoners in custody at that hour. It wasn't respectable or even modestly paying work, yet occasionally Károly felt like the mayor of a small city. Inside the copper-fortified cages he opened was an unscientific sampling of Budapest's misguided, misfortunate, or mistaken: thieves, con artists, killers, men with too many scars or too few teeth. But regardless of who they were or what they'd done, the inmates had their rights, and if they didn't get their walk, every one of them knew he had only to yell, "International Court of Human Rights at Strasbourg," and wait for the rattle of the keys. Times had certainly changed in the decade since the fall of communism. Didn't Károly just love it.

When he reached cell no. 312, Károly saw a familiar figure through the slot window of the thin, cafeteria-green door. It was Attila Ambrus, prisoner no. 43, wide-awake and standing stiffly in a military posture, as if he were guarding the room. He was thirty-one years old and phone-your-friends handsome: wide shoulders, strong jaw, a scruffy new mustache on his thick upper lip, and a bemused look in his hazel eyes that said, "I know where *everything* is buried." Attila's expression, and even his pose, had a barely perceptible wink to it that you had to ignore if you didn't want to get caught smiling back. It was a classic Hungarian this-isn't-a-wink wink and Attila had it down pat. But twenty-seven hours into a thirty-two-hour shift, his zookeeper didn't have the energy for even a yawn. "Three-twelve," Károly announced, opening Attila's door while another guard arranged the black metal cuffs on Attila's wrists.

For a fleeting moment, Károly had a thought: What was Attila doing in jeans and a bulky long-sleeve shirt on such an oppressively hot day? This was a jail for the accused awaiting sentencing or trial. Normally in summer, the inmates dressed in shorts. Then again, Attila, a former pelt smuggler who'd managed to make twenty-six desperate, booze-fueled heists look like performance art, wasn't much like the others. Sure, he had the mystery scars, the childhood horror stories, and the unquenchable yearning to be somebody. But he also had paparazzi and a coterie of women delivering cured meats and fresh pastries. Yes, he bribed the guards with cash and cigarettes to turn their heads when he returned from visiting hours with soda bottles stinking of his signature spirit, Johnnie Walker Red. But he was discreet about it. He seemed to have his own sense of right and wrong. And since he'd never given the guards any real trouble, Károly had concluded what Attila assumed he would: the so-called Whiskey Robber was a model prisoner.

Attila's cellmate, a fraud, declined to get out of bed that morning for the voluntary exercise call, so Attila alone was ushered into a single-file line, which, when Károly finished unlocking two more cells, included eleven men from six units. They marched outside into the concrete courtyard, by then half draped in gauzy sunshine, and continued along the outdoor corridor, where the empty exercise chambers awaited. Each cell was assigned one of the six open-air boxes. Attila, every well-honed muscle and overstressed vein twitching with anticipation, soundlessly stopped at the fourth. The sit-ups, the push-ups, the leg-sits, the years of studying ways out of unpromising places, were about to be put to their biggest test; the stomach cramps had started hours ago. At last, his walk-box door was opened and then closed behind him, and he turned to put his hands through the slot so one of the guards could remove his cuffs. God, did he need a drink.

Typically, Attila used the ten-minute fitness allotment to jog circles around the roofless, bare, racquetball-court-size room. He was, after all, a professional hockey goalie for Budapest's best-known team. And by his calculations, which were incessant, 192⅓ laps around the perimeter was roughly five kilometers, or 3.1 miles. But Attila wasn't about to make any unnecessary movements today. His legacy, not to mention his life, depended upon the exactitude of his next series of actions. Attila's round face tightened and his combable eyebrows dropped toward his eyes as he breathed deeply and squinted at the cerulean sky. He figured he had nine and a half minutes.

He pulled up his cream-colored overshirt and his dark undershirt. Beneath them, wrapped tightly around his trim waist, was a pink, red, and blue rope made from the strips of four sets of bedsheets, shoelaces from three pairs of sneakers, and thick strands torn from two towels. He tied a slipknot into the line and threw it lasso-style over the thirteen-foot-high wall. On the second try, it caught on the post of a wrought-iron railing in the guard plank above. With the other end of the rope in hand, Attila stepped back until the cable was taut, gathered his strength, then took a running jump against the wall, hauling himself up to the brim of the jail's interior courtyard.

Phase one complete, but he still had to get into and out of the administration building, which faced him from across the yard.

At 8:54 A.M., the black-and-white monitor inside the central guard station displayed a pair of feet stepping along the thin path atop the walk-box wall in the direction of the brown brick guard tower that stood sentry over the courtyard. On most days, due to staff shortages, the tower was empty. As Attila had chanced, today was no exception. When he reached the unmanned post, he looked down at his open-mouthed fellow inmates and put his index finger to his lips. Then his figure vanished over the far side of the wall.

Attila Ambrus, who had turned a six-year robbery spree into a serialized satire of the times, was at large again.

The emergency decree sealing Budapest was issued at 10:50 A.M. All avenues and highways in and out of the city were roadblocked. Police helicopters hovered low and beelike over the sullen, stately buildings. Then, just as the coast guard set out to check every vessel on the Danube River, the hardest rainstorm in decades began pounding the region. Summer in Budapest was over.

Upon hearing news of the jailbreak, Margit Szabó, Attila's aunt who'd helped raise him in Transylvania, suffered a near-fatal heart attack. But most people who knew the fugitive former gravedigger did not require medical attention.

Lajos Varjú, the former chief of the robbery department who had unsuccessfully tracked Attila for five years before dejectedly leaving the force, had warned police two months earlier that Attila would attempt an escape. "They didn't want to listen," he said to anyone who would.

Éva Fodor, Attila's fire-haired former girlfriend who had secured his Hungarian citizenship with a perfume-bottle bribe, then nearly swept him from the crime game with a suburban bartending offer, asked herself: "He's smart enough not to show up here. He is, right?"

László Juszt, the colossal, albino-like host of the hit television show *Kriminális,* veered dangerously close to thrombosis. He was unable to air the latest development in the Whiskey Robber saga, as his top-rated show had been banned from the airwaves following his own arrest on charges of revealing state secrets.

The actress Zsuzsa Csala, who had made headlines by offering (along with roughly a thousand others) to adopt Attila's Bernese mountain dog, Don, when Attila was arrested six months earlier, awoke to the jungle sounds of eight policemen foraging in the bushes of her back-yard. "Even if I did know something," she contemplated telling them, "do you think that I would tell you?"

Bubu, Attila's brothel-size former hockey teammate who would soon carry a business card reading UNEMPLOYED HOCKEY PLAYER, laughed so hard, he almost choked on a plate of pig's feet.

Gábor Orbán, another of Attila's teammates and his longtime rob-bery accomplice, settled in for a long day of questioning in his jail cell: "That's right," he told a commando unit. "I'm not surprised at all. But that doesn't mean I knew."

István Szopkó, the credit fraud specialist who'd become Attila's cellmate only the previous day but had known the Whiskey Robber legend for years, told police what they already knew: "With him, any-thing is possible."

And George Magyar, Attila's former-mayoral-candidate lawyer, began to formulate his press statement: "It is unlikely the police will ever find a trace of my client," he would say. "He is much too precise."

All of them, except for Attila's ex-accomplice and cellmate (who were already behind bars), were shadowed by undercover agents and were among the 214 Whiskey Robber associates whose phones were tapped in the apparent hope that authorities might outmaneuver "the century's most persistent, cautious, and most wanted" bank robber.

Thus began the largest manhunt in postcommunist Eastern Europe's history.

first Period

One

Hungary has always been unlucky.

In the approximately eleven hundred years since the handlebar-mustachioed Chief Árpád rode into the Carpathian basin in 896 and founded Hungary, the country has been plundered so relentlessly that defeat could be considered the national pastime. In 1241 the Mongolian Tatars swept in, killing a third of the population; the Turks arrived in 1526 on a 150-year bender in which they pounded Hungary into their Ottoman Empire; at the end of the seventeenth century, the Hapsburgs of Austria cut in and swallowed Hungary whole.

The only heyday in Hungary's modern history arrived in 1867 after a compromise was struck with Hapsburg emperor Franz Josef. Though Hungary was not put in charge of anything but its own land, the agreement granted it title credit in the Central European geopolitical blockbuster of the nineteenth century, the Austro-Hungarian Empire. Landlocked Hungary became co-chair of a global power that stretched all the way west to present-day Switzerland, north to the contemporary German and Polish borders, and east and south through parts of what is now Ukraine, Romania, and Serbia. Six years later, in 1873, the formerly rival twin cities of Buda and Pest, separated only by the serpentine Danube River and at least two social classes, swept their differences aside and married to form a new Hungarian capital, Budapest.

United for the first time, the new city raced into the European spotlight, unveiling the continent's first subway system and setting in motion a renaissance in business, architecture, and culture that would enable it to compete with the Romanian capital, Bucharest, for the title "Paris of the East." In the parlor levels of Budapest's brand-new balustrated five- and six-story Belle Epoch residences, more than six hundred coffeehouses overflowed with some of Europe's finest artists and intellectuals. Hungarian Ferenc Liszt (later known by the German, Franz) was composing symphonies, the expansive new Budapest Commodity and Stock Exchange opened for business, and on old Pest's Danube bank, a massive neo-Gothic structure that would become the second-largest government building in Europe (after Britain's House of Commons) was under construction.

It was a heady time, and in short order it would come to a fantastic end. After fighting on the wrong side in World War I, Hungary was so royally fleeced by the postwar treaties that some Hungarians challenge the assertion that Germany was the Great War's big loser. Indeed, no other country was stripped of as much territory as Hungary, nor had Hungary ever been so humiliated in its whole humiliating history than it was at Versailles, where the infamous peace accords were cooked up. In one round of fountain pens, on June 4, 1920, Hungary went from being part of the most dominant kingdom of Central Europe to a smudge on the map, crammed between seven bordering countries. Two-thirds of Hungary's territory — including its beloved Transylvania — was lost, along with the hope of its people and, seemingly, its planetary relevance. Later that year when international war-relief organizations doled out food and clothing, Austria received 288,000 tons; comparably sized Hungary got 635. Needless to say, involuntarily gaining independence from the Hapsburgs did not lead to Hungarians dancing in the *utcas*. In fact, an alarming number of the country's remaining 10 million citizens began diving into the Danube River, securing perennial world-class status for Hungary's hari-kari rates, alcohol consumption, and swimming teams.

But the pleasures of twentieth-century life were only beginning for Hungary. After twenty-five manic-depressive years that included a brief communist takeover followed by the bloody right-wing reign of Admiral Miklós Horthy (who made Hungary a kingdom without a king, ruled by an admiral without a fleet), the Germans came calling with an offer that Hungary was desperate enough to accept. In exchange for Hungary's support of the Nazis in what would soon become World War II, Germany promised to restore to Hungary much of Transylvania, the hunk of rugged land containing the fecund Carpathian basin that would eventually, thanks to Attila Ambrus, be called "a nest of Robin Hoods" and that Hungary had forcibly ceded to Romania after the First World War. But Transylvania would not be returned. Hitler decided instead that while he was mopping up the rest of Europe, he might as well occupy his two-bit ally Hungary. In 1944 Hungary frantically tried to switch sides, but it was too late. Within a year the Nazis, with shell-shocked Hungary's complicity, had killed 440,000 of Hungary's 800,000 Jews, destroyed all six of Budapest's bridges, obliterated much of its famous architecture, and absconded with the thousand-year-old bejeweled holy crown of Hungary's first king, Stephen.

The Soviets rescued Hungary from the Nazis the following year in an operation that by its own trigger-happy ending left Budapest with just 30 percent of its majestic prewar buildings intact. Then, Soviet leader Joseph Stalin calculated Hungary's tab for services rendered by the Red Army: everything. Russian troops were installed and communist rule from Moscow imposed. Hungary became part of the western hem in the Iron Curtain. Transylvania remained inside Romania, which also capitulated to Soviet communist rule.

During communism, Hungary's factories produced much of the Soviet bloc's lightbulbs, televisions, and those ubiquitous Eastern Europe roadside decorations, the Ikarus bus. The cost of a one-room apartment in Budapest was approximately eight years of average wages, an unachievable savings. Families fortunate enough to live in multiroom dwellings were forced to take in strangers as roommates. The price of getting a phone line was extraordinary patience: the waiting list was twenty years long. The countryside remained a predominantly green, if discouragingly impoverished, agricultural land. But in Budapest, where one-fifth of Hungary's population lived, as well as in the smaller cities, the air was filthy from cheaply manufactured, blue-exhaust-belching Soviet- and Czech-produced cars, and the rivers were poisoned by unregulated industry.

There was a brief flicker of hope in 1956, when a group of young Hungarians managed to stage the historic first, and largest, uprising against Soviet communist rule. For twelve days Budapest was transformed into a shooting gallery as sniper-fired machine guns pointing out of apartment- and cinema-house windows picked off Red Army soldiers. Molotov cocktails delivered in jug-shaped liquor bottles set Soviet tanks ablaze like cake candles. It was, briefly, euphoria. Hungarians relayed the urgent word to America and the West that they had seized control of their capital and needed reinforcements to hold the city. Time was of the essence. But Western Europe and America, which had encouraged the uprising via radio broadcasts, were too busy to take a call from Hungary. They were fighting off an impending conniption over a Soviet-financed dam in the Suez Canal, which, a few people could tell you, was located in Egypt. The SOS from Budapest was answered not by American aid but by a line of Soviet tanks that rolled into the city like a funeral procession. Twenty-seven hundred Hungarians lost their lives, two hundred thousand more fled the country, and within a few short months Hungary once again felt as if it had been pronounced dead.

For those who remained, however, the failed uprising was not wholly without benefit. It was such an embarrassment to the Kremlin that rather than risk another rebellion, the Russians opted to give more latitude to János Kádár — the Hungarian leader Moscow had installed — than to any other leader in its eastern orbit. As a result, Hungary was the least oppressive place to live in its communist neighborhood. The media remained hopelessly state-owned and -controlled, but Hungary was the only Eastern bloc country that allowed people to listen to shortwave foreign radio broadcasts about what flourished beyond the Curtain. Unlike in Romania, where President Nicolae Ceauşescu ran his country like a police state, Hungary allowed monitored meetings between dissidents and Western reporters and had no known political prisoners.

This isn't to say insouciance reigned in Hungary's sixteenth-century Turkish bathhouses. Even if people weren't being hauled off regularly, there were enough incidents of the Political Investigation Department haranguing intellectuals to remind the populace that harboring aspirations of anything but a gray, unsatisfying life was useless, and possibly even hazardous to one's health. As it is with such subsistence, Hungarians mollified themselves with theories of relativity — in their case, the pronouncement that their country was, as they put it, "the happiest barracks on the (Soviet) bloc." And as time went on, Hungary began to edge toward free market capitalism, albeit painfully, without interference from the Kremlin. In order to shrink the spiraling $13 billion budget deficit it had accrued over years of corrupted fiscal policies, the Hungarian government began shaving social services such as health care. To curb inflation, it caused an outcry by raising prices for bread, flour, electricity, and other staples. Slowly, Hungary's leadership broke with Soviet practice, signing worldwide trade agreements and conforming to enough human rights conventions to qualify for International Monetary Fund aid. In the early 1980s, citizens were even permitted to open their own businesses.

By the time Soviet leader Mikhail Gorbachev's progressive policies of *perestroika* and *glasnost,* or "economic restructuring" and "openness," arrived to the USSR in the mid-1980s, Hungary was setting the pace for Eastern Europe's march toward Westernization. While Attila Ambrus was warding off knife-wielding Romanian bunkmates in a desolate Transylvanian juvenile detention facility, Budapest was welcoming an Adidas sports store and Eastern Europe's first McDonald's.

As the end of the 1980s neared, it was clear that even bigger changes were coming, and so — for the first time in most people's lifetime — was the unknown prospect of true Western-style opportunity. This is where our story begins.

Two

The day he arrived was one only he would remember: cloud-covered, sticky, unending. Attila stood beneath the small black Departures board suspended between tracks seven and eight from the sloping, steel-beamed, grimy glass ceiling of the Keleti train station. People streamed around him like a river over a rock. *Bocsánat,* they said. *Excuse me.* According to the train schedule, a traveler could even go to Vienna, at least if he had the right papers. Attila was content just to ponder it. Four hours ago, he should have died. *Bocsánat,* he responded, smiling.

Some of the women smiled back. Not bad, this guy with the soft whisker-sprouting face, standing unharried in the vortex of Budapest's primary transportation hub. He carried nothing but his determination. Attila's straight dark bangs, carelessly pushed underwear-model-style to one side, could even have passed for cutting-edge; new fashions were arriving quickly now that some of the Western boutiques had been allowed to stake their claim of Budapest real estate. But . . . was that a pair of overalls? It was hard to tell exactly what he was wearing. His clothes were striped with black grease, as if he'd just stepped out of an oil well. Sorry, but they had a train to catch.

He didn't care. He didn't want to go anywhere. Attila Ambrus had long known that if he ever got to Hungary, he would never leave. Sure, it was still communist terrain, but he was finally among his own — a very Hungarian Hungarian who had never, until today, been to Hungary. To his eager ears, even the most banal statement that afternoon was a *shrstk-hat-chop* sonata, the syncopated conflagration of consonants, accents, and unabashed umlauts an auditory orgy.

Daylight faded. He walked down a stairwell to the city mall, a dingy concourse beneath the street lined with kiosks offering the best vendibles on the market: at the music booth, Madonna, Jefferson Starship, and *Komár László Sings Elvis Presley* cassettes; at the feet of wrinkled women with bulbous noses and black shawls, waist-high sacks of sunflower seeds; and at the newsstand, crossword-puzzle books with naked women on the cover and a selection of Hungarian-language newspapers, trumpeting the impending arrival in Budapest of U.S. deputy secretary of state John Whitehead. Earlier that day in Berlin, Whitehead had implored East German authorities to tear down "that gray, monstrous snake," the Berlin Wall.

Attila swiped a postcard: Budapest at night, when you saw only what they illuminated — the windows of the stately former Hapsburg palace twinkling like a thousand cubic zirconias over the electric golden garland that outlined the Széchenyi Bridge. With a pen borrowed from the nearby subway ticket counter, he wrote on the back of the card, *Itt vagyok* — *I'm here* — and stuck it in his back pocket to mail later.

When night fell, the proprietors padlocked their wooden booths and went home. The Gypsy women tied up their sunflower sacks and curled into the station's dank corners. The cool cement hall was almost quiet when a lone busker on a violin appeared at the subway entrance playing the theme to Attila's favorite TV show, those Communist Party–approved darlings of contemporary Eastern Europe, *The Flintstones*. There were no police around and those he had seen earlier appeared neither armed nor dangerous. Relieved, Attila sat down against the wall, singing himself a lullaby: *Let's have a doo time, a dabba doo time. Let's have a gay old time!*

In the morning he awoke in a slump at the edge of a people stampede with a stiff neck and a six-part question. He went outside to where the cabbies were lined up in black-and-white-checkered Russian Zhigulis and let it fly: Where might he find some food, clothes, money, a job, an ID, and a place to live?

The answer to all six was 55 Népköztársaság, just a few doors down from the infamous Communist Party headquarters building, from which a summons could still be interpreted as a memo to cancel your plans and pack a toothbrush. As the Thursday workday began, Attila set out into the linty fall air. The city was like a bustling ghost town, an inhabited shell of the place it had been at the turn of the twentieth century, when it was the fastest-growing city in Europe. Bullet-pocked five- and six-story fin de siècle limestone buildings loomed over the sidewalk like uncalled witnesses to the carnage of the 1945 Soviet "liberation" and the unsuccessful 1956 uprising. It was never quite clear if the scars remained as a warning or as evidence that there were no quick fixes in the lands of the Red Star.

Most of the street names were Russian, which Attila assumed explained why he had to zigzag back and forth in order to maintain the direction in which he'd been pointed. On the looping, traffic-choked avenues, ottoman-size automobiles and the occasional brightly colored BMW or Mercedes coursed like clots through damaged arteries. On the diagonal side streets, boys on bikes went bumping along the uneven black stone and men smoking Multifilters stood in patches of sunlight.

When he reached Népköztársaság (which was only a year away from reclaiming its original name, Andrássy) he turned left onto the wide, leafy boulevard that was modeled after Paris's Champs-Elysées. Above him, the crenellated windows of the baroque attic roofs looked out from their curved perches like sunken eyes. Walking in the opposite direction of the statue-filled Heroes' Square, where Chief Árpád and the seven other founding fathers of Hungary rode stone horses, Attila passed the renowned Művész café and confectionery, whose patrons debated the merits of democracy while employing aluminum spoons to shovel sugar into their espressos; the nineteenth-century Opera Pharmacy, where pitchers of water sat on the counters for those who couldn't wait to take their medication; and the neoclassical State Opera House, roosted atop a swath of marble steps, behind a statue of Liszt. Every few minutes a banana-yellow tram, linked to a network of elevated cables, clanked to a stop and deposited its passengers onto a cement island in the middle of an intersecting avenue, there in the convenient, high-occupancy, and fashionably invadable neighborhood of dead central Europe.

At number 55, Attila stopped. Under a small red, white, and green

Hungarian coat of arms, a sign read, BEVÁNDORLÁSI HIVATAL — Immigration Office. He'd made it.

"Excuse me," he said to the woman sitting behind the counter on the second floor.

"Take a number."

He looked around. The small room was empty. Nevertheless, he took a numbered square from the stack of paper and sat down on a bench.

A few minutes later, with the atonal fervor of the condemned, she called his number. "Fill this out," she said, handing over a two-page form and a pencil.

> Name: Attila Ambrus
> Place of birth: Csíkszereda, Romania
> Date of birth: October 6, 1967
> Member of associations: UTC KISZ
>   (Communist Youth Association)

And so on.

At the bottom of the second page was a paragraph stating that if he renounced his foreign citizenship, he could not be involved in any political activities in Hungary and that he would respect the laws of the land. Below it Attila volunteered, "Hereby I state that I do not want to return to Romania. Never again. I would like to live in Hungary as an upstanding man. I accept that I cannot get involved in any political stuff."

He left only one question blank: Have you ever been prosecuted before?

He signed his name in tall half-cursive lettering that leaned exaggeratedly backward as if laboring in a headwind, then brought the form back to the woman. Told to wait, he returned to the unforgiving bench.

And waited.

And waited.

And waited.

Three hours later a man in an olive green Party uniform with silver buttons down the front appeared from behind a door and asked him to follow. All too familiar with state-sponsored hospitality, Attila had already begun making mental notes of potential escapes from the building, and as they walked, he added a couple more windows and a likely back hallway to his list.

He was ushered into a windowless room with a desk upon which two small flags sprouted from a coffee mug — one bearing the communist Hammer and Sickle, the other the horizontal red, white, and green stripes of Hungary. The dark wood furniture whispered, *Shoot me.*

"Mr. Ambrus," the officer said, sitting down behind the desk and pointing for his subject to take a seat. He had Attila's forms in a brown folder, marked by his case number, 0224-877-6.

"Yes, Comrade," Attila answered.

Comrade? Was this peasant serious? "You are from Erdély [Transylvania]?" the man asked.

"Yes, Comrade," Attila said.

"Why do you make this request for temporary residence in Hungary?"

"Because I would like to stay in Hungary and live here," Attila said. "And with time I would like to get Hungarian citizenship."

"How do you plan to make a living?" the officer asked, unmoved.

"I would like to work," Attila stated. "In Romania there's no point trying to make ends meet." Bureaucrats, Attila thought. Did he need to spell out *hell* for him, too? Attila assumed he knew only bits and pieces of current events, but from what he understood, even the United States had condemned Romanian president Nicolae Ceauşescu for his human rights abuses against the Hungarians living in Romania. He'd heard it himself on an illegal shortwave radio, tucked comfortably in a patch of beech trees, on the far-reaching signal from Radio Budapest. Now he wondered if he'd taken the news too much for granted.

"Have you ever been prosecuted before?" the officer asked, eyeing Attila.

"No, Comrade," Attila said, lying.

The man paused, then continued. "Do you have a profession?"

That was a tough one. "After school I went to work as an electrician," Attila said, stretching the traditional definitions of *school, work,* and *electrician.* "But not long afterward they took me to be a soldier. For a year and four months I was a member of the Romanian army. After that I started to work again, but even then it was my intention to live in Hungary. And I succeeded because I escaped. And now I'm here. . . . In Hungary!

"*Bocsánat*," Attila added, apologizing that the last two words — *in Hungary!* — had jumped out of him like a victory toast.

"So you did not come on a visa, then," the man noted coolly. "Did you come across the border on foot?"

"No, Comrade."

"How did you come, then?"

Attila shifted in his seat. According to the Radio Budapest report he'd believed, Hungary was admitting all of its Hungarian brethren who made it out of Romania, with or without the paperwork. But it was a tenuous time. A few months earlier, in May of 1988, János Kádár, the apparatchik who had led Hungary for the past thirty-two years, had been ousted by the forward-thinking Hungarian *nomenklatura* in favor of a bickering collection of reformers and opportunists, each hoping to make history as the man to lead Hungary from communism. But not all of Hungary's Communist Party tentacles were ready to play dead. In June, Budapest police had beaten about a hundred people who were trying to publicly commemorate the thirty-year anniversary of the death of Imre Nagy, the former Hungarian prime minister who was hanged for his role as an instigator of the 1956 uprising. And while Attila pondered his fate that morning in the airless immigration office, Hungary's neighbor to the north, Czechoslovakia, watched as Moscow sacked its newly appointed reform-minded leader in favor of another iron-fisted lackey.

Romania, as Attila could report, was even less predictable. The country of 23 million had become the closest thing there was to a police state in communist Europe. Ceaușescu's secret police force, the *Securitate,* patrolled the cities in machine-gun-toting militias and had one in every seven citizens working for it as an informant. Food was closely rationed: each household received a cup of oil and sugar and one pound of an item referred to as meat every month. Even in the notoriously frigid winters, homes were allowed only two hours of heat per night. Some had taken to calling their country Ceauswitz.

Of course, it wasn't only the ethnic Hungarians who were living in fear and misery, but they had the right to be especially terrified. Transylvania (population, 7 million), where almost all of Romania's 2 million

Hungarians lived, was a highly prized and historic piece of land that both Hungary and Romania claimed was the birthplace of their culture. And Romania, an independent state only since 1878, believed its ancestors, the Dacians of Rome, had lived there seven hundred years before Hungary's Chief Árpád. If you were one of Romania's Hungarians circa 1988, there were an increasing number of reasons you might suddenly disappear from society, among them the crime of speaking Hungarian.

Ceaușescu's recent treatment of Hungary's displaced nationals had so enraged Hungarians in Hungary that some favored going to war with Romania over Transylvania. Ceaușescu seemed ready. He had shuttered his embassy in Budapest and evicted Hungary's Transylvania-based consulate from Romania. So although there was in fact a program in Hungary, with Red Cross funding, to resettle Hungarian refugees, or *menekült*, from Romania, the Hungarian authorities were necessarily suspicious of anyone associated with Ceaușescu territory. Sure, Attila spoke good — if somewhat anachronistic — Hungarian. But so might anyone with no identification and an ulterior motive.

The door swung open and an older man entered the room. Same drab uniform except for the addition of blue ribbons on the shoulders and a stiff officer's cap. Attila stood as the man moved behind the desk and sat down beside his poker-faced confederate.

"Sit," he told Attila brusquely. "Mr. Ambrus, I've been reviewing your application form for a temporary residence permit."

He handed Attila a clipboard and asked him to write down his account of how he had arrived in Hungary. *Kérem*, he added. *Please.*

The room's only exit was the door on the other side of the desk, where the officer across from Attila sat. Attila didn't know what he'd done that had raised the suspicion of his interrogators, but he had little choice now but to tell the saga of the past few weeks again and hope for the best. He picked up a pencil and wrote down his account while the officials watched. Then he passed the clipboard across the desk. The senior officer read through the pages with a wan smile, then put the clipboard back down and leaned forward on his elbows. "Listen, *Comrade,*" he said to Attila. "Do you expect us to believe this story?"

Three

Attila had been, as he told the immigration officer, "recommended for a team of church painters" along the Hungarian-Romanian border three weeks earlier. Painting churches in the far western reaches of Ceauşescu's Romania was a fast-growing industry in 1988, though neither the Romanian authorities nor their Hungarian counterparts had yet to spot the trend. What qualified a sanctuary for cosmetic repair was not necessity (though often the case could be made) but rather that the house of worship be — as it invariably was — the tallest structure in its border village. Thus, the painters, almost all of them Hungarian and almost none of them painters, could ascend to the steeple for guidance as to which method of flight over the *zöld határ*, or "green border," was least likely to result in their death.

Approximately fifteen thousand Transylvanian Hungarians had made it into Hungary since the beginning of 1988; untold hundreds of others met a dark end trying. Some folded themselves into the trunks of cars and were spirited through the checkpoint; in the winter, some wrapped themselves in white sheets and slipped wraithlike into border-hugging woods; others poured industrial oil all over their bodies and hoped they would float when they hucked themselves into either the Kőrös River in the western Romanian city of Oradea, the Maros in nearby Arad, or the Tisza in northern Romania, the most circuitous of the three, which twisted first through Ukraine before passing into

Hungary. Everyone wanted out. Romania's most famous Olympian, gymnast Nadia Comaneci, soon added to her training regimen a five-hour crop crawl that ended in Hungary.

Whatever method was employed, however, scouting had become mandatory. The mad dash through the cornfields between Romania and Hungary had become too fashionable for its own good: Ceauşescu had volleyed back with a new law that vegetation along his borders not exceed three feet in height and an order that his already tetchy border guards shoot to kill. In one enlightening 1987 incident, a fleeing twenty-eight-year-old Transylvanian Hungarian was chased by Romanian guards on horseback, who shot and killed him *after* he had crossed into Hungary.

Attila Ambrus had already spent what felt like a lifetime running from unsympathetic forces, never getting farther than the next quagmire. In June of 1988 he had returned from the latest, a sixteen-month stint as a slop-cook corporal in the Romanian army, as he'd stated in his immigration interview. What he hadn't mentioned was that he'd done his military service in the noxious southeastern Romania steel factory town of Galati — like most Romanians with criminal records. While there, Attila was occasionally let out of the kitchen to haul backbreaking railroad ties and, twice, to spend freezing, foodless weeklong stints in a twelve-foot isolation pit for talking back to his commander in Hungarian instead of Romanian. When his tour of duty ended, he boarded a bus for an eight-hour ride north through the rocky, soaring Carpathians to the eastern Transylvania capital of Csíkszereda. When he got out in the shadow of the surrounding green foothills of the Hargita Mountains, Attila found a city so desolate and defeated that he almost didn't recognize it.

To most of the world, Transylvania may as well be Timbuktu in a lightning storm, but to Attila it was home. He was born in Fitód, a village of five hundred just outside Csíkszereda, in 1967, the same year Ceauşescu ascended to one of the only Communist Party posts he hadn't yet occupied: president. Attila moved to the city nine years later, the same year the bulldozers started showing up. With forty-eight hours' notice, four-hundred-year-old churches, homes, and taverns were turned into pet rocks. This was Ceauşescu's economic revitalization plan, which, he said, was going to connect Transylvania to the rest of Romania by turning seven thousand mostly Hungarian villages into 250 supreme agro-industrial complexes. Even translated into archaic

Hungarian, the message was clear. He was going to pave paradise and put up a housing block.

And, to a large degree, that's what Ceauşescu had done. The architectural style of the thirteenth-century all-Hungarian city of thirty thousand had gone from ornate castle to concrete shoebox. But at least when Attila had shipped out for his army duty, there had still seemed to be ways to get by. Now, everywhere Attila looked, hundreds of people were queued up for food or pay they weren't likely to receive. The Securitate marched through town with machine guns, questioning people at random and clearing the streets by nightfall. If you wanted to end the day at home, you answered their questions in Romanian, which, thanks to his two years in a state-run penal institution, Attila now spoke fluently. Indeed, if you were smart, you were forgetting your Hungarian entirely. Hungarian books were disappearing from the schools, as were the remaining Hungarian-speaking teachers. The Hungarian-language newspapers were ceasing publication. Parents were no longer allowed to give their children Hungarian names, such as Attila. Even the name Csíkszereda was no longer allowed to be uttered; the city went only by its seldom-used Romanian name, Miercurea-Ciuc.

Attila was planning to stay with his aunt and uncle, who had raised him after his grandmother died when he was nine. But Aunt Ninny and Uncle László no longer felt they could ask their now twelve-year-old daughter to sleep in their bed so cousin Attila could have the couch. Instead, Attila took a cot in a log cabin dormitory provided by the same electrical company — Romania's only electrical company — that employed his estranged father and hired Attila as a maintenance man, one of the only gigs available to someone with a Securitate classification as a "class enemy," or in plain language, a do-no-gooder. Thus began a streak of twelve-hour days digging ditches for electricity poles and occasionally, out of boredom, climbing them, then retiring to his cot by eight o'clock when the lights went out.

Life was pretty much intolerable but for the fact that within a few weeks he fell in love for the first time with a blue-eyed girl named Katalin, whom he met while hovering thirty feet above her family's backyard in the city's rural outskirts. Like Katalin, Attila had also grown up in a tiny neighboring village in which there were no cars, electricity, or running water; six hay bales constituted a bed; bathing was an event that took place once a week in a sawed-off wooden barrel; and the bathroom was a creaky outhouse. In the snowy winters, when the temperature regularly stayed south of negative ten Fahrenheit, they both learned how to hold it in. After so many pent-up years, Attila needed to let it out. Disregarding the only rule of the land (that you not trust anyone), Attila told Katalin all. She heard about the two-room Fitód home he had shared with his father and grandmother until her death; how much he hated his mother for running out on his family when he was only a year old; how the first and last time he sought comfort from his father was at age four, when he ran to him after being picked on, only to be slapped across the face and called a sissy by Dad.

Attila also disclosed to Katalin his propensity for mischief. At age seven, he'd been arrested for climbing too high in a tree. He had made a string of vegetable-field pillaging missions to feed the fifty-plus hungry pet rabbits he'd kept in his father's tiny back lot. And there was his never-exposed method of pilfering the recyclable bottles from behind the city supermarket and re-returning them for lunch money. He had also played hockey for the prestigious boarding school outside town before being expelled for short-circuiting the electricity on exam day. By reputation, he was a regular Transylvanian Dennis the Menace until the summer following his expulsion. Then sixteen, he was caught stealing musical instruments belonging to a popular local wedding band from a basement pub. Attila's Hungarian name, admitted guilt, and dearth of influential advocates made him easy prey for the authorities. He was held for two months inside the Csíkszereda basement jail, then shipped off for a two-year stay at a juvenile detention facility on the grim Moldavian border. About his time there, he wouldn't say anything.

Katalin, then nineteen, was working as a tailor in a knitting factory, but whenever possible, she and Attila would skip work and go to his aunt and uncle's apartment, hoping to find no one home. Thanks to those afternoons and Ceaușescu's ban on contraceptives, Katalin was soon pregnant. After hearing the news that he was to become a father, Attila offered Katalin the ring his grandmother had given him before she died, and asked her to marry him. Life wouldn't be easy, he told her. With the heft of his Securitate file, his chances of earning a livable wage were about as good as his being named a member of his favorite band, AC/DC. But he wanted a real family and told her he would find a way. Katalin accepted. But then without warning a few weeks later, she returned Attila's ring. She wasn't ready to be married, she told him.

Against Attila's wishes, and at risk of arrest, she aborted their child in a cornfield, and with it Attila's last hope of salvaging a future for himself in Romania.

That summer Romanian television broadcast only two hours a day, one of which was devoted to hagiographies of Ceauşescu, "the most beloved son of his people," who mailed himself forged seventieth-birthday cards from England's Queen Elizabeth and Spain's King Carlos, then published them in the Romanian papers. But the Hungarian government had recently erected a gigantic broadcasting tower near the Romanian border so that those with illegal radios in Transylvania could get information from the freer world. Attila borrowed what money he could from his uncle László and managed to procure the use of a radio. During his workdays, he made sure to find an electrical glitch in a remote location where he could tune in. On the newscasts were reports of the bloody student-led protest in China's Tiananmen Square, the successful Moscow nuclear disarmament meetings between U.S. president Ronald Reagan and Soviet leader Mikhail Gorbachev, and even — aha! — the growing international support for the Hungarians in Transylvania. In August 1988 the U.S. Senate unanimously passed a bill halting all economic benefits and trade with Romania and specifically condemning Ceauşescu for his human rights violations against the Hungarian minority. Even PLO leader Yasir Arafat's top deputy condemned Ceauşescu, saying his treatment of Transylvania's Hungarians "undermined Romania's credibility." But there were no lessons or hints over the airwaves on how to get out.

On the morning of Friday, September 23, 1988, Attila left his dormitory and went to the cinder-block apartment where he'd done much of his growing up. He told his uncle László he needed to speak to him alone. Securitate informants were known to be crawling all over the building; László had recently been called to the city office and cited for singing a Hungarian folk song in his living room. László asked his wife to put on a record for the enjoyment of anyone who might be listening and went with his nephew into the cramped rectangular kitchen.

Before Attila could start, he heard Ninny crying in the other room. She liked their record collection but she had a feeling what the music signified that morning.

"I have to leave," Attila whispered to his uncle.

"I know," László mouthed, nodding slowly. "I know." He and Ninny had just spoken about the eventuality; they knew about Katalin and they knew their nephew. And as much as it hurt to acknowledge, they also knew that Attila's chances of staying out of jail, or even alive, were probably just as bad if he remained in Romania as they were if he attempted an escape. It was time to let him go. "Do you have something arranged?" László asked.

"I was recommended for a team of church painters," Attila said, "through Csibi" — his mother's brother, János Csibi, who still lived nearby and always had his ear to the ground.

László opened a junk drawer and fumbled through a stack of black-and-white family photographs. "Take these," he said to Attila, trying to hold back his tears. He was a small man, and when he wrapped his arms around the nephew he considered a son, they reached around his mid-section. "You're going to make it," László said, hardly sure.

Attila hugged him back, remembering the Sunday dinners after which Ninny would give him a candy, how proud his relatives had been when he earned a hockey scholarship to the boarding school outside town, all the times they'd picked him up from the hospital with broken bones and concussions and bused three hours to visit him at the juvenile detention center. "If I don't see you," Attila said, "thanks for everything you and Ninny have done for me."

"Drop a postcard," László said, starting to cry. "Tell me something about the city. Just remember not to sign it."

"I promise," Attila said, without a tear. He was on a bus that afternoon.

～

The village of Curtici, an agricultural hamlet just a little more than half a mile from the Hungarian border, had lost its bucolic feel in the past few years, since it found itself inside the "exclusion zone," the five-mile pad on the western edge of Romania that Ceauşescu had declared off-limits to nonresidents without special permits. Uniformed soldiers were everywhere. Citizens could be asked to show their IDs getting on or off a bus or train, and — particularly if their names were Hungarian — they had to be prepared for an unexplained detention or, if they weren't well-practiced sycophants, arrest.

Attila phoned the church when he got close. The priest told him nervously that the paint crew he had been expecting had left suddenly for Arad, a larger hub city twenty-five miles east — nowhere near the border. When Attila found them there a few days later, he heard the full story.

Over the previous few weeks, while touching up another Curtici chapel, the five-man team had befriended the local border guards. One day two of the painters brought some drinks to the least belligerent of the sentinels and asked if they were hungry, because the painters were going to start a barbecue. The guards, who weren't exactly living like voivodes themselves, were grateful. All that was needed, the Hungarians told them, was some wood for the fire. Could they help gather a few sticks, since the paint crew wasn't allowed in the fields? The guards obliged, set down their rifles, and headed for a patch of trees. At that moment, two of the painters made their break. They grabbed the guards' weapons and sprinted into the field toward Hungary. As far as the others knew, they had made it.

It had been exhilarating but also posed a difficult question for the rest of them: now what were they going to do? There weren't many more churches in the area that hadn't already been solicited by an exterior design team, and it didn't take an advanced degree to understand that the border guards would henceforth be leery of itinerant Hungarian church painters. But since three weeks' painting experience was still the group's most marketable skill, they hustled a job touching up the towering early-nineteenth-century Hungarian cathedral in the center of Arad, where they could regroup.

For the next four weeks, Attila lived in a tiny two-room apartment with the crew. They spent their days painting in silence and their nights drawing up escape plans in silence.

On October 6 Attila was watching from one of the top spires of the church as a Hungarian parade marched down the boulevard in commemoration of the lives of thirteen Hungarian generals who helped lead the 1848 uprising against the ruling Hapsburgs. The revolt had been part of what Karl Marx and Friedrich Engels then called the "Springtime of the People," as uprisings swept fadlike through France, Germany, and Italy. Several of the Hungarian leaders had been executed in Arad. As Attila looked on, a group of Romanians stormed the parade, throwing rocks at the marchers and screaming, "Hungarians, go home!" He resolved once more that he was prepared to die in order to get out of Romania. It was his twenty-first birthday.

Three days later he put on all the clothes he owned: sneakers, a pair of pants under his overalls, a white T-shirt, and a sweater. His knife went where he normally kept it, in his sock. Instead of reporting for work, he caught the tram to the Arad train station. He took the train west to the end of the line and got out at a town he hoped was close to the border. Securitate men were all over the station. If they asked him for ID or where he was going, he had two options: he could show them nothing, or he could tell them nothing, and in either case he would be finished. As he approached the exit, he kept himself positioned neither too close nor too far from the clusters of people heading for the doors. When the crucial moment came, he looked one of the guards in the eye, nodded, and said, *"Buna dimineata!"* — *Good morning* — in formal, unaccented Romanian and kept walking. He was not stopped.

As the sun rose on its westward arc toward Hungary, Attila slipped into the cornfields behind the station, crouching and crawling in search of the border. It took until the following day before he could see in the distance the checkpoint on the international cargo train route. The air was hot and there was nowhere to find shade. The pollinated fields made his mouth feel like a receptacle for gauze. He shed his sweater and shirt and lay low to keep out of sight of the wooden tower about 110 yards ahead, hoping the dogs wouldn't catch wind of his armpits. When each train passed, he carefully noted the time, direction, and speed and repeated the numbers over and over so he wouldn't forget. He slept in the field for one more night, hoping to catch the next day's slow-moving ten-fifteener.

As morning dawned, his stomach began to cramp. At last, the train appeared in the distance. He got up from the ground and readied to time his run so that he would be shielded from view of the checkpoint as much as possible and still be at full speed when the train passed him. Before he knew it, he was racing diagonally out of the field. But the window of time he'd given himself was too small. When he reached the tracks — legs churning, the train roaring over his right shoulder — he realized he couldn't keep up.

Then, out of the corner of his eye, he saw a handrail sticking out from the front end of one of the cars. As it passed, he lunged and grabbed it with both hands, the force of the train pulling his arms ahead of his legs, first lifting his body horizontal to the ground, then swinging it back down and smashing him against the side of the car. He held on as his body steadied enough for him to reach out one foot and then the other onto the metal grating between the two cars and gain purchase on the connecting platform. He needed to be beneath the grating on which he stood, lying flat along the wide bar that held the cars together.

The border checkpoint was approaching. He got on his knees on the edge of the platform with his back to the fields and gripped the steel below him. He looked like a gymnast on the parallel bars — arms locked, teeth clenched, as he prepared for a swoon and a swing that would either propel him safely under the connecting platform and above the couplings or, if his form was less precise, onto the tracks, where he would be instantly killed. Attila pushed his torso up and swung his curled knees back over the edge of the train, then quickly and forcefully pulled his legs back in and shot them straight out along the platform beneath the one on which he'd just stood. He could feel his thighs drift across the black metal slab that functioned as the connector to switch the cars. As his legs settled on this slab, he forced his body to follow, belly-up, by pushing with his arms against the bar he was holding, like a reverse chin-up. There was just enough room to balance himself on his back. But his body. . . his body was slipping on the grease as the train chugged along the rails toward Hungary. If he were to lose his balance now, it would be a short, quick tumble to a gruesome death. He held the metal platform with his hands and pushed his feet against the grating above him to steady his trunk. The train would surely be checked and probably even inspected, but he hoped it would not be examined for people flattened corpselike between two cars, hanging so low to the tracks that a muscle twitch could remove a limb.

And all of this to get from one communist dictatorship to another.

A few minutes later the train slowed to a stop at the checkpoint. Attila held his breath as footsteps approached, paused, and then, after what seemed like an eternity, passed. Finally the train began moving again. Supine and six inches off the ground, Attila Ambrus entered Hungary.

Four

Budapest
The following week

Attila's James Bond escape yarn and Hungary's deep distrust of Ceauşescu were more than sufficient for the immigration office to tag him as a potential spy or budding reprobate. As a result, instead of being given a room in one of the city's new housing blocks for Transylvanian refugees, Attila was assigned a bed in a policemen's dormitory, where he could be more closely monitored. It being communism, he was also assigned a job — a bad one. He became an electrical assistant at a glass factory, where he was paid slightly less than the average $150/month Hungarian wage to make sure a truck-size glass-cutting machine didn't overheat. Daylight hours weren't so bad. It was having to go to sleep among two hundred communist cops every night that undercut the logic he'd prevailed upon when weighing whether to throw himself at a moving train. Didn't these Hungarians understand he was one of them? Apparently not. Every few days someone from an official post approached his bunk and, after a short chat, asked him to describe the industrial swamp pit of Galati where he said he had done his military service (which he could do) or where Romania's power grids were (which he couldn't do).

During his breaks at the glass factory, Attila disappeared into the sports pages of the precious Hungarian-language newspapers, each filled with stories of Hungary's championship pro hockey team, UTE (Újpesti Torna Egylet, or Újpest Gym Association). In October, UTE had won a European championship tournament in the world's C division, two competition levels below that in which the global puck powers from the Soviet Union, Sweden, Canada, and the United States played. And in one week in November, the Budapest-based UTE club won three straight games over its foes in the eight-team Hungarian professional league by a combined score of 42–4.

Attila loved hockey even more than he loved the Transylvanian delicacy pig's feet. Aside from playing goalie at the private school, he used to sneak into every game at Csíkszereda's four-thousand-seat indoor hockey arena, where Romania's only all-Hungarian professional team played. And as much as he loved hockey, he hated his current job. So, one afternoon at lunch, Attila went to a pay phone and dialed the number of the UTE facility. "I'd like to speak to the general manager," he said. "This is Attila Ambrus."

By the time Gustáv Bóta picked up, Attila's new phone card was nearly creditless. "Can I help you?" Bóta asked.

"Hello, Comrade. I'm Attila Ambrus from Transylvania," Attila said. "I'm a goalie and I'd like a tryout."

Bóta paused. *Comrade?* Who called anyone "comrade" anymore? In the decade or so since Hungarians had received the unofficial all-clear to start using "Mr." and "Mrs.," the communist honorific had all but disappeared from the lexicon. "Ancsin? . . . Flóra?" Bóta said, attempting to match the voice on the other end with one of the jokesters from the team but encountering only silence. "Well," he said, composing himself, "we actually do need another goalie." Everyone in hockey knew the illustrious reputation of the all-Hungarian hockey program in Csíkszereda. Bóta hadn't heard of this Ambrus fellow, but news didn't transmit out of Transylvania in people years. Bóta told Attila he'd pick him up the next morning and take him to practice. In the meantime, Attila decided to keep quiet about his colossal lack of competitive goaltending experience.

The following day, when the UTE general manager pulled up in front of Attila's dorm in a bright orange two-door Soviet-made Lada, he was surprised by the diminutive size of his new recruit. Hungarians weren't behemoths to begin with, but the Transylvanian variety usually came a few sizes bigger. True, for goalies, size mattered less than reflexes, and there were plenty of international greats under six feet tall. But Attila looked about five feet eight and a little on the thin side. Then again, at five feet four and a dead ringer for the bearded, rosy-cheeked Sneezy of the Seven Dwarfs, Bóta wasn't one to judge on sight. Surely, he figured, Attila would make up for his height in speed and smarts. And he would fit in the car.

Attila folded himself into the Lada, and he and Bóta lurched through the curving, narrow streets with the fashion and firepower of a toaster. It didn't take Bóta long to realize that Attila's "comrade" comment had been no joke. His passenger spoke in an archaic Hungarian dialect that Bóta couldn't always follow. When Attila mentioned his love of the forest surrounding his home in Csíkszereda, he didn't call it *erdő* — he called it *rengeteg*, or, in Budapest Hungarian, a "big pile." When Attila said his boss at the glass factory was *lópokróc*, or a "horse rug," Bóta could only guess it meant that he was rude. It was like talking to a Hungarian Shakespeare.

Half an hour later, after negotiating stop-and-go traffic and passing the dilapidated, white wooden row houses near the sports complex in the city's northern suburb of Újpest, Sneezy and his Transylvanian catch pulled into the UTE parking lot. The light gray November sky illuminated a locale Attila had only read about in the papers — UTE's hulking ten-thousand-seat soccer stadium and barren bleacher-ringed hockey rink. (UTE fielded teams in several sports.) Attila was surprised to see that the latter didn't even have a roof.

Bóta and Attila walked to the far end of the rink, where they entered a brown silolike building with the distinct bouquet of urine. At the end of the hall, Bóta showed Attila in to the small square locker room. Black-and-white team pictures hung at odd angles on walls painted in purple and white, the UTE team colors. A couple of dozen players ranging from eighteen to thirty with buzz cuts and in various stages of undress sat on wooden stools. "This is Attila Ambrus," Bóta announced to the group. "He's going to be trying out as a goalie today."

A few of them grunted. Attila went around in a circle, reaching out his hand to each of them. "Hello, Comrade, I'm Attila Ambrus from Transylvania," he said. He got about halfway around the room before someone finally asked, "Who the fuck is this bumpkin?" Even Bóta couldn't hold back his laughter.

The only extra skates the team could find for Attila were three sizes too big. Attila picked some newspapers off the floor, crumpled them up, and shoved them into the toes. Asking for a helmet, he reflexively used the Romanian word, *kasca*, which was what they'd called it back in Csíkszereda but which was nonsensical in Hungarian. The room exploded into laughter again.

Once out on the ice, it didn't take long for the players to recognize the new kid's level of talent: Zero. It had been six years since Attila had stood in front of a hockey net. He was flailing and diving all over the ice like a soccer goalie on roller skates. A few of the players started a contest to see who could hit him in the face mask the most times. His hand-me-down helmet was so old, it provided little protection. The third or fourth bull's-eye broke his nose. As the shots continued to batter his face, chest, legs, and arms, George Pék, the team's captain, skated over to Bóta, who was standing in a stupor on the side of the rink. Pék was a tall man, a former cop whose ice-blue eyes and blank stares endowed him with the authority of someone who operated on the fringes of anger and insanity. And he'd seen enough. "Whatever this guy is doing," Pék said to Bóta, "it has nothing to do with hockey."

Sneezy blew his whistle and tried to wave Attila over, but Attila ignored him. No matter how many pucks flew past him or into him, no matter how many times he flopped onto the ice, he kept returning to his hermit-crab crouch in front of the net as if the scrimmage in which he purported to be playing were the national title game. And so, partly out of morbid curiosity, Bóta let Attila play on until, two hours later, his whistle ended practice. Pék skated over to confer with Bóta and Dezső Széles, the head coach, at the side of the rink. "It's simply amazing," Pék said, "that there is a person on this planet who wants to be a goalie for our team so badly even though he clearly has never had anything to do with hockey before in his life."

The decision was unanimous. Attila was offered an immediate position with the team. He had what it took.

Three months later Attila sat alone in the locker room with his head in his hands. The brown linoleum floor was strewn with tape, sneakers, and the plastic hospital cups the team doctor had brought around earlier on a tray like hors d'oeuvres. "Don't forget your antifatigue pills, boys," he'd said. "Same as the Russians use."

The rest of the team had already headed out to the ice, and the raucous commotion that had attended their entrance rumbled through the building's thin walls — horses braying, people screaming, unimaginable objects thunking. In twenty minutes UTE was to play its crosstown rival, FTC (Ferencvárosi Gym Club), in Game One of the Hungarian national hockey championship, and from the sounds of it, Attila was about to wade into the biggest battle of his life.

Ice hockey was popular across much of Eastern Europe, with the Soviets consistently among the world's best. It was one of the few things Hungarians admired in the Russians. Hungary couldn't come close to duplicating their talent, no matter how many steroids the team doctor mixed into their energy drinks. Nonetheless, Hungary boasted a modest but respectable pro hockey league, and even though it drew smaller crowds and fewer televised games than soccer, Hungarian hockey's rabid fans didn't seem to notice. Anytime UTE played FTC — much less Game One of the finals — it was a good bet that two or three dozen supporters would leave the premises in paddy wagons. In fact, the hostilities in the stands often seemed to be of greater interest than the game. When the two teams had played a month earlier, the contest had to be called off in the third period when the FTC fans wouldn't heed their own team's exhortations to please stop hurling fireworks at the UTE goalie.

As the crowd noise grew, Attila slowly got up and went to the entrance to the bathrooms, casting a longing glance at the fetid stalls. Anna, the team's cleaning woman, had recently decided that her job title did not carry with it the requirement that she do the work it described. The eau de toilette was motivation enough for Attila to get to the ice. He headed back into the changing area, grabbed two heavy purple equipment bags, and began the long walk through the dim corridor.

As Attila was now all too aware, UTE contests had the capacity to provoke a particularly vehement rage among the public, and not just because the team had won six of the last seven Hungarian championships. In Hungary, all of the professional sports teams — much like everything — were run by the government. But the branch of the government that ran UTE was the Interior Ministry, the agency in charge of the police, who were probably the most spectacular of all *rohadt bolsi* (rotten Bolsheviks) the country had to offer. Some Hungarians, particularly loyal fans of the green and white FTC — "the people's team," run by the Agricultural Ministry — even thought of the purple-shirted UTE as the police team, though in reality the UTE roster rarely featured more than one or two actual cops.

Had Attila known any of this earlier, he would never have phoned UTE. To him, hockey had always represented rebellion. The fans at the Csíkszereda hockey games he attended were so maniacally anti-Ceauşescu that the Csíkszereda arena was known as the only place in Romania that the Securitate was too afraid to enter. They waited outside while inside, four thousand inebriated Transylvanians chanted the Hungarian anthem and other jingles at the opposing Romanian players, such as "Next time you'll have to bring your passport to get in here!" While the Romanian referees were under orders from Ceauşescu himself to prohibit Csíkszereda from winning the important games, if they were too egregious with their calls, they risked being held hostage inside the arena and getting beaten senseless by the locals.

But as much as the idea of being associated with the police troubled him, Attila couldn't do anything about his connection to UTE now. Once the team's staff saw just how little he had — he was confined to his dormitory every weekend because that was when he washed and dried his only outfit — they immediately began the requisite string pulling, paper shuffling, and mild-to-moderate Interior Ministry rank pulling to get the immigration office to approve a formal work transfer from the glass factory. That accomplished, Bóta even arranged for Attila to move out of the police dorm and into a closet at the UTE facility, where he was now living rent-free. It was a lot better than sharing a roof with the police, though Attila now shared something even stranger with his former bunkmates: he, too, was an employee of Hungary's Interior Ministry.

Not that that was going to be of any help to him in the coming hours if war broke out at the stadium, which was the way it was beginning to sound as he approached the double doors at the end of the long hallway. With one quick rocking motion, Attila smacked the entrance-way open with the bulky purple shoulder bags.

The late-afternoon fog was low and thick, as if he'd stepped into a cloud. All he could see were arms swinging and horse legs kicking, the prechampionship game riots already at full tilt. The open-air rink was less than fifty yards away. He lowered his head and began to run. "Get him!" someone shouted. "He's bringing reinforcements!" Before he could react to the erroneous accusation of ferrying battle supplies to the front lines, people and police horses converged on him from all directions. Attila was forced to the ground and subdued by that most contemporary of crowd-control techniques, beating by leather-sheathed police sword. "They're not reinforcements!" he screamed. "They're hockey sticks for the game!"

As if it mattered. He lay back down with his forehead on the cement and took it. *A decent beating,* he thought, but he'd had much better. When the UTE captain, George Pék, found him sometime later, he was lying in a semicircle of broken sticks.

"Get up," Pék said, pulling him by his arms. László "Gogi" Gogolak, one of UTE's starting forwards, was there, too. He threw a bloodied towel at Attila. "The game's starting in five minutes," Gogi said. "Get a move on."

Attila brushed himself off and headed to the metal shed behind the south goal. A few minutes later came the soundtrack that regularly accompanied his arrival on the ice. It wasn't cheers or a catchy theme song, but a noise like a sick animal coughing, followed by a tinny ping like the thawing of a frozen pipe, and then the sputtering hum that denotes a piece of, well, machinery with an engine. It was the ice-starching automobile, the Zamboni, starting. Then came the cheers, borne by the confirmation that there would in fact be a game that night — as soon as Attila, black and blue and behind the big wheel, finished clearing the ice.

In a haze so dense that the goalies couldn't see each other across the ice, UTE prevailed, 5–2, in a Game One showdown that featured nearly two dozen penalties, three ejections, and two thousand fans in a traditional Hungarian-style frenzy. The daily sports newspaper *Népsport* remarked of the sellout crowd the following day, "There was the typical chanting we can't print, but the cheers made use of an entire zoo as well as the players' whole family genealogy."

The Zamboni driver did not yet merit attention.

⌒

The remainder of Attila's first championship series continued in much the same vein: riots, dirty bathrooms, Zamboni duty, ejections, police beatings, and even some hockey. Attila did not see any playing time — his ability to take abuse still far outweighed his ability to stop shots with something other than his proboscis. His official position with the club was team janitor, with a salary of 6,000 forints (about $120) per month and responsibilities that included cleaning the rink, repairing the spotty electrical service, keeping track of equipment, and, at night, working as a security guard at the entrance to the complex. But Attila felt he had played some part in what unfortunately had been a bad series for UTE: FTC won the championship, three games to one.

Little by little, Attila was acclimating himself to his new surroundings. Bóta entrusted Attila with the only key to the pool in the basement of the UTE complex, should he ever feel like swimming alone. Attila was also learning his way around the city's convenient three-line subway system by visiting every church in town that was advertising free meals for Transylvanian immigrants. He still thought about Katalin, and his uncle László and Ninny, but for the most part, he was too busy working and finding his next meal to dwell on his unmoored existence.

He did make one friend: Zsuzsa Hamer, an overweight middle-aged clerk at the grocery store across the street from UTE, whose hubcap-size bifocals were always slipping off her nose. Zsuzsa had taken to Attila after listening to his frank and unaccusatory (toward her, at least) complaint that the chocolate milk the store carried was never cold enough. Every day when he came in after practice, she tried to gently extract his story, but he was so resistant that it took her months. Then one slow evening she finally got him talking, only to find herself blubbering along like a psychiatric patient. It was the part about his mother that really got her. The only memory Attila had of his mom was of an afternoon when he was about six. For years, he had begged his father to let him meet her, and finally his dad had agreed. They boarded a horse-drawn cart and trotted over to the nearby village where she was living. Attila was afraid to approach the house, but Károly Ambrus pushed his son up to the window. There was his mother, naked with another man. Attila ran back to the cart, crying, while his father shouted, "Happy now?"

Zsuzsa began hiding milk for Attila in the grocery's coldest refrigerator and inviting him to dinner at her cluttered apartment near the UTE stadium. Her husband, who worked several jobs, was rarely home, and Zsuzsa's ten-year-old daughter, Sylvia, looked up to Attila like an older brother. Sometimes late at night Attila would sneak Zsuzsa and Sylvia into the UTE complex, where he would give them skating lessons and play tag with them on the shadowy rink with only the moonlight as their guide. They were the closest thing to family he had.

Attila could only assume his aunt and uncle had received the Budapest postcard he'd stolen from the train station, but since they didn't have a phone, he had no way to contact them. He did know that things had gotten even worse in Romania since he'd left. It was all over the Hungarian news that Ceauşescu had been building a barbed-wire fence along the Hungarian border to keep his people in. Meanwhile, Hungary was lurching ever closer to freedom, even if it was in ways that didn't yet benefit Attila: Russian was dropped from the list of compulsory classes in the schools, travel restrictions were lifted, and, most significantly, in early 1989 opposition parties were allowed to form.

The resident of UTE's closet had other concerns. A few months after the hockey season ended, István Bereczky, the former army general who oversaw UTE for the Interior Ministry, called Attila to the stadium unexpectedly. Bereczky knew that on Sundays he could usually find his factotum down the street at the Transylvanian diner, Csülők (the Hoof), where they fed the UTE janitor for free. And he was right: Attila was there, enjoying some pig's feet and his sixth or seventh home-fermented, 150-proof plum *pálinka* (a Hungarian brandy), when Bereczky summoned him to the phone and told him to come back to clear the ice for some skating lessons. Shortly thereafter, Attila pulled out of the UTE tool shed astride the wheezing Zamboni.

The rink was nearly empty, just a few girls standing around in pink and baby blue leotards, looking at him riding high in his motorized saddle like the Lone Ranger. He thought about standing up on the seat or at least waving. Turning the wheel hadn't entered his mind.

The boards along the north end of the stadium never knew what hit them. Nor did Attila, who, after piloting the blue and white machine straight through the wall, found himself flying headlong toward the third row of bleachers.

Bereczky, a former national team ski jumper who was now a vodka-swilling drunk, was not trained to find humor in calamity. He ordered Attila to collect his sweater and vacate the storage room. Only the intervention of Bóta, Pék, and Gogolak stopped the general from firing Attila from his janitorial duties entirely.

A week later Pék, on whose couch Attila had subsequently been living, told his boarder that he'd found him a new home. He drove Attila to a little place near his house, just a few miles from the hockey stadium. "I think you're going to like it," Pék said as they pulled up in front of the building.

Attila took one look at the rectangular structure with the holey door and said, "It's a horse paddock."

"A *former* horse paddock," said Pék, getting out of the car. "See," he said, pushing open the barn door. "They've put in a floor."

Five

At times, Hungary itself felt a bit like a former horse paddock, as it shoveled out from under the stinking debris of communism. In May of 1989, just after Attila was ejected from the UTE closet, Hungary's move to open its western border with Austria enabled thousands of trapped and persecuted East Germans to flee through Hungary to the West. (Few Hungarians utilized the newly open border; they had been allowed to travel with some limitations for several years.) Six months later East German officials watched as their citizens tore through the Berlin Wall with their own hands, a scene that inspired bedlam across Germany. In contrast, when the Hungarian politburo officially agreed in October 1989 to dissolve the Communist Party and declare the country a republic, the red star atop the Hungarian parliament was extinguished without fanfare — no victory chants, not a single highlight-reel image.

The lack of drama belied some real anxieties. Having become accustomed to seeing their hopes dashed every time they were raised, most Hungarians had already marked their farewell to communism earlier that summer by holding not a party but a carefully choreographed funeral service. Two hundred fifty thousand people crowded into Budapest's statue-ringed Heroes' Square in June 1989 for a reburial ceremony for former Hungarian prime minister Imre Nagy, a supporter and symbol of the 1956 anti-Soviet uprising, who had been executed for his role. Attila was not among those present for the Nagy service. He was in a cemetery on the other side of the city. In order to help make his rent on the horse paddock, he had taken a second job as a gravedigger.

From Attila's vantage point at the bottom of a wormy pit, life was pretty good. He may have been six feet under, but at least it was Hungarian dirt. Most of the natives, however, were looking ahead with a combination of exhilaration and fear, as if a collective decision had been made to enter a Formula One race without ever having driven a car.

At the start line in March of 1990, when Hungary's first democratic elections in forty-five years were held, fifty-two political parties were on the ballot. The results were read on Hungarian television by sportscasters. While Czechoslovakia was rallying around the charismatic former playwright Václav Havel, and Poland behind the outspoken labor leader Lech Walesa, Hungary crossed its fingers as József Antall, a former medical science museum curator who emerged as the country's new prime minister, admitted he wasn't sure how or even if he could steer his country in the right direction. (Neither could he determine the time, as his watch had been swiped by Parliament guards prior to his inaugural address.) "Moses probably also had doubts, or he wouldn't have gone up the mountain for guidance," Antall said, not so reassuringly.

In this case, the mountain Antall intended to scale was across the Atlantic Ocean: America. The profligate United States was the standard to which all of former communist Eastern Europe aspired, that exalting country whose capital markets would shape global discourse in the millennium's final decade. "The prime criterion for anything," wrote Hungary's most prominent — and formerly dissident — writer, George Konrád, "is, How does it work in America?" In October 1990 Antall made a six-day trip to the States to find out. He met with former spy chief and then-president George H. W. Bush in Washington, former film star and president Ronald Reagan in Los Angeles, and, in New York City, business titan Jack Welch, whose General Electric Company would soon own a controlling stake in the Hungarian state electric concern. "We aspire to let the United States play a predominant role in making investments" in Hungary, Antall proclaimed during the visit.

Wish granted. By the end of 1990, more than a thousand U.S. companies had flooded into Hungary — among them Citicorp, General Motors, Price Waterhouse, US West, and Ralston Purina — to take advantage of the tax-free operating incentives and bargain-basement labor force. Australian media magnate Rupert Murdoch bit off two Hungarian periodicals (turning them into brassy tabloids), and British publisher Robert Maxwell helped himself to the former official communist state organ, *Magyar Hírlap*, intending to turn it into one of the country's first new legitimate journalistic endeavors. Despite being the smallest country in the region, Hungary found itself — by virtue of its location and its comparably developed infrastructure — the designated entry point for the biggest and most unscrupulous gold rush in years. Western boutiques such as Estée Lauder, Benetton, and the vaunted Levi Strauss were turning Váci Street, Budapest's downtown pedestrian shopping avenue, into Rodeo Drive minus the balmy weather, palm trees, and rich people. With the average Hungarian salary at $200 a month, the only humans in Hungary who could afford to shop on Váci were the tourists, members of the mushrooming expatriate population, or the select few natives connected to the former Communist Party who were bequeathed lucrative businesses formerly owned and operated by the Hungarian government. (Meet the new boss, same as the old boss.) Inflation quickly started to spiral upward, and much of the country began to feel about as under control as Attila's final, *pálinka*-fueled Zamboni ride.

Here was an idea. Hamstrung by the exorbitant foreign debt that had been acquired under communism, the new Hungarian government decided that "in the entrepreneurial spirit," it would begin renting out rooms in Parliament.

The closing of factories that had once manufactured products for the now-collapsing economies of the former Soviet bloc facilitated the arrival of some other capitalist by-products: unemployment and homelessness. The situation wasn't as bad as in places like Moscow (still in communism's final throes), where the streets were stocked with the destitute and the supermarket shelves stood bare. Average Hungarians still had food, but the longest lines at the Budapest butcher were for the cheapest cuts, chicken necks. In a place that had formerly provided its citizens with not just jobs and homes but health care, rigorous education, three years' paid maternity leave, and more sick days than a malingerer could misuse, a lot of people were feeling queasy.

The UTE gang read in the local sports pages about NHL hockey star Wayne Gretzky buying a new $3.2 million home in Beverly Hills, where he could be "closer to the stars." Meanwhile, the sloping,

wooded hills that rise up over Budapest from the west were being colo-
nized by Eastern Europe's nouveaux riches, who were building walled
compounds complete with landscaped gardens, moats, and airplane-
hangar garages in which to park their luxury sedans and sports cars.
Theirs was a class to which these professional athletes, and the vast
majority of their countrymen, weren't sure they would ever belong.
Most of the UTE players lived on top of one another in two-room
apartments in the gray cinder-block high-rise clusters that littered the
outskirts of the city. Twenty-five percent of the population, Attila
included, were living in poverty. Except for the overalls, T-shirt, and
sweater he rode in with, every piece of clothing Attila owned was a
hand-me-down. While Czechoslovakia's playwright president Václav
Havel was championing "living in truth," Attila was still living in his
teammates' underwear. He rolled up his pants four and five times so
they didn't drag along the ground and used a piece of string as a belt.
Other than the fact that they all had holes, none of his socks matched.

But there was some upside to the country's economic distress. As
state funding for sports was slashed to almost nothing, Hungary's best
sportsmen began heading westward in search of places where "payroll"
wasn't code for "manager's wallet." The ripple effect was not insub-
stantial. In April of 1990, for example, after two seasons as a janitor,
UTE employee Attila Ambrus was promoted to second-string goalie.

⁓

It would be a couple of years before Attila actually saw action in a real
game, but for the time being, it was enough for him just to see his name,
once synonymous with trouble in Transylvania, on the roster of one of
Hungary's most revered sports teams. And despite the player defec-
tions, the 1990–91 season was shaping up to be a good one, assuming
you were a fan of comedy, concussions, or the circus. The other way to
look at it was that the league had gone to hell.

One of UTE's informal assistant coaches was the father of the forward Gogi. "Old Gogi," as he was known, had done a coaching stint in
Moscow years earlier, and through his well-maintained connections
he'd managed to lure three former Soviet hockey stars out of retirement
to join UTE for the year. Among the theories proffered to explain why
in God's name these Russian icons would agree to add this asterisk to

their career stat lines were that Budapest was two or three degrees warmer than Moscow, that the goulash was tangier, and that Old Gogi was a KGB agent. Alexander Maltsev, Sergei Svetlov, and Valeri Vasiliev (aka "the Russian Bear") — who were so grizzled that they played without shoulder pads — quickly became known around the Hungarian hockey league as the "Three Musketeers." They burnished quite a different reputation in the UTE locker room as the incomprehensible geezers who hobbled around on bum knees and guzzled vodka from tall glasses before taking the ice.

There was another key addition to the roster that season: Transylvanians. Two of them, and they came knocking on Bóta's door together in the spring like a "guess what?" act. "Bubu," said one, reaching out a hand the size of Bóta's femur. "Karcsi," said the other in a voice like a chipmunk's.

Ceauşescu was dead. The previous December a Hungarian pastor had incited his western Transylvania congregation to take up arms against its oppressive dictator. The revolt quickly spread across the country, culminating in the capital, Bucharest, with a live, televised Christmas Day finale in which the "genius of the Carpathians" and his wife, Elena, were presented with bullets to their heads. It was the bloodiest of Eastern Europe's 1989 revolutions, resulting in an estimated several hundred dead. Afterward, thousands of Transylvanian Hungarians, including Bubu and Karcsi, came charging over the newly porous border into Hungary.

As it happened, Bubu and Karcsi were both from Csíkszereda, and Attila, despite being almost three years older and having lived outside the city for much of his teen years, knew their hockey reputations. With Attila's urging, Bóta reluctantly agreed to try out Bubu and Karcsi, hoping he wasn't going to wind up feeling obligated to add two more janitors to the roster. But as soon as he saw the new Transylvanians play, he realized they were the real things.

Károly "Karcsi" Antal skated around UTE's defensemen as if they were gates on a slalom ski course, and his finger-dislocating slapshot would soon make him one of Hungary's leading scorers. For his part, at six feet five and 280 pounds, Jenő "Bubu" Salamon earned the nickname *Gép Játékos*, or "player machine," because of his bionically heedless approach to the sport. The program listed Bubu as a defenseman, but not unlike Anna the cleaning woman, he was unburdened by titles —

or the rules. When Bubu wasn't sitting in the penalty box — which he did more than anyone in Hungary that year — he played his own game. Chasing after a tiny round disk was not of interest to him. He preferred instead to focus on a particular style of throttling that he had nearly perfected. The process, beginning with stick abuse and followed by gloved-hand combat, was perpetuated on the opposition as soon as the whistle blew and in the following order: best player to worst player. By the third period, Bubu expected to be well into the second line.

Bubu's value to UTE was inestimable. No one wanted even to imagine how pained they would have been if he had shown up on another team's doorstep first.

The three anachronistically accented Transylvanians became UTE's other indecipherable Three Musketeers. They were "cooked and boiled," as they said, presumably meaning "inseparable." Weekdays were all hockey and work, but on Saturday afternoons the Transylvanian trio moved into a back corner table of the Hoof and didn't leave until early morning. No orders needed to be placed: the waiters knew to bring *nyers hús,* or meat tartare, for Karcsi; *sokat,* or "a lot," for Bubu (he wasn't picky); *disznóláb kocsonya,* or pig's feet in aspic, for Attila; and an extra round of whole purple onions for the table. The three of them commiserated about days wasted in red kerchiefs trying to impress their group leaders in Ceauşescu's Communist Youth Association, the Boy Scouts for the blasphemed. Bubu told Attila how one of Csíkszereda's worst Securitate men — *persze,* of course, Attila remembered him — had been stomped to death during the revolution, right in front of the town jail, a building that each of them, it turned out, had once inhabited long enough to become proficient in the xylophone-like language of tapping on iron bars.

Attila regaled his new friends with childhood tales, such as the time he earned the dubious distinction of being the only person ever excommunicated from the small Catholic church that his entire village of Fitód hiked over the hill to attend every Sunday. He and two other boys had been assigned to guard the valuables in the church the day before Easter, which happened to be the same day that the country's only television channel was showing *Tarzan.* One of the village's homes had recently been equipped with a black-and-white television, so the boys agreed to guard the church in shifts so they could watch parts of the film. Attila drew the first shift and reported for duty. When his friends didn't return to relieve him, he was so angry and starving that he gobbled up the bulk of the church wafers, gulped down a bottle of wine, and then passed out on the dais, only to be discovered by the priest. Bubu and Karcsi pounded the table. *This guy.* They loved him.

When the plum *pálinka* started kicking in, it was time to sing "The Sparrow of Hargita." Who had an accordion? A cappella or accompanied by a willing diner with a harmonica handy, they croaked out the tune until they cleared the place, were too drunk to keep singing, or some combination thereof. Afterward Attila usually slept on the floor of Bubu's convenient new bachelor pad, the police dormitory near the stadium. Ceaușescu was gone, but Hungary's mistrust of anything Romanian wasn't.

Back at the hockey arena, UTE was struggling to get in playoff shape. Attila wasn't quite ready to see game action, but Pék and Bóta were intrigued by his development. Whether emboldened by his new Transylvanian confederacy or by two years of intense physical conditioning, the janitor now spent as much practice time screaming as he did suffering. If someone wasn't working hard enough, he got a mouthful from behind the face mask of Attila Ambrus. *How could you miss that play? Am I going to have to make it for you myself next time? That's your man!* Attila ended most practices bloody, bruised, or at least buckled from exhaustion. He became such a regular at the Interior Ministry hospital — chipped clavicles, eye gashes, dislocated fingers — that the staff finally just gave him a ministry ID so he didn't have to bother signing in each time.

But injuries and ailments notwithstanding, Attila was the only member of the team who never missed a practice. No one — neither the players nor the coaches, some of whom had played with the big boys in Russia — had ever seen someone as competitive. And despite his relatively diminutive size, Attila was the second-fastest player on the team after Bubu and possessed the quickest reflexes. But it was Attila's entertainment value, as much as his fanaticism and textbook goalkeeper lunacy, that endeared him to his teammates. Listening to Attila's entreaties to play poker in the sludge-gray cafeteria after practice, one might have thought he was offering free tickets to the moon. When someone asked him a question, he didn't just answer, he began by saying, "I'm going to tell you . . . ," as if his explanation were the start of an epic novel. More often it sounded like the stuff of fairy tale. A thick plume of smoke emanated from the roof of Attila's childhood home, which doubled as the village's pork smokehouse. And when his mother left the family, his father had retained custody of Attila by bribing the town judge with a pig.

By the time the season started, no one called the Zamboni driver Attila anymore. He was, from that point on, the "Chicky Panther" (*Csiki Párduc*), or just Panther for short, a reference to his roots in the Transylvanian mountain town of Csíkszereda and his catlike speed and reflexes. It would turn out to be an apt nickname. Like a cat, Attila Ambrus would have many lives.

Six

Professional sports had never paid much in Hungary, but under communism at least there were perks: government-approved sportsmen could get out of their military service, and if they were good enough to make the national team (as many of UTE's players were), they might return from international tournaments with only outpatient injuries and a suitcase stuffed with Levis and Marlboros to sell on the black market. Now, however, if they wanted to make a real buck, they had to find a second job. Pék was trying to make a go of opening a 24-hour convenience store; Bóta attempted to become Europe's shortest pimp. Some of the players printed T-shirts to sell at a lake; others started driving their cars as cabs.

If most of the team were part of the new lower-middle class of the emerging capitalist caste system, UTE's Transylvanian trio were lodged somewhere between classless and philistine. Before and after practice, for loose change, they washed and vacuumed their teammates' cruddy cars, cleaned the apartments where many of them still lived with their parents, and carried things around for them like bellhops. When the other players went out to the clubs at night, they never invited Bubu, Karcsi, or Attila to join.

The rejection both was and wasn't personal. A resentment of Transylvanians was brewing in Hungary as their sudden mass immigration and willingness to take jobs at lower pay was making already scarce jobs even tougher to come by. During practice, some of the players teasingly began to call Attila a *bozgor*, a nasty Romanian term for a homeless person. Unfailingly, this unleashed in the janitor a fury beyond his control. Regardless of the offender's body mass, the Chicky Panther would chase whoever it was, sometimes all the way into the locker room, and batter him until others could pull Attila off. Attila broke a few noses that way, including his own (again). And thus was revealed our young hero's Achilles' heel: the insinuation of irrelevance.

Attila always did his best to brush aside the hard feelings the following day, but his all-too-predictable reaction to the *bozgor* slight made it something of a parlor trick to send the unsuspecting Panther into instant paroxysm. Attila began detecting other slights as well. For instance, many of the UTE players were falling out of their chairs trying not to laugh when he, Karcsi, and Bubu argued in their antediluvian accents about the proper thickness for salami or how many times Ceauşescu shot a bear in Csíkszereda. To their teammates, they were a joke.

Though he tried not to let it show, Attila was crushed. In Romania he'd been nothing but a lowly Hungarian. Now finally *in Hungary,* he was living in a horse paddock with no hot water, was still waiting for Hungarian citizenship, and, at least by some measures, was nothing but a lowly Romanian. He didn't need his teammates' sympathy. He just needed their acceptance.

Attila had never cared about appearances before, but he became obsessed with winning the respect of his peers. He had his bowl-cut brown hair chopped into the popular military-style crew cut, stopped doing grunt work for his teammates, and the next time General Bereczky asked him in front of others to pick up the trash around the stadium, he quit his job as UTE's janitor, shouting, "I don't need to be your field hand!" at the highest-ranking Interior Ministry official he knew. It felt great, but when he turned to see his teammates slinking away from the scene, he was quickly reminded just how tenuous his entire existence was. Though he was too ashamed to admit it to anyone but Bubu, Attila was the only player on the UTE squad who wasn't paid a player salary. His only income had been from his custodial work.

One of the team's retired players, János Egri, who had become the announcer for the five or six UTE games per season that were broadcast by the country's only television station, witnessed the Zamboni-obliterating goalie's second, and potentially ruinous, confrontation with

General Bereczky. In his playing days, Egri, a slender argyle-sweater-wearing man of strategic action, had made a decent living doubling as Hungary's first television game-show host (for *Játék a Betűkkel!*, or Scrabble). He'd made his connections, and he felt sorry for Attila, who surely had none. True, the Chicky Panther was marginally insane, Egri thought, but he was a good egg. Egri talked the general down, then pulled Panther aside after practice a few days later.

There was a three-story apartment building he knew of in the south part of Buda that needed a live-in super, Egri told Attila. It was on the opposite end of the city from Újpest, an hour and a half each way to the hockey stadium — the tram and two subways. But it was a good neighborhood. Residential. And Attila could live there rent-free as long as he kept up the small grassy grounds, the eight-space parking lot, and the stairwells. "You could make it work," Egri said as they sat in the empty bleachers, watching the junior team practice. Attila had just one question, but it stumped the game-show host. "What do you mean, does it have hot water?" Egri replied.

It was time for Attila Ambrus to enter the modern age of plumbing.

The basement-level one-room apartment on Villányi Street that Egri found for Attila was a groundhog hole with parking compared with the gated palaces with moats that were going up in the undulating Buda hills just miles away to the north. But it came with — yes — hot water, a bathtub, a door without holes, and a ninety-year-old woman on the fourth floor who would provide an unexpected link to love and language lessons.

Margit, whom Attila quickly took to calling Ninny (a term of endearment he'd used before only with his aunt, also a Margit, back in Csíkszereda), had a thing for her new super ever since she saw him taking out the trash in a sweatsuit. He was polite, too. She asked if, for a small retainer, he would help her do her food shopping and walk her to the post office once a week so she could pay her bills. Attila saw her book-lined apartment, which featured not just Hungarian but English titles, and made her a deal. If she would teach him English and help him learn to speak Budapest Hungarian, he would even take her to get her wig done.

A few weeks later, on her own initiative, Ninny placed a personal ad on Attila's behalf in *The Express,* Budapest's free weekly classified newspaper: "Gentlemanly, smart, handsome young man, learning English, in search of a nice, well-educated girl." Attila didn't have a phone, so Ninny left her own number. The day after the paper came out, a woman named Judit Milos rang. Ninny listened to her details ("rich, blah, blah, rich, blah, English teacher"), then told Judit how lucky she was. Her ideal man would call her back shortly. Then Ninny buzzed the super.

As promised, Judit found Attila sweet, intelligent, and not the slightest bit arrogant for an athlete. Attila was smitten as well. Judit was twenty-six years old with short red hair and an excellent command of English, as Ninny had required. She had a few extra pounds in her thighs, and her breasts were a little big for Attila's taste, but she wore fox fur coats, was a graduate of Budapest's prestigious ELTE university, and was from a well-heeled family, the daughter of a construction engineer who also owned a confectionery factory he'd won in one of the government's privatization tenders. That could only mean Judit's father was important and connected, two things never before associated with his daughter's new boyfriend. Judit's family even had a small summer place at Lake Balaton, the Hungarian Hamptons, sixty miles southwest of the city. It was like a dream for Attila. Opportunity had finally come knocking on his life's door, and it would soon lead him to the top of a profession few (including Attila) knew existed.

Although his experience in the ways of wooing had so far been confined to chatting up Katalin about her family's electrical output from thirty feet up a wooden pole, Attila did his best not to blow his chances with Judit. On their dates he always remembered to bring flowers, as per the Hungarian tradition, whenever he saw her, which wasn't often, given the extra work he'd taken on in order to make enough cash to keep dating: Egri got Attila a third gig with his wife, an applied artist, and Attila spent months with her building an ornate glass chandelier, which was eventually hung in the supersize McDonald's adjacent to Budapest's biggest train depot, Nyugati Station. He also took jobs doing everything from walking dogs to selling Parker pens door-to-door to stocking shelves with Karcsi in a toy warehouse to working as a security guard at Hungary's National Savings Bank, OTP. He regularly toiled from 5:00 A.M. to 11:00 P.M. six days a week, with two hockey practices in between, then showed up exhausted on Sundays at Judit's apartment near the heart of downtown's construction-burdened

Deák Square business district. "I got you an electric knife," he would say; another week it was a tennis racket; another time, an afghan for her armchair. He liked Judit a lot, could maybe even love her if he could figure out what she wanted from him.

Between Judit, his half a dozen jobs, and his unsalaried hockey career, the last thing Attila needed was a letter like the one he received in November. His aunt and uncle, with whom he'd by then corresponded a couple of times, must have given his new address to his father, because there was a piece of mail in his box from Károly Ambrus. Károly hoped to visit for a long weekend and gave the date of his planned arrival in two weeks. For Attila, this was like receiving news that all the details had been arranged for his head to be squeezed in a vise.

Attila didn't know his father well, and he tried not to remember anything about him at all. Yes, Károly Ambrus had bribed the town judge with a pig to keep custody of his only son. But he'd also beaten Attila every time he got drunk, which as far as Attila could recall was something like always. He hadn't seen his father in years, but it was still his gruff *pálinka*-coated, Carpaţi-cigarette-burnished admonition that kept Attila awake at night: "You're going to die a gray nobody!"

Attila spent a week cleaning and preparing his apartment. He put all of his hockey team photos on display, borrowed some history and travel books from Ninny, and waited for his father's arrival. The stocky, hook-nosed Károly Ambrus had once commanded significant respect in the Hargita Mountain Valley for his job as one of the chief electricians charged with bringing electricity to that cold, dark corner of the world. When a graying, slower-moving version of that man showed up at the door, Attila shook his father's small hand. "*Apám,*" Attila said, using the formal word for *father,* "you're going to see the whole city. But before we go, I must inform you that it is not advisable in Budapest to mention Székelys" — the name of the particular tribe of Transylvanian Hungarians to which the Ambruses belonged — "or Erdély," Transylvania.

"I understand," said Károly, who had never been to Hungary.

Attila and Károly traveled the city by subway and tram. They went to the Royal Palace on Castle Hill above the Danube River, where until World War I the Hapsburgs spent their summers. They visited the seven-hundred-room Hungarian parliament, with its ludicrously unusable 12.4 miles of staircases and which, despite the fact that Hungarians

Ede Teller, Jenő Wigner, and Leó Szilárd had been among nuclear energy's pioneers, was still cooled in summers by ice blocks and fans. And they toured plenty of unimpressive museums whose ocher facades and arched mosaic-trimmed entranceways gleamed grime gray. At night Attila found some new *csárdás,* or traditional Hungarian restaurants, with the live Gypsy music both he and his father loved (and cots in the back for patrons unable to make the trip home). Attila did not introduce his father to Judit, or anyone else.

Károly could see from Attila's limited pocket change, ill-fitting clothing, and sparsely furnished apartment that although his son was making a mighty effort to appear otherwise, he was struggling to make a go of it in Hungary. He didn't expect Attila to admit it. If there was any trait he and his only child shared, it was hardheadedness. Károly could still remember Attila, bloody-nosed after he'd administered a good slapping, running back inside to yell at him, "I'm going to be somebody! You'll see! I'm going to be famous! I'll make you proud!"

Károly had plenty of his own memories to cry about: his wife, Klára, leaving him when Attila was a year old; finding his only brother's dead body a few months later on that electric pole where he'd sent him to work in a storm; eight years later his mother's untimely death from pneumonia, when Attila was nine. Károly had made a mess of things, no doubt, but he was getting older now and, in his own strained way, wanted to do something right. As hard as it was, he refrained from drinking during his stay with Attila, and on the night before he left, as he and Attila changed for bed, he asked his son to sit down because he had a surprise. "I want you to have my car," Károly said, referring to his Dacia, the Romanian equivalent of a Yugo, which he'd driven twelve hours over the mountains from Csíkszereda.

It was a generous and, in some ways, enticing offer. Though Attila didn't yet know how to drive, he desperately wanted a car. But he also knew that driving a Dacia was an unambiguous sign of two things: first, you were broke; and second, and perhaps even worse, you were a Romanian. Relishing the opportunity to strike back at his father with the only power he'd ever been granted, Attila refused. "In Hungary, that is not a car," he said.

That night, Károly and Attila lay awake in Attila's lumpy fold-out sofa bed, stubbornly passing Károly's last hours in Budapest in silence. When the first light glinted from the apartment's only window in the upper corner of the kitchen, Károly rose, collected his things, and left without saying good-bye. It seemed to both father and son a fitting end to a stilted trip and a stunted relationship.

When the Christmas holidays rolled around, Judit invited Attila on a ski vacation with her family to a resort they frequented in Zell am See, Austria, outside of Salzburg, near Hitler's famed Eagle's Nest. Attila had never been west of Hungary, or skiing for that matter, nor did he have a passport. But Egri came to his rescue again, spiriting Attila down to the Hungarian consulate and using his celebrity *Scrabble* influence to spell out "Give this guy a travel visa and skip the crap about the fourteen-day waiting period."

Attila had his reservations about the trip. He'd met Judit's parents a few times and, despite his efforts to appease them, was afraid they, too, thought of him as a *bozgor.* One night when he was having a steak dinner at their Budapest home, Judit's mother asked Attila why he wasn't eating much of the meat, to which he'd replied as delicately as possible that it wasn't his favorite type. "What do you know from meat?" Judit's mom had responded coldly. *Right,* thought Attila. As if he hadn't grown up in a smokehouse.

But the ski holiday turned out to be unexpectedly fruitful. The weather was so frigid and relentlessly overcast that hardly anyone wanted to go outside, so Attila spent most of the days with the mountain to himself. By the end of the first afternoon, he was almost able to make it down the piste without turning. At night, he collapsed in exhaustion, curling up with Judit in the backroom pub and ordering his beers by metric length in waist-high beakers. Above them on the walls like cave art were dozens of bear, deer, and ram skins.

The inn's owner was a heavy, ruddy-faced man named Hansi, who liked to chat with his guests about their day, their favorite Heffeweisen, or the type of hooker they would like for the evening. Hansi, whose family — like many of Austria's — had once lived in Hungarian-speaking regions before the post–World War I fire sale, spoke enough Hungarian to get by, and one night when Attila and Judit's family were eating dinner he stopped by their table. By Attila's deference to Judit's parents on the Budapest small talk, Hansi guessed that he wasn't part of the city clan. Hansi's curiosity was piqued, and before the group finished dessert, he was tableside again.

"So, where are you from?" he asked Attila.

"Transylvania," Attila replied, since Judit's parents already knew and he sensed something in Hansi's familiar peasant face and evident interest in him that seemed worthy of a powwow. Indeed, for the first time in Attila's life, his birthplace couldn't have been more auspicious. A short chuckle escaped Hansi's lips as he glanced distractedly around the room, then swooped his large head toward Attila's ear. "Can you get me some pelts?" he whispered in passable Hungarian.

Attila looked up at the fur-covered walls and racked his mind for whom he might go to for such a thing. He came up with nothing except a vision of himself flush with deutsche marks. "Why not?" he said, securing the first business deal that would change his life.

Seven

The apple red Opel Astra careened into the lot with a squeal. It slowed, then turned out again, making a tight loop around the parking area before pulling up next to the hollowed-out cement block that served as the stadium snack bar. A group of players — Bubu, Pék, Gábor Lantos, and some others — were enjoying a pre-practice feast of *zsíroskenyér,* or bread with fat, fifty forints, or three cents a slice, from the girl at the counter.

The Opel didn't look familiar, but the driver, the players soon noted with incredulity, did.

"Hello, boys," Attila said with a wide grin as he climbed out of the driver's seat. "Don't we have a practice to go to?"

There were a number of responses such a comment could have elicited. The one that surfaced came in the form of a question.

"What did you do, knock off a bank, Panther?" Bubu asked. Given that beneath Attila's sweats was most likely someone else's underwear, it didn't seem an unreasonable query. But by 1991, Budapest had become a place where the fortunes of even a disgraced Zamboni driver could change overnight. The privatization process — by which everything from factories to hotels was dealt away to the best-bankrolled or most-connected bidder — was making multimillionaires of former

apparatchiks. Minting was also available to anyone who had the sagac-
ity to recognize a demand without a supply — be it for bananas, girls,
leather, heroin, twentieth-century furniture and electronics, or maybe
even Transylvanian animal pelts.

The massive influx of Western capital had transformed Hungary
into a remarkably fertile business center — as well as a magnificent dreg
drain in continental Europe's big sink. Budapest was full of crooks.
Employment opportunities unheard of during the law-and-order days
of communism were springing up everywhere, particularly in wholesale
merchandising such as drug running, arms dealing, and car swiping.
Pimping and prostitution was also a growth sector. And if you could
make your cash here, you could launder it at any of the growing number of local banks conveniently unencumbered by any laws regulating
the previously nonexistent financial service industry.

Budapest's reinvigorated underworld and its fast-growing tentacles
were soon of enough concern to U.S. interests that each of the top
American law enforcement officers made official visits to the Hungarian
capital: CIA director William Webster, FBI director William Sessions,
U.S. Attorney General Richard Thornburgh, and Drug Enforcement
Agency director Robert Bonner all sampled the goulash. László Ton-
hauser, the unfortunate new head of Hungary's organized crime division, explained to them his untenable predicament. "If I start to take out
of circulation a couple of big entrepreneurs who are leaders of criminal
gangs, I will be labeled anti-entrepreneurial," he said.

But ideology crisis was only the beginning of the problems for the
Hungarian police. With the government wary of funding a police force
previously viewed as the right arm of an oppressive state, the Interior
Ministry, responsible for crime-fighting, was forced to subsidize its pal-
try budget by renting out its employees and sniffer dogs to private security companies. Some police precinct houses in Budapest couldn't
afford to pay for their electricity. There were only a few cars to go
around, and none of them were as fast as the ones speeding away from
crime scenes.

Rather than stay on for approximately $100 a month, many of the
more capable cops left the department for the private sector, leaving a
remarkable group of individuals in charge of stemming the country's un-
foreseen crime epidemic. The force was a farce. In 1990 alone, more than
a thousand of Hungary's cops were themselves arrested on corruption

charges. The rest of the newly hired gang were merely incompetent, overmatched, or miserable.

Lajos Varjú, a twenty-eight-year-old constable working the burgeoning pickpocket beat, would eventually, and somewhat unfairly, become famous for being all three. He was a short, thick, barrel-chested man with a black mustache, bushy eyebrows, and a shock of dark bangs that hung over his high forehead like a just-crashing wave. Though he laughed easily, Lajos was serious about his work and had the unpredictable intensity of someone who might perform an unexpectedly long Cossack dance at a wedding. In reality, he had no such physical abilities, but he was game enough to give anything a try. Why not? He'd grown up on a southern Hungarian horse farm, spent his post-high-school years hauling furniture around a warehouse, and after only a year in uniform was well on his way to becoming the highest-ranking detective in Budapest's robbery department. He didn't know how to be a cop, either.

But Lajos had learned a lot in a short time just from observing the scene that unfolded daily in the park beneath the window of his fifth-floor office in Budapest's downtown police headquarters. If you wanted bagmen who could collect unpaid loans, ferry prostitutes around town, or perform other sundry duties on short notice, you pulled your tinted-window vehicle up to the far side of the park in Erszébet Square, the 24-hour lawbreakers' mini-mart. This dynamic establishment was staffed primarily by members of the new and bedraggled Csíkszereda mafia, fresh out of Transylvania and seemingly oblivious to the fact that they'd set up shop on the police headquarters' front lawn. The group constituted one of the most unimpressive collections of small-time gangsters since Don Knotts and Tim Conway formed the Apple Dumpling Gang. Once, Lajos had to chase a guy he'd arrested earlier in the day back through the park, where the man was laboring to get away while still handcuffed to a metal bench he'd dragged out of the station house. Another arrestee was found by one of Lajos's colleagues suspended Spiderman-style inside the police building's heating ducts. The Erszébet Park gang was so bizarre that Lajos began calling the place Planet of the Zorg.

None of it was what Lajos had expected to encounter in law enforcement from watching dubbed *Columbo* reruns. But if he thought any of it seemed strange, it was only because he had no inkling just how absurd a career in Hungarian law enforcement could get.

⌒

The 850-mile pelt-smuggling route from eastern Transylvania to the Tyrolean mountains of Austria was fraught with potholed roads and corkscrew turns that would make even a donkey nauseous. Dominated by stretches of unlit two-lane streets clinging to cliff overhangs and dotted with the occasional Gypsy selling pumpkins or, not infrequently, themselves, the pelt smugglers' thruway was not to be confused with the autobahn. It was twenty-two hours of hell, done, in Attila's case, in one uninterrupted charge, alone, without music, and with the thick stench of rotting flesh emanating from the trunk.

Immediately upon returning from the ski trip to Hansi's lodge, Attila had begun plotting such a trip home to Transylvania to find pelts. For starters, he needed a visa. He also would require a car.

He had cobbled together enough money from his odd jobs and by borrowing from teammates to purchase a ten-year-old brown Russian Lada Samara for 100,000 forints ($1,400) from George Pék's father, who ran the garage at the Interior Ministry. It would be arranged so that someone would forget to remove the Interior Ministry license plates from the vehicle, giving Attila a premium insurance policy against being pulled over by kickback-hunting traffic cops. Lesser strategists might also have recommended he learn to drive. But when the Romanian consulate's approval for Attila's travel visa came through, our man opted to set off for points east before someone levied another processing fee. He figured he would learn to drive as he went.

The 450-mile ride to Csíkszereda took Attila ten hours, but not because he kept stalling at the traffic lights in Budapest. The big holdup was the line of horse carts moving like low-budget parade floats through the snowy mountain passes. When Attila finally got to his aunt and uncle's apartment, they were so overjoyed he'd returned that they let him gobble down his food standing up without bothering him with any questions. At his request, they hadn't told his father he was coming.

Csíkszereda didn't seem to Attila particularly different without Ceauşescu. There were no Securitate marching around, of course, but the place looked as gloomy as ever. Romania's economy was so bad that people were using their bank notes, or *lei*, as toilet paper, which they could no longer afford to buy. Just three streets away, Attila's father sat jobless and alone over an empty *pálinka* bottle in his dark third-floor apartment, indifferent that the room's only lightbulb had gone out hours earlier. Food was scarce and still strictly rationed. Attila's uncle — who was making an unlivable pittance operating a crane at construction sites — put victuals on the table thanks to handouts from farmer friends. Needless to say, Uncle László had an interest in helping his nephew get his smuggling career off the ground. It was one of his contacts who sent them, on a snow-dusted January day, north over the hills to Csángóföld, in search of "Uncle Béla," the pelt king.

Split by roaring rivers and shaped by jagged cliffs on one side and rolling fields on another, Csángóföld is the Transylvania of Transylvania. It is so remote and untouched that livestock rule the roads and avuncular pelt monarchs can take hours even for locals to find. As Attila and László rode through the winding boulder-strewn byways and past the creekside wooden shack villages, they spun off down auxiliary routes to avoid pig and sheep flocks and passed carriages full of peasants whose language they could barely understand.

The misturns and misunderstandings were to be expected. Much of Transylvania was so snow-saddled and inaccessible that over the centuries it had become, and has remained, something of a real-life Oz populated by little-known tribes: Saxons speaking German, Germans speaking Schwab, Gypsies speaking Roman (not to be confused with Romanian), Székelys speaking an ancient form of Hungarian, and Csángós speaking their own Hungarian-Romanian blend. To the rest of the world, they may as well have been vampires.

Attila and László had at least one thing in common with Béla the Csángó pelt king. They were each from one of the two primary tribes of Hungarians still living in Transylvania: Béla's Csángós, and the Székelys, from whom Attila and László descended. The similarities between the two groups, however, end there.

The Székelys are the only tribe of Hungarians that traces its lineage all the way back to Attila the Hun, who conquered the Carpathian basin nearly five hundred years before Árpád's ninth-century arrival. As the oldest known ancestors of the Hungarian people, the Székelys feel they played a special role in the country's history that is too often over-

looked. Imagine a Scotsman who is always carping about the unattrib-
uted inventions and contributions of his people (the kaleidoscope, the
bicycle, the decimal point, the television . . .). Multiply the Scot by a
factor of ten and feed him fifteen *pálinkas* at a bar in Tomorrowland.
That's a Hungarian (the Rubik's cube, 1956, nuclear fission, the carbu-
retor, the croissant . . .). Now consider that the Székelys are "the most
Hungarian of Hungarians," or a Hungarian squared. And it started
with a tough from the fifth century named Attila, who achieved such
renown that generations of Hungarian parents named their children
after him and generations of English-speaking people incorrectly assumed
that the Hungarian people are called the Hungarians after him. (*Hungarian* is actually derived from the Turkish word *onogur,* meaning ten
tribes, close enough to the seven that Chief Árpád united to form Hungary; the Hungarians call themselves Magyars, or, in English, Men.)
Even though Attila the Hun died a rather unglamorous death at forty-
seven by nosebleed, his fearless warrior reputation was passed on to the
Székelys and led to their all-important assignment by future Hungarian
kings as the country's border guards. In exchange for the Székelys'
courageous (and not altogether successful) service over several centuries
of war, the Székely tribe was accorded special rights, such as tax exemption and, not infrequently, early and gruesome death.

Battle losses in the thirteenth and sixteenth centuries to the Mongolian Tatars and the Ottoman Turks nearly led to the extermination of
the Székely nation, as the tribe was known. Then in 1764 the Hapsburgs
swept through Transylvania, killing thousands of Székelys in a bloody
nighttime attack. The remaining Székelys dispersed throughout the
Carpathian basin, founding towns with such imposing names as God
Help Us and God Receive Us. Along with folk music and woodcrafts,
the fabled warrior tribe soon developed a line of memorable tombstone
epitaphs, including "I'd rather be dead and lying down here than alive
like you standing up there."

After Transylvania was turned over to Romania in 1920, a move-
ment for Hungarian repatriation reignited Székely pride. A Székely
national anthem was written, and the entire eastern part of Transylvania, including Csíkszereda, became and is still known as Székelyföld,
or Székelyland. But the Székelys found they could only watch from the
intricately carved woodwork as Romanian history books were rewritten to show that the Székelys were descendants not of Attila the Hun

but of the early Romanians who had lived in the area in the second century, a view that supported Romania's claim to Transylvania. A pleading 1940 essay "The Székleys Are Magyars" is a mere hint at the tribe's desperation for recognition and Attila Ambrus's heartache at being called a Romanian even in Hungary.

The Csángós, on the other hand, had done everything in their power to remain hidden from the rest of the world. Few people, including the Csángós themselves, are positive of anything regarding their history, but the prevailing local wisdom is that they were originally Székelys who split from the tribe in the thirteenth century because of their unwillingness to fight against the Tatar invasion. Instead, they wandered away — or *csatangol*-ed — into the hills and forests beyond Székelyföld, where most of them now live in what has become known as Csángóföld.

After sliding through snow and dung for hours and inquiring discreetly in their best Székely-inflected Hungarian Csángó dialect at places like the Vadász (Hunter) Bar, Attila and László arrived at last to the base of a large hill in the middle of Nowhere, Nowhere. A small wooden house stood on the side of the road, in front of which was a tall, lithe man doing nothing. Attila and László got out of the car and cautiously approached.

"Are you Béla?" László asked.

"No," Béla said.

"But we were told you were Béla," Attila said.

"No," Béla said.

"Do you know Béla?" László said.

"No," Béla said.

"But you look like Béla," Attila said.

"No," Béla said.

"How would you know, if you don't know him?" Attila said.

"I said I don't know him," Béla said.

"We know," László said. "But how do you know what he looks like, then?"

"I don't," Béla said.

"Right, you already said that," Attila said.

"I did not," Béla said.

An ice-chilled wind was sucking away the day's last light. Attila turned the conversation to the pan-Transylvania-accepted topic of *pálinka,* a sip of which he sorely needed. As chance would have it, the Csángó in question was carrying a flaskful in his jacket pocket. They drank as darkness began threatening and the last of the day's hay-filled horse carts jerked over the bridge.

"Hello, Béla," two men yelled from the road.

After a minute, Béla looked at his Székely visitors. "What do you want?" he said.

"*Szőrme.*" Pelts.

Béla said nothing. He had recently returned from a freezing overnight excursion to his special spot in the woods. There, his regular three "chasers" had performed well, scaring an ark full of animals into the clearing over which Béla presided, rifle-sighted and ready, in a wooden fort built forty feet up a lone tree. Of course, it was illegal. But he was a damn good shot.

Béla turned and started walking toward the steep snow-covered hill, past the small house, through a fence, over the blackening field, and toward a red barn Attila and László hadn't noticed behind a shroud of spidery bare weeping ash. They followed.

Béla threw the latch, sucked in a chestful of air, and pushed open the gate. Almost half a century in the business, and he still wasn't used to the smell. Up and down both sides of the cavernous barn, hanging by their haunches on metal hooks, were about a dozen bears, wild boars, deer, rams, and badgers. It was like being backstage at *The Lion King.*

The size of the car was estimated, the price was negotiated, the handshakes were delivered, and one bearskin complete with head was salted and stuffed beneath some blankets into the Lada's little trunk.

⌒

A few months later Attila showed up at Uncle Béla's again, this time driving the UTE hockey van so that he could transport up to ten pelts, if Béla had them available. Attila bought bears for between 10,000 and 20,000 forints ($145 to $290), rams and boars for about 5,000 ($70), and deer for 3,500 ($50). He then turned around and sold them to Hansi in Austria at a 300 percent markup. Sometimes a single trip's profit, minus expenses, could be up to $1,600.

The drive was a haul, but Attila quickly discovered that delivering animal pelts across three borders had much more cachet than cleaning ice hockey rinks and digging graves. Except for the door-to-door Parker pen and paper sales, which he continued only occasionally and on his own schedule, Attila gave up his other jobs. He was around more for Judit, and he could afford to take her out to concerts (Rod Stewart: she loved it, he hated it) and shows (*Hair:* he loved, she hated). Attila didn't hide from her that he was an animal-pelt smuggler; he was proud to be part of the global economy. He was feeling happy and, finally, at home in Budapest, a once-dreary city that was exploding in Technicolor. Patches of the Danube riverbank were dressed and undressed in scaffolding as teams of authentic painters methodically converted the exhaust-stained apartment carcasses into desirable addresses decked in yellows, pinks, and blues. Big black Mercedes sedans and red Pontiac Firebirds cruised the serpentine streets, making the compact Zhigulis and Trabants look like an uncared-for set of collectible Matchbox cars. The old communist street names were X-ed out with red paint and new names placarded to the corners of the city's buildings. The former East German cultural center reopened as a Porsche dealership.

Money, once such a shameful symbol of Communist Party loyalty that it was enthusiastically renounced, now required flaunting in order to make the same important point: that obviously it was meaningless to you. The best way to illustrate this in Budapest circa the early 1990s was by pushing a stack of chips across a table at one of the sparkling new casinos, eleven of which opened to great fanfare in Budapest between 1991 and 1993. The grandeur of these wildly popular gambling halls, replete with marble colonnades and reflecting pools, was fit for ancient Rome, or at least modern Reno. One of the best-attended casinos, suitably named the Las Vegas, was opened by Sylvester Stallone and the Hungarian-born Hollywood film producer Andy Vajna (the Rambo movies, *Terminator 3, I Spy*) in the basement of the Hyatt hotel just off the Danube River. Over a three-month period in 1992, the Hungarian newspapers reported, the Las Vegas contributed more tax money to the Hungarian government than the entire metallurgy industry had in about a decade.

There were three types who frequented the casinos: foreigners (particularly the Americans, Western Europeans, and Chinese, all of whom were snapping up an inordinate percentage of Hungary's resources at bargain-basement prices); the nouveau riche Hungarian politicos and businessmen (who were well connected enough to steer whatever wealth was left in their direction); and the immaculately groomed gangsters, many of them Russians (who had more elaborate methods of making money and who moved from table to table like a buffalo herd under the protection of armed shepherds in sunglasses).

Attila, who was flush with pelt money, also became a casino regular, though he was hard to pigeonhole. The tuxedo-topped-and-lingerie-bottomed waitresses came to know him as UTE's Panther, who wore silk Italian suits and copious amounts of aftershave, liked his Johnnie Walker straight up, and always sat alone. Of course, they weren't fools. Anyone who could waste an evening pissing away a few hundred thousand forints (about $4,000) at the roulette table clearly couldn't be making a living as a professional athlete. But it didn't matter. All that was required to be accepted into this exclusive club was money — and Attila had it.

As UTE's 1991–92 season rolled around, it was becoming harder to ignore the grim realities of the Hungarian hockey league. This was partly because the NHL was now available on cable television in Hungary, and watching it for up to four seconds was enough to generate an epiphany that the Hungarian league was penniless, bereft of sponsors, devoid of all but a few quality players, and required fans to freeze their asses off outside on a metal bench in order to see live. If there was a bottom of the barrel, Hungarian hockey seemed to be occupying it.

Not surprisingly, the Three Vodka-Swilling Musketeers had staggered back to Moscow after helping carry UTE to a respectable but disappointing third-place finish the previous season. Even without them, however, the team was showing some promise, at least on the nights the schedule was accurate in its suggestion that a game would in fact take place. Advance ticket purchases were not advised. One contest was called off when the UTE Zamboni broke down and an attempt to tie towels to the back of a Trabant and drive it around the rink proved unsuccessful. Another game ended seven minutes into the second period when the lights at the UTE stadium went out. But the problems weren't only at UTE. A club out in the eastern Hungarian plains town of Jászberény had lucked into a sponsorship from the Swedish refrigerator company Electrolux (which had bought up the local factory) but announced midway through the season that it could no longer afford to cool its ice to playing temperature.

For the first time, team road trips on the red Ikarus buses with the vertical double-set headlights were more than just a cheap way for the players to loosen their teeth. They could also have their spirits destroyed simply by gazing out the vehicle's barely transparent windows at the omnipresent IKEA billboards along the road. On the left side of the ad was an image of Karl Marx's book *Das Kapital;* on the right, a photo of the IKEA catalog. At the bottom it read, "Which one will make your life more beautiful?" The real question was how IKEA expected to do any business when the cost of a couch, $450, was equal to three months of the average Hungarian's salary.

Theoretically, the UTE players were still being paid, though their weekly cash allotments were now distributed approximately monthly. All of them were hustling at least one other job to support themselves. Taxi driving wasn't proving to be the easiest buck; one debt-burdened cabbie some of the UTE guys knew drove to the front of Parliament, doused himself with gasoline, and burned himself to death. George Pék, the UTE captain, stuck with trying to make his 24-hour mini-mart profitable. Bubu found employment that occasionally obliged him to field phone calls at the stadium and sprint from practice yelling, "I have to take care of something quickly!" No one had time for card games after workouts anymore. Only Attila, who hung around in the UTE cafeteria, seemed to have any free time, pumping coins into the complex's new toy, a slot machine. "Watch this," he'd say as the guys passed through. "I won on the last one."

The players found Attila's bit about smuggling animal pelts amusing, but they didn't believe he could make any real money trading in dead animals. Most likely, Attila's teammates figured, the Chicky Panther had found a stable second career running guns or drugs like the others with flashy cars and name recognition at the casinos. It was a real party at the gambling halls to hear Attila tell it — free drinks, loose women — but in truth Attila could go whole nights there without speaking to a single person but the croupier. Judit didn't like to go, and sometimes when Attila returned home after a long night, pockets empty, he couldn't remember why he did.

Even though the shiny new Opel Attila drove made it clear that he was now in a higher income bracket than most of his teammates, Attila went out of his way to make sure they didn't begrudge him his new-found status. There was nothing more important to him than his UTE team, and to prove it, he began inciting his teammates to question his loyalty. What did they want him to do? Run ten laps? He'd run twenty. Buy drinks? Everyone in shouting distance of the bar had a round coming. A thousand leg-sits? Start counting. (Of course, after completing the last challenge, he had to take a few days off from practice, since he was too sore to stand.)

Attila's archmaniac on the squad was, perhaps unsurprisingly, his attention-starved Székely companion, Bubu. (Karcsi was now married and, though he continued to be among the league leaders in scoring, was generally considered too lazy to chew gum.) Attila and Bubu had a number of ludicrous, vomit-inducing physical duels, such as distance canoe racing during the UTE summer training camps at the Interior Ministry's Lake Balaton compound. But the two most famous contests between the Székelys took place in the fall of 1992 at the Atlantis pool hall, a dingy red-carpeted dive on an industrial boulevard lined with gas stations and fast-food restaurants. Both matches were well publicized around the hockey grounds by way of diatribes, epithets, and profanity-laced proclamations of billiard supremacy from the contestants. Standard eight ball was the game.

The first match (billed as a three-of-five, but ultimately amended to the strict Transylvanian-style fourteen-of-twenty-seven) was won by Attila. As soon as the final ball dropped, the small crowd pushed forward to watch Bubu begin serving out his impossible wager, a thousand push-ups. He was well into the four hundreds by some reports when his body froze like a crossing guard mannequin and he crashed to the floor on his side. By the time the ambulance arrived, Bubu's rigor mortis–like symptoms had worsened and he exited the Atlantis on a paramedic stretcher, arms extended toward the ceiling, screaming, "Please, quickly, I think I'm having a heart attack!"

As is often the case with billiards injuries, it was only a muscle tear. It was also great publicity for the rematch, which began a few weeks later after the Friday-morning practice session. Attila had also been to the hospital twice in the interim (sprained knee, chipped clavicle), so it was decided that the grudge match would be a gentleman's game: the wager was cash, which heightened the pressure on Bubu, since his life savings fit snugly into his left shoe.

The match would go on for three straight days. Attila kept the owner's palm full of thick tips to see to it that the Atlantis remained open through the night. The competitors ventured out of the hall's confines only for fresh air and slept on tables in separate corners of the building for a couple of hours each night. Both mornings Bubu was awakened by a pool stick to the gut.

"Is it true you've surrendered?" — Attila.

"Not likely." — Bubu.

By dinnertime on Sunday, Attila had polished off a few gallons of whiskey and purchased seven pool cues from the owner, the remnants of six of which were splintered and scattered around the hall. He was down 600,000 forints ($7,500), his TV, VCR, and stereo. "Double or nothing," he said.

Double was agreed to mean Attila's Opel, which had been illegally parked in front of the Atlantis's entrance for the past fifty-six hours. Some of the witnesses, who had been in and out all weekend, were summoned back for the final game. Girls were prohibited, Attila declared, to no objection from Judit, who had gotten bored and left after the first day of competition. (It was Bubu's girlfriend Attila found objectionable, whispering hexes on him each time he lined up a shot.)

Attila wouldn't even get to take a shot in the final game, however. Bubu ended it with one thunderous break, in which he either heroically sunk the eight ball, winning in extraordinary fashion, or tragically sunk not only the eight ball but also the cue ball, losing in extraordinary fashion. Both he and Attila simultaneously raised their arms in triumph as if they'd just picked a lock safeguarding a tunnel of meats, and began to sing the Székely anthem. ("Our ancestors crumble to dust through these wars of nations, as cliffs on rough seas. / The flood is upon us, oh, overwhelming us a hundredfold; Lord, don't let us lose Transylvania!")

After order was restored, the de facto judges at the Atlantis declared that the cue ball, which had dropped into a side pocket on Bubu's break, had done so because of a tap from Attila's hand. Though Attila would forever dispute the decision, Bubu was declared the victor. Graciously, he let Attila keep his Opel, but he waltzed out of the basement apartment on Villányi Street with the super's television, stereo system, VCR, and an IOU for a fistful of cash Attila didn't have.

Finding himself suddenly without financial prospects wasn't Attila's only problem. His glamorous high-flying life was a mirage. He was living from pelt delivery to pelt delivery, dead broke by the time of his bimonthly excursions to Csángóföld. Béla's prices were rising, and so were the costs of gas, Uncle László, Romanian prostitutes, Hungarian prostitutes, Hansi's prostitutes, Judit's pop concert tickets, and, worst of all, bribes for the border guards. Sometimes when he emptied his pockets at the bar, calling out for another round, he was spending his last forints. He was so self-conscious of the way his car looked that he had it washed every day even if it meant skipping dinner.

Perhaps worst of all, Attila had all but lost the thing that most defined him: his unpaid day job as UTE's backup goalie. UTE's hockey season had been going well enough that General Bereczky had decided he was going to do everything in his power to ensure that the team reclaimed the Hungarian championship. So, a call had been placed to Sergei "the Champ" Milnikov, the legendary anchor of the Soviet Union's 1988 Olympic gold medal–winning team, who agreed to fly in from Moscow in January to be UTE's starting goalie for the remainder of the season. Since so many foreign players had been imported into Hungary over the past few years, the league had instituted a team limit of three. No one had to tell Attila what that meant. Bubu, Karcsi, and the Champ would get to play in all the games. Attila, as long as his official papers listed him as a "temporary resident," would once again be relegated to practice goalie/cheerleader in just a few short weeks.

The outlook wasn't promising. But as Attila chewed over his hockey and pelt-smuggling tribulations, he realized there was one remedy that could cure both problems: citizenship. The real obstacle preventing him from profiting in his pelt business was the Romanian border guards. They kept jacking up their prices for safe passage — and given that on the outward-bound leg, he was carrying illegal goods and not carrying a passport, he had no choice but to empty his wallet. He'd been on the waiting list for citizenship for four years now. He needed a passport, pronto.

Having hung around with people from the Interior Ministry for the past few years, Attila had become a keen observer of the way things were dispensed with in Hungary. Whenever he got a speeding ticket, which was not infrequently, he went to the liquor store, bought two bottles of Finlandia and Jack Daniel's, and took them to General Bereczky's office. Bereczky, who at some point had decided he found his madcap goalie charming, always appreciated the possibility of being stutter-step smashed by 10 A.M. So, on Attila's days in need, he would show up at Bereczky's office around breakfast time, hand over the bottles with a wink, and wait while Bereczky put down his cigarette and picked up his "K" phone, for *közvetlen* (direct), which was wired into Interior Ministry headquarters. "In the matter of Attila Ambrus, ticket number [X]," the general would say, "why don't we just remove that page from the system." Then Bereczky, whom Attila now called Uncle Pista, would hang up, exclaim, "Okay, there's no speeding," and prepare for the toast.

But Uncle Pista didn't do passports. After searching his memory for someone he could reliably turn to on the delicate topic of citizenship subornment, Attila recalled that he'd given skating lessons about a year earlier to a girl whose father worked at the immigration office. When her dad had come to pick her up, Attila had made a point of introducing himself. Just before the New Year, Attila got the guy's number and phoned him up with his proposition. What he needed was citizenship papers and a passport, he said. That was a risky proposition, he was told. But for 100,000 forints ($1,300) it might be possible. "Done," Attila said.

Unfortunately, it wasn't going to be done easily. Aside from Bubu, Attila now owed both Pék and Gogolak for loaning him a couple of hundred thousand forints (a few thousand dollars) to get his car keys back from the Las Vegas Casino, which had been holding them as collateral for a miscalculation Attila had made on black 17 at the roulette wheel. Attila was going to have to make one more chancy trip to Béla without a passport. After UTE's 9–2 loss on Friday, January 15, there was a one-week spell between games during which time Milnikov would arrive in Budapest and Attila would take off for Transylvania. At the Thirsty Camel pub after the game, Attila managed to shake 50,000 forints ($650) out of two more teammates to fund the journey. "You'll have it back plus ten percent in a week," Attila promised them, sipping someone else's drink. And no, they didn't need a new fountain pen.

On Saturday afternoon Attila went to see the UTE groundskeeper. As per the usual agreement, he handed over 10,000 forints ($130) for the keys to the hockey van — bags, sticks, and helmets included, under which he would hide the pelts. He would leave late that night and have the van back before practice Monday morning.

After squaring away his transportation, Attila jumped back into his Opel, headed to the Margit Bridge, where he crossed into curvy Buda, and drove south toward the volcano-like Gellért Hill, behind which he lived. He was going to pick up Judit in an hour for dinner, then send her home in a taxi, ride back to the stadium for the van, and hit the pelt road. He had 40,000 forints ($520) in his pocket, thirty-eight hours to the next hockey practice, forty-one hours until he could sleep, and less than a week before he would make yet another career change.

For the moment, Attila Ambrus was still a nobody. Soon, he would be a legend.

second Period

Eight

Budapest
One week later
Friday, January 22, 1993

It wasn't pretty. Two hours before Sergei Milnikov's much-anticipated Hungarian hockey debut, his backup's backup, UTE's third-string goalie, Attila Ambrus, was holed up in the bathroom of his apartment, puking his guts out. An hour earlier he'd gone out dressed as a clown. That was the kind of week it had been. Nauseating and not that funny.

It started the previous Saturday night. Just as Attila was about to hit the pelt road to Transylvania, his Romanian border guard contact told him over the phone that neither he nor any of the other border guards with whom Attila had arrangements would be able to honor those accords any longer. They had all been fired in a huge scandal he would probably read about in the next day's papers, something to do with whether they shot a trucker because he was unwilling to pay the extortion surcharge or because he was reaching for a passport that in a certain light resembled a Tokarev 9mm.

It took a couple of days for the reality to set in. Attila's pelt career was over. So were his days as a Parker pen salesman, not that he would miss it; he hadn't been very motivated about hawking office supplies recently, but he'd liked to keep some merchandise in the car should he stumble upon someone in need of a tablet. But on Sunday someone had broken into his car and stolen everything. Now on top of his other

debts, he was out 50,000 forints' ($650) worth of frilly paper and foun-
tain pens, nearly the cost of replacing his shattered car window.

By the time Milnikov showed up at the UTE training facility on
Tuesday, it was difficult to say which UTE goalie was more miserable.
The Russian champ nearly broke down in tears when someone let slip
that the ragtag outdoor rink he was suffering through his first practice
on — in a poorly timed driving rain, no less — was the same "stadium"
where the team's games were played. Attila, meanwhile, was promising
to pummel anyone who found it a laff riot that he was yet again the
third-string goalie, behind Milnikov and the regular netminder, Gábor
Gézsi. After practice Milnikov went to sulk alone in one corner of the
locker room while Attila set up a receiving line in another as Pék, Gogolak, and a couple of other teammates all filtered by to remind him about
that borrowed money he didn't have. Oh, and that morning Attila
had received word that the deal for his citizenship papers had fallen
through; that his $1,300 wasn't going to be returned didn't require
explication.

The dilemma Attila faced on Wednesday was not for the restless or
ruminative: he could be piss-poor and potentially beaten bagman silly
by week's end or he could be stinking drunk in an hour. He chose judi-
ciously. As Bill Clinton of Hope, Arkansas, raised his right hand to a
Bible on the steps of the U.S. Capitol, Attila Ambrus of Csíkszereda,
Romania, resolutely foraged through a discount wig bin at Budapest's
4 Tigers Chinese flea market. He couldn't stop thinking about tomorrow, either. It would be quick and easy, he figured, pouring himself
another whiskey back at his apartment. He was going to rob the post
office down the street, the same place he'd taken Ninny from upstairs at
least a dozen times before she'd died the previous October. Everyone in
Hungary paid his bills at the post office, cash only. And a lot of people
kept accounts there, like at a bank. But there was no security guard, no
camera, and little chance of a working alarm system. He would enter in
disguise, wave around the fake gun he'd just bought at the flea market,
ask for the money, then walk — not run — out the front door, hail a
cab, and go home.

When he woke up, spinning, the following morning — Thursday —
Attila was excruciatingly unable to formulate any better ideas about
how to recoup the money he needed to pay his debts by the Saturday
deadline. And after a grueling workout session — aside from having to

face a roster full of creditors, Bubu kept pestering Attila to challenge Milnikov to a goalies' leg-sit duel — Attila went straight home and started drinking again.

It wasn't as if he'd never stolen anything before, though he'd assumed when he got to Hungary that those days were over. But if he'd been wrong, which he was now willing to consider, he had to be right about this: he could never be caught again. He could still smell that musty Csíkszereda basement slammer where he was treated to an almost daily beating with a police baton and a few stomach-turning trips down a hill stuffed inside a wooden wheel. And on his left arm, he carried an eight-inch scar from an incident at the juvenile detention facility that he had blocked from his memory.

Attila spread a piece of paper across his writing table. On it, he drew a map of the neighborhood and then a detailed diagram of the post office, a small linoleum-floored room with three glass-encased teller windows built in solid molded wood. From the street schematic, he determined the best escape method to be a stroll down the block and into the tunnel where the no. 61 tram stopped on its way to the westernmost hub in Buda on the M2 subway line, Déli station.

His stomach hurt. He sat down on the pullout bed he hadn't folded up since the previous week. There wasn't any hockey practice in the morning because tomorrow was a game day, so he had all night to get in the mood. He wasn't sure if he could go through with it. But as the evening wore on and the bottle of whiskey drained, his fears receded along with his thoughts of Judit, and his mind settled on a simple, sensible idea: the money sitting in that post office wasn't the government's money, it was the people's money. *Our money.* The politicos had had more than their fair share. And as long as Attila didn't hurt anyone in the process, he reasoned, the only harm that could come from his grabbing a piece was if he was caught doing so. Where the hell was that map? He picked up a red Parker stylograph and drew a dotted line marking his preferred escape route.

The only mirror in Attila's studio apartment was in the bathroom, down a hallway from the small, square living quarters. He spent the next several hours spinning around the corner of the hall with the toy pistol in his right hand, saying, "Freeze!" to his reflection. It was his Travis Bickle "You talkin' to me?" moment, if slightly less convincing. At the flea market, Attila had bought dress shoes three sizes too big in case the police checked for footprints, and half the time he twirled around the hall toward the mirror he tripped and fell into the wall before he could spit out his line.

It was morning already when he hatched the notion of shaving his normally scruffy face and leaving only a mustache, which he darkened with some mascara Judit had left in his bathroom. God, he thought, taking a look at himself after rosying his cheeks with her rouge and lipstick, what time *was* it? He still had to do his hair. He yanked the shade off his desk lamp and set it on the bed. Then he grabbed a long, curly brown-haired wig and threw it over the shade. He poured himself another drink, pulled his chair up to the bed, and, with a tube of gel he'd bought at the market and a pair of scissors he'd appropriated from a kitchen drawer, began styling.

Fortunately, he'd bought more than one wig.

Attila startled awake and looked at his digital alarm clock: 3:30. In half an hour, the post office would close for the weekend. He jumped up and began trying to pull on his pants, then misbuttoning and rebuttoning his shirt. He could never tell what kind of weather it was outside because his basement apartment had only one small window way up in the top corner of the kitchen. He selected an all-purpose black raincoat from his nearly bare wardrobe, then stepped to the front door and craned his unrecognizable head into the hallway to make sure no one was on his way down the stairs in search of a screwdriver. Fortunately, the coast was clear, because — as he soon realized — the shoulder-length straight brown wig he'd fallen asleep in was now jutting out on one side like a Mohawk. A comb-thru proved useless. Irritated, he stomped back to the freestanding closet, fished out a bright red ski hat with floppy ears and a pointy top, and yanked it down over the wig.

Outside, it was Romanian-childhood overcast and UTE-bleacher cold. The boulevard gurgled with slow-moving vehicles; the sidewalks hiccupped with winter-wrapped citizens — some carrying sacks of groceries with which to cook a warm, paprika-spiced dinner, others the knowing smile of someone about to trade his layers for a waist-tied genital apron and let his ass hang out at the nearby Gellért or Rudas bathhouse. Then there was Attila, cursing himself for drinking so much, as he stumbled down the street on his way to knock off the post office.

His intended target was on the east side of the wide boulevard, about ten blocks north of his apartment, nestled between an interior-lighting shop and an ABC supermarket in a row of one- and two-level storefronts. Attila slowed as he approached the post office to get a good look through the glass door at how many customers were inside. Then he walked quickly to the corner, where he stopped, turned, and began counting patrons as they went in and out. Time, he could only assume, was limited; he'd forgotten his watch. Just when the customers appeared to have vacated the premises, he received a good sign. The post office's only male employee stepped outside without a coat and hurried into the crowded butcher shop farther up the block.

Attila had to will his legs to move. His oversize shoes felt like heavy clogs. Even with two pairs of thick socks, he felt every slap his loafers made on the cold, hard cement. Finally he reached the post office and tried to push open the door. But it wouldn't move more than a few inches.

"Sorry," came a woman's voice from the other side. "We're closed."

He looked up. It was Mrs. Geromos, the woman who'd sold him lottery tickets and had helped Ninny fill out her payment receipts and forms.

"But I have to mail this letter to my girlfriend today," Attila pleaded, hoping she wouldn't recognize his voice.

"Sorry, you'll have to come back on Monday," she said, giving the slightly ajar door another nudge.

Attila shoved his foot between the door and the frame. Mrs. Geromos was starting to object when he followed it with his shoulder, busting the door open and knocking her back into the room. "Freeze," Attila said, stepping inside, but the gun was so small that he couldn't find it in his pocket. Finally his fingers settled on the utensil, and he pulled it out and thrust it into the air. "This is an armed robbery!" he declared, half expecting to hear the opening beats of a well-paced musical score.

Mrs. Geromos looked more annoyed than afraid. Institutional robbery didn't happen very often in Hungary. And whatever this guy with the schoolyard ski hat and toy gun thought he was doing, he was making her late for her weekend. Attila, bowing his head so Mrs. Geromos wouldn't recognize the parts of his thickly made-up face not covered by his hat and earflaps, motioned for her to go around through the wooden half door to the back. He followed, high-stepping so as not to trip over his shoes again.

There was only one other employee in the office, and by the time Attila got around to the other side of the counter, she was hiding under her desk. "Why are you doing this?" the voice asked when the feet appeared at her station.

Was there a silent alarm? Was she stalling? "Shut up," Attila said. "Please."

He pulled a yellow and blue duffel bag with the Joe Camel insignia emblazoned on the side out of his other coat pocket and began rummaging through the cash drawers. A lot of small bills and worthless coins. When he finished with the drawers, he asked, "Where's the safe?" since that's what they did in the movies.

The woman pointed at a small steel box on the floor the size of a Bundt cake. He nodded. She opened it. Empty.

It suddenly felt like a month since he'd knocked Mrs. Geromos over with the door. Perhaps he should go. "Don't move," he yelled, backing up with his two-dollar cap gun raised. He returned to the front and let himself out into the cold air, then pulled the glass door closed behind him. A combination lock was produced from his pants pocket, and he bolted the door shut as if he were an employee. *Just walk,* he told himself. He got about ten steps down the sidewalk when he heard a window slide open and two women's voices scream, "Robber! Robber! Catch him!" That did it. Attila took off like the Chicky Panther toward the train station tunnel, where he chucked the wig and hat into a trash can and, still running, eliminated most of his mustache with a disposable Gillette and saliva. He kept up his sprint past the station's oven-warm bakery, an overstuffed antique-book store, and back through the wintery apartment-lined residential side streets to his building, where he bounded inside his flat and promptly puked.

For the first time, the Whiskey Robber had struck.

⌒

Attila's three minutes of work in the post office netted him 548,000 forints (or about $5,900). And even though he'd been sick afterward, he'd made it to the stadium in time to watch Milnikov's victorious 4–2 debut over Alba Volán from the bench. He'd even joined the team at the smoke-filled Thirsty Camel afterward, where he had bought the second, third, and fourth rounds. He couldn't help himself. He was ecstatic — perhaps too much so, he worried on his way home. But despite his pronounced upward mood swing, none of his teammates seemed to have the slightest idea that anything was amiss with their third-string goalie. To them the Chicky Panther was bananas. Nothing to see here.

With the proceeds from the robbery, Attila paid off his debts, repaired his broken car window, and surprised Judit, who had recently complained about her billowing thighs and ass, by offering to pay for liposuction. Attila also got Bubu, who was now in catastrophic debt himself, to accept Attila's offer to buy back his TV, stereo, and VCR at a quarter of their value. With all the suspicious money spinning around, Attila's brief bout of solvency was hardly newsworthy — even, unfortunately, to him. Except for the fact that he got his tenuous existence back in order, almost nothing changed for Attila. Over the next few weeks, Milnikov helped UTE to a decent 18–8–2 record, but the team was once again eliminated in the semifinals of the national championship series. And when the season ended, Attila found himself in a familiar place. He was almost broke.

In the mornings he drove up to UTE for weight training and conditioning workouts, which were now run by his friend George Pék, who had taken over the coaching duties while General Bereczky tried to shake some money out of the Interior Ministry to hire a new coach. The rest of Attila's days were free, and he wasn't sure what to do with them. He and Karcsi kicked around ideas for starting a videotape rental, car importation, or furniture-repair business. Bubu wasn't around much; it seemed he was always taking care of something quickly. Sometimes, if the team manager Gustáv Bóta invited him, Attila went to play tennis at the Interior Ministry club, where he envisioned one day being not only a member but the reigning club champion. Already, in only his first year playing, he'd become one of the club's best players.

During the evenings Judit wasn't tutoring English, she and Attila went to the movies with her friends — lawyers and business professionals with regular paychecks and a command of English, who seemed to Attila knowledgeable about everything. Occasionally they even took him along to the "American night" cocktail parties sponsored by the U.S. companies at the ritzy foreign-owned downtown hotels. One time at the Hyatt, Attila won the top prize (a six-course dinner for two) in a Hungarian sports trivia contest. But no one seemed interested in networking with a Transylvanian hockey goalie. Attila knew he wasn't like them, but he kept dressing in suits and spending his money as if pretending for long enough might make it so. He began reading the newspapers and promised Judit, who still thought his pelt business was thriving, a trip to an exotic surprise location. Anywhere sounded good to him; he'd never been on a plane before.

On the nights Attila didn't stay at Judit's, he whiled away his insomnia in his sparkling red Opel, acquiring another kind of education. Budapest's narrow downtown streets thumped with hypnotic bass beats emanating from basement-level techno clubs. At traffic lights, vendors stood draped head to toe not with newspapers but with every variety of porn publication imaginable. Outside the neon-lit casinos near the Hungarian Science Academy, women in unbuttoned black mink coats over bikinis handed out drink tickets for the establishments whose call Attila could avoid only by staying inside his car.

Some nights Attila would turn a familiar corner and find himself on a street he'd swear he'd never seen. Stereo and discount-furniture stores that had opened only months earlier were zapped and reopened as computer and imported leather joints the next. Ferenc Liszt Square, famous for its cafés, now had another claim to fame: across the street stood the world's largest Burger King.

The traditional, intellectual Eastern European cultural scene — opera, classical music, folk dance, art film, satirical theater — was supplanted by new movie theaters showing foreign films such as *The Untouchables* and the bank heist thriller *Point Break*. Some started referring to the changes Hungary was undergoing as the *amerikanizácioa* or Americanization, as if it were a state of consciousness that had been intravenously introduced. As with a Happy Meal or a Peanut Buster Parfait, most people knew it wasn't good for them, but it also wasn't easy to turn down when dangled in front of their faces.

Meanwhile, day by day, protective fences and security cameras were being installed around buildings and warehouses. In the first five months of his tenure, the new Budapest police chief had his car stolen. Twice. Hungary's suicide and alcoholism rates soared. Among those who took their own lives in 1993 were twelve of the thousands who had been lured into a failed Ponzi scheme to raise and sell ringworms.

Disillusionment with capitalism's side effects was hardly unique to Hungary. The former Soviet republic of Ukraine, which abuts northeast Hungary, watched inflation hit 10,000 percent in 1993. The cost of a loaf of bread sometimes doubled from one day to the next. In Poland, which like Hungary was offered up by Western pundits as a model of democratic transition, a group of protesters marched on the U.S. embassy in Warsaw with signs reading, "We are gradually becoming Los Angeles blacks, living in poverty among luxurious hotels and shining supermarkets." Yet the highest measured level of discontent in the first several years of the postcommunist era was not among the Ukrainians, the Poles, the Russians, or the Romanians. It was in Hungary, purportedly the most progressive country of them all, where by 1992, more than 40 percent of the population concluded that they preferred communism to the so-called free market capitalism that they were, according to the Western press, enjoying.

Attila had never thought of himself as a politically minded person. But it was hard not to wonder what the $2 billion of U.S. corporate investment in Hungary, which the Hungarian government had touted as a triumph for its people, had done for him besides presenting the opportunity to bet the house on a round of roulette. In the neighborhood near the Las Vegas Casino, where Attila got his Opel waxed, the local mayor backed a foreign company's $1.2 billion proposal to build an office tower with luxury shops and apartments that required knocking down part of the historic old Jewish Quarter and displacing thousands of people. "Why sell to foreign interests?" complained one resident at a raucous town hall meeting on the issue. "Local entrepreneurs should be given a fair chance." Half of Attila's teammates had resorted to setting up fictional international businesses just to get the tax breaks offered to foreign companies.

To make matters worse, Hungary's privatization process was beginning to look more like a crash course in cronyism and money laundering than an equal opportunity method of redistributing state-owned holdings into public hands. Valuable buildings and companies formerly owned by the communist state were being bestowed (for little or even nothing) on the ruling political party and its allies, after which they were sold for hundreds of millions of dollars — to yet another branch of the government. With that as the new prototype, some Hungarians began referring to the postcommunist era as *szabad rablás,* or "free robbery." It was a term that had last been used in Hungary at the end of World War II to describe the Nazis' pillaging of Budapest before the Russians chased them away. The gravity of those final bloody days of the war was far greater than the sinister but somehow weightless aura of nascent capitalism. But there was one distinct similarity: it was every man for himself. And that was a sentiment with which Attila Ambrus had always identified.

During one of Attila's late-evening/early-morning drives, a building on Hűvösvölgyi Street up in the northern part of the city suddenly jumped out at him. It was an interesting edifice, he thought, and not only because it was a post office and he was veering into debt. It was also because the structure was located on the opposite side of the district from the police precinct station, a distance he discovered required three minutes and twelve seconds to cover going eighty miles per hour at 3:00 A.M. During heavy traffic times, it would take at least twice that long. Plus, when he popped in for a look at the place during business hours, twice, he saw only female employees, whom he imagined would be less fussy about unorthodox requests for withdrawal. This robbery business wasn't going to be a regular thing, Attila rationalized; he just needed to get back on track so he and Karcsi could get their legitimate endeavors up and running. And his last gig had been so easy. He'd really have to screw up to get caught.

Nine

Police Headquarters
Budapest
March 14, 1993

Major Lajos Varjú's morning walk through the halls of the Budapest police headquarters — that is, when he didn't wake up on the torn-up couch in his office — was like going through a surround-sound exhibit of modern Hungary. Up and down the main corridor, leading from the employees' side entrance to the elevator, were the previous night's roundups, scuffed-up, stinking, and handcuffed to anything nailed down. Hungary had the highest incarceration rate in Europe, as anyone who followed the Great Paprika Scare might deduce: when lead was discovered in a batch of paprika powder (a staple of the Hungarian diet), fifty-nine vegetable vendors were arrested with remarkable alacrity, thirty-nine of whom were prosecuted for a cornucopia of crimes that had nothing to do with the lead poisoning. Not surprisingly, human-rights advocates were taking a renewed interest in the Hungarian judicial system.

Between 1991 and 1993, several hundred Hungarian cops were charged with crimes ranging from accepting bribes to running drug smuggling rings. The country's second-highest ranking police official, General László Valenta, earned from his colleagues the nickname "The 12 Percent," for the amount he was said to expect funneled into his pocket from every car, equipment, and construction contract he negotiated on behalf of the police department. And the Budapest police chief was reprimanded for "violating secret internal regulations" by the national police chief, who would himself soon be suspected by coworkers and the media of having ties to what had suddenly become Europe's most volatile mafia scene.

Hired in 1989, during Hungary's retooling of its communist police department, Lajos Varjú had been around just long enough to be accepted by the remains of the old guard and not quite long enough to be fired by the new guard. He was outstanding in that he actually cared about fighting crime and, on occasion, could make his thirteen-man robbery squad believe it was capable of doing so.

Lajos was what some in Eastern Europe might have called a cop's cop in the same way that those in professional sports describe certain coaches as players' coaches. Which is to say he loved to drink. Boxes of Gosser beer were kept under his desk. Some days on break, his whole team would fill a flask with whiskey and go down to the McDonald's on the corner to see how many drinks they could put down over Big Macs and fries. (The record was fifteen shots and three beers.)

The robbery department offices consisted of a ramshackle two-room command post decorated with a couple of desks, wooden chairs, a threadbare dark brown couch, and, taped to one wall, a rogues' gallery of photographs and case files that Lajos's team had little chance of solving. By American standards, it was News of the Weird fodder: a guy ripping off his mother's Herend porcelain elephant, a gang of Gypsies smuggling restaurant napkins. Armed robbery was still rare, though in the past two months there had been two such incidents involving post offices. The second had occurred the previous afternoon.

On every day but Sunday, Lajos held his group meetings at eight o'clock. On this Saturday, as usual, there was no one there to listen to him, so Lajos's assembly took place only as an interior monologue. He slumped back in his chair and looked out at Planet of the Zorg, now crowned by an insistent royal blue TDK sign atop the nineteenth-century former City Hall.

Around 8:30 Lajos's men began to file in. There was Zoli, who was as big as a communist statue but ran on sight of a Chihuahua and was pass-out drunk after a single shot. Lajos Seres, the team's crack crime analyst, was known as "Dance Instructor" because he taught ballet in his spare time and occasionally showed up for his police work in a tuxedo and top hat. "Bigfoot" was six feet seven and had kicks so big that he moved as swiftly and efficiently as an Ikarus bus. And then there was Lajos's loyal stumplike sidekick, five feet three Tibor Vági, who had an unparalleled gift for rendering police cars utterly unusable, often through the misapplication of the gas pedal or emergency brake, and thus went by *Egy Rakás Seggfej,* or Mound of Asshead.

Among the thirteen of them, they had less than twenty years of police experience, three going on fewer squad cars, four guns, and six Polaroid cartridges to last them another twelve months of crime scenes. The pay? Twelve thousand forints ($130) per month, about half a buck an hour. Some of Lajos's charges kept pigs and chickens in the countryside to supplement their supper tables.

By 8:45 Lajos's men were fighting over chairs and spilling their coffee, half of them bogarting cigarettes, the other half complaining about the smoke. These were the usual signs that a meeting would soon come to order.

"The next one to talk is going to be the doorman tomorrow," Lajos said, prompting a break in the action.

"Lali, do you have a cigarette?" Bigfoot asked.

"No, I don't have a cigarette," Lajos said. "Mound just took my last one."

"Yeah," Dance Instructor said. "Why don't you get it from him? Or would it be too difficult for you to catch him?"

"Let's go," Lajos said. "What does everyone have today?"

The room went silent.

"Does somebody want to tell me what's going on?" Lajos said.

"Have you read the papers?" Zoli asked.

"I was here until two in the morning with this robbery," Lajos said. "I didn't have time to browse the news."

Someone handed up a copy of the popular tabloid *Kurír,* and the group braced for Lajos's reaction.

At the top of page three was the headline:

NO TROUBLE, IT'S A BANK ROBBERY

"What should a well-situated gentleman do in the early afternoon on a Friday," the article began. "Naturally, he will supplement his monthly payments with a little private work."

Lajos didn't have to read any further. The country's cynicism had been ballooning, and with elections only a year away, the government had hired the American public relations firm Hill & Knowlton to try to repair its negative image. Unless his gang tripped over a clue quickly, Lajos would have to find something important to do outside the office on Monday morning when the police chief held his weekly department head meeting. The brass would not tolerate any bad press like this.

Lajos didn't get mad often, but when he did, he transformed the fifth floor of HQ into a well-lit haunted house: doors slammed shut and a domino chain of screams went off up and down the hall. Fortunately, it was Saturday and the only souls Lajos could incite were sitting in front of his face. He threw the newspaper down and stood up. "I want everyone on this case — now!" he shrieked. "I want this guy caught today!"

All thirteen of Lajos's men descended like cops on the post office site at Hűvösvölgyi, in the western part of Buda, where the robbery had taken place. The office's employees were summoned and reinterviewed. The thief had apparently come by taxi, during rush hour, and entered in sunglasses just before the office closed. He'd bought a lottery ticket and filled it out at the counter, apparently waiting until the other customers cleared out. Then he produced what one employee said appeared to be a gun from his coat pocket and shouted, "It's a robbery! Everyone in the back. Chop chop."

Lajos compared the description of the perpetrator from this robbery with that of the one two months earlier at Villányi Street. The thief was described as "good looking," "athletic," "agile," "disciplined," "didn't waste any movements," "obviously wearing a wig," and, oddly, "polite." Most significantly, Lajos noted, witnesses from the Hűvösvölgyi job said the man had gotten into the back by leaping up and grabbing the six-foot-high glass teller booth partition and hurtling himself over it like some kind of poleless Olympic vaulter.

Lajos had a hunch. There was a military barracks down the block from the Hűvösvölgyi Street post office that housed about fifty Hungarian servicemen. Lajos wanted them all checked out. Sure enough, one of them had failed to show up for work the previous day. His picture was collected and shown to the post office employees. "It's him," one of them affirmed. By nightfall, Csaba Bencík, a Hungarian border guard, was in custody.

After reading his excellent review in *Kurír,* Attila got up off the bench next to his favorite newsstand and walked down to a travel agency near his apartment. It was time to book his first overseas trip. He could afford it. His three minutes of work at the post office had netted him 667,000 forints (or about $7,200), and now he was finally going to take Judit somewhere dreamy. The travel agent recommended the beautiful country of Tunisia. She had a special deluxe package for two she could offer. "Sold," Attila said.

Since he still didn't have a passport, Attila got Egri to take him down to the visa office again. A week later he and Judit were flying to North Africa, an experience Attila found ill-defined by the movies he'd seen. His aircraft was in dire need of a paint job and reupholstering, and the stewardesses all had runs in their nylons. Attila felt sorry for them. Malév Hungarian Airlines, he thought, must be the Dacia of the sky. He chatted up the flight attendants and tipped them well after every drink order — the people's money circulating back through the people's hands.

As for Tunisia, the ruins of Carthage were breathtaking. But so was the stench emanating from the city and the hellhole of a hotel he'd been swindled into believing was a deluxe accommodation. The bed was Flintstones hard, there was no TV, and the buffet food was inedible even to a fan of pig's feet. Judit, who looked better than ever thanks to the thigh and butt work Attila had paid for, was aghast. After the second night, Attila paid to move them to the nicest hotel in the city, right on the beach, but even that was humiliating because he had to ask Judit to make the arrangements since he didn't speak French, Arabic, or English. They played some tennis and went swimming in the ocean, but it wasn't the romantic excursion he had envisioned. By the time they returned, Attila was more insecure about his relationship with Judit than ever. And, once again, he was almost broke.

On his daily drive to the off-season training sessions at UTE, he began to notice a Budapest Tours travel agency, conveniently situated on a corner not far from the Újpest subway stop. He was still fuming about the Tunisia trip — and the travel agent who had clearly assumed he wouldn't know the difference between deluxe and decrepit. After UTE's morning weights session on May 3, Attila decided to stop in at the travel agency to inquire about trips to, say, Croatia. The only employee, a Ms. Csépai, handed him some predictably lovely brochures. "Thank you," Attila said. "I'll come back later after I talk to my girlfriend."

He left to make a few diagrams and returned a couple of hours later, unrecognizable as the customer who'd been in that morning. Another chump was in the midst of forking over a wad of cash — credit cards were still almost nonexistent in Hungary at the time — so Attila took a seat in an armchair and waited for him to leave. Once he did, Attila stood, pointed his little gun at Ms. Csépai, and more than evened his score with the travel industry. He left with 1.166 million forints ($12,500).

"You asked to see us," Mound of Asshead said, entering Lajos Varjú's office with Zoli, Dance Instructor, and the department's two newest members, Gábor "the Fat" Tamási and twenty-one-year-old rookie József Keszthelyi, the ice-blue-eyed lady killer.

"Indeed," Lajos said. He told them that after they'd all gone home the previous evening, he'd received a call from a certain Sándor Pintér, the national police commander and a towering figure in Hungary who was getting more press lately than he liked. Commander Pintér had a question for Lajos that sounded reasonable enough: How was it that a robbery of a travel agency could take place fifty-five yards from a police precinct station? The answer, Lajos learned, was that the precinct's alarm call systems were not yet linked to Popeye's pub, where the station house cops had apparently decided to hold their afternoon meetings. The authorities had become aware of the Budapest Tours robbery only when a Ms. Csépai sent a fax to police headquarters several hours later, informing Budapest's finest that she still remained hopeful she could leave the office one day, though for the time being she remained locked inside.

Mercifully, most of the media hadn't gotten wind of the Popeye's part, but Lajos's favorite tabloid *Kurír* had the robbery covered.

URI RABLÓ, or **GENTLEMAN ROBBER,** was the headline.

According to the article, "the good-looking dandy" walked into the travel office and "haphazardly took out his revolver from his inside pocket. This was in reality a cigarette lighter, but the one-person staff saw some similarities and therefore quickly lifted both her arms in the air. . . . He almost unknowingly raked in the money . . . and then while wishing the office manager all the best and kissing her hand, he swiftly left the office."

It wasn't a post office job, but Lajos could see that the robbery had all the markings of the other two recent hits his team had investigated. Similar body type, polite manner, cat-quick movements, a tiny fake-looking gun, and a proclivity for interning the employees. The perpetrator also hadn't bothered to wear gloves, perhaps assuming, Lajos feared, that the robbery department's crack staff wouldn't be able to come up with a single fingerprint suitable for analysis. (Which, of course, it hadn't.)

"Did I say you could sit?" Lajos bellowed as his team began to settle into chairs. They stood.

It was time to shape this group up. Last week, Zoli, the 250-pound pansy, had to be carried back to HQ by two of his colleagues because he'd passed out from two glasses of champagne at a party down the street. What if Commander Pintér had walked into the robbery office the following morning, when Zoli was snoring away on a cot in the middle of the floor, wearing lipstick, high heels, and a garter belt on his head? What would Pintér say if he knew that Mound of Asshead had recently neglected to administer the parking brake on one of their only cars and that when he and Lajos finished an interrogation at a house on top of a hill, they had to dig the mangled vehicle out of a juniper bush at the bottom of the hill?

"It's time to get serious around here," Lajos said. "I want a full analysis of this Batman. I want to know how he's flying all over Budapest robbing, and we don't know anything about him. If you don't know how to do it, go rent some *Columbo* videos. And, Dance Instructor," he said to his expertish crime analyzer, "do your thing."

Budapest wasn't exactly New York City. Though the population had increased after World War II as communism created more jobs in the city than in the countryside, the majority of the capital's 2 million denizens were people whose families had resided in and around Budapest for generations. Asking around in the right places was still the industry standard for finding someone.

But when Lajos's men tried their regular street sources, they came up empty. No one in Planet of the Zorg offered anything but amusingly accented drivel. Police sketches were made and published in the papers, but the facial descriptions were too varied. None of the sketches looked alike. Few tips came in; none checked out. Lajos was as frustrated as they all were. Instead of Batman, he began referring to the thief as the Lone Wolf, since he seemed to be working not only alone but in a vacuum.

Then, that summer, the perpetrator did exactly what any good investigator hopes. He got greedy.

~

While living on Attila's floor, eighteen-year-old László ("Laczika") Veres figured out that his cousin Attila had a lot of things figured out. Two weeks earlier, László had left the tiny Transylvanian village of Fitód, where he'd grown up down the path from Attila, with the hope of simply one day becoming your average László. But now he wondered if he'd been shooting too low. Attila was no great hope as a tyke, but here he was in Budapest, eating at restaurants, dating a girl who spoke English — and today was proposing a plan to net a million forints ($10,800) in one afternoon. "It's nothing," Attila said. "It's just standing at a door." If László hadn't been so homeless and unemployed, he might have declined on the grounds of terror and self-doubt.

Little Laczika was not a formidable presence. An out-of-work carpenter, he was five feet ten but thin as an American-style hot dog. Hardly the optimal choice for an accomplice, but he was trustworthy — and someone had to watch the door if Attila was going to step up and do a real bank job. The "gentleman robber" had a reputation to live up to. "Laczika, listen to me," Attila said. "All you do is stand and hold this." He handed his cousin a toy gun. Simple.

On the afternoon of Friday, June 18, the Fitód cousins busted into the Nagykáta and Vidéke savings bank on Pesti Street in the far eastern part of the city near the airport. László wore a new red hairpiece from 4 Tigers; Attila, who entered first, went with a blond number he'd cut and sculpted to look like an ad he'd seen in a women's fashion magazine.

"Robbery!" Attila yelled, running up and down the waiting area, waving his miniature pistol. There were only two customers in the bank, both of whom started laughing. Attila looked back at László. His cousin was standing motionless in the entranceway like an emu in headlights. *Hoppá, Laczika!* Uh-oh. Attila raced over to one of the sniggering patrons and pointed his cap gun at his head. "Old chap, this is a robbery," he said. "Do as I say." The look in Attila's eyes alone was enough to get both customers to hit the floor without another peep.

Attila and László made it home safely by a mosaic of public transportation routes about which Attila had spent the previous night quizzing László. After berating his cousin for his pitiful wax-museum robbery performance, Attila shook out the contents of his Joe Camel duffel, and the cousins dropped down to their knees on the red-and-black-checkered carpet. Beneath the black-bearskin-covered wall, they divvied the bills into piles like Monopoly money. It was nearly 3 million forints ($32,000), half of which Attila gave to László, who suddenly didn't care if Attila and Karcsi ever actually acquired any of that furniture he'd been promised a job repairing. Neither did cousin Attila, who made Laczika pledge, for real, not to spend any of his loot for at least three weeks so as not to raise suspicions of a connection to the city's latest heist. László promised.

The following afternoon, however, László returned to Attila's apartment in a sparkling new crimson-colored Jeep Wrangler. *Hoppá!* Then Attila wasn't going to wait, either. He went out and bought a souped-up new red Mitsubishi Eclipse from a guy who ran a nearby "car repair" shop that occasionally offered bargain merchandise. Judit, who was in England for most of the summer with friends, would love it. The news clipping from *Kurír,* headlined GRADUATING BANK ROBBERS — during the cousins' robbery a group of eighth-graders were marching for their commencement ceremony across the street — went under the sink.

Six weeks later the bewigged cousins entered another financial institution, the Pilisvörösvár bank on Ágoston Street, on the bottom floor of a ten-story concrete communist-era apartment block. For the first time, Attila was carrying a real gun, an old Russian Tokarev 9mm pistol, which he'd procured through a contact at 4 Tigers. He had no intention of firing it at anyone or even anything, which he knew would only mean more jail time if he was ever caught. But given the effect his gumball-machine pistol and petrified assistant had had the last time, he needed the insurance. His line of work was just like any other. He couldn't expect to be successful if he couldn't be taken seriously.

Attila's resolve was put to the test right away. Inside the Ágoston Street bank was a fast-growing genus of Budapest life, an armed guard.

Attila had never had to deal with a lethal obstruction before, but he had prepared himself, and László, for such an eventuality. The bank was, after all, a private commercial institution unrestricted by Hungarian government-size budgets. In the case of a guard, László had been commanded to create a distraction, perhaps by asking the man a question, so that Attila could pounce upon and disarm him. Instead, however, László fainted at the guard's feet.

It was, at least, unexpected. The guard bent down to help László, which provided more than enough of a distraction for Attila to bumrush him and snatch the gun from his belt holster. But, like László, the robbery never really got off the ground. One of the tellers hit an alarm that buzzed like a deafening busy signal inside and outside the bank. Over that racket, Attila was getting an earful from one of the tellers about his career choice. "This is the problem with this country today," she scolded him. "Everyone thinks they can take something for nothing."

"I don't have time to argue about ethics," Attila finally shouted back. "Where's the safe?" But it was already too late. The police sirens were audible in the brief pauses between the bank alarm's wails. Attila pulled László up off the ground, and they broke for the door and then raced down an alleyway toward the train station. They made it home, but Attila's Camel bag held just 398,000 forints ($4,300), by far the smallest of Attila's five scores. Attila laid into László all night, and when Attila awoke the next day, there was a note from his cousin at the foot of the bed, reading, "Please don't be mad, but I had to go home." Without working a day, Attila and Karcsi's erstwhile labor force drove back to Fitód in an automobile worth roughly as much as his hometown.

The pitiful robbery hadn't merited even a mention in the papers, which was no way to end the summer. There were still a few weeks before Judit returned from England and the two-a-day hockey practices began in preparation for the upcoming season. Attila drove out to the police dormitory, where the only other person in the city he really trusted was living. He roused Bubu from his cot and told him they were going to the Hoof. "It's on me," Attila said. The two Székelys sat at their regular table in the back, and Attila started in about their days in Ceauşescu's Communist Youth Association, the Pioneers. "What do you want?" Bubu said.

"All you have to do is stand and hold something," Attila responded with a tragedy-ahead grin. The big guy was afraid. The government was beginning to blame the crime wave on immigrants. Fifteen thousand people, many of them Ukranians and some of them Hungarian Romanians without papers, would soon be deported as part of a police crackdown. Whatever Attila was up to, it was clearly prosecutable. Bubu had picked up his share of work from Planet of the Zorg, but he wasn't ready to entrust Panther with his geographical future. Like Attila, Bubu didn't have his citizenship papers yet, not to mention that he was still living with a few hundred cops. Without hearing any more, Bubu had to decline.

Attila's only other option was Karcsi, who owed Attila a few hundred thousand forints (about $3,500) for loans Attila had given him to get a videotape sales business off the ground. Attila didn't even have to buy Karcsi lunch; he had him at "doorman wanted/excellent pay." But Attila had selectively forgotten that the reason Karcsi was always broke was that he was too lethargic to do anything that required work. Of course Karcsi liked the *idea* of bank robbery, but after hearing more, he told Attila that (a) he wasn't taking public transportation to get to the bank and (b) he wasn't memorizing a labyrinthine maze to get back home. Karcsi told Attila that unless they drove to the site in Attila's roadster, he was out. It didn't leave Attila much choice. Now that Karcsi knew what he was up to, Attila had to do at least one gig with him to minimize the risk of Karcsi's ever turning around and ratting him out. Attila agreed to the requests on two conditions: that Karcsi wear a wig of Attila's choosing and that he walk and not run back to the car when they were finished.

Given his concerns about Karcsi, Attila chose another post office, this time one in the eastern part of the city near the flea market where he bought his wigs. He wanted to minimize the margin of error, and as long as the target was owned by the government, he figured he could at least be sure no one had approved paying for a guard. And he was right.

However, someone had purchased a silent alarm system, which rang back to police headquarters soon after he and Karcsi entered. Attila was oblivious, busy showboating for his teammate by doing a running headfirst circus tumble through one of the open-window teller's booths, then faking a Ukranian accent with the four-person staff.

("Could I please have the keys to the safe?" he politely inquired of one employee.) Then he stuffed his bag with the money and, apologizing, locked the employees in the bathroom. The whole thing took about three minutes, after which he went back to the front to find Karcsi frantically waving his arms at nothing. There were no guards or police in sight. "You're free to leave now," Attila told him. Karcsi bolted for the door and, despite his earlier promise to walk back to the car, broke into a dead sprint, yelling, "Hurry up! Come on!" all the way down the street. Attila didn't see what the fuss was about. Small thanks to another petrified accomplice, the haul was a new personal high, 3.4 million forints, or more than $18,000 per man.

Ten

Budapest
Fall 1993

Attila was now responsible for six of the city's thirteen major robberies since the year began (or five, according to the special report Dance Instructor put on Lajos's desk on September 13; they were a little behind). It was an average of almost one a month. By Thomas Crown standards, his swag was hardly worthy of a red flag, but in Hungarian hockey circles it was enough to make the handsome Transylvania-born Chicky Panther out to be a man of wealth and mystery. On paper, he was at least a sizable conundrum within a notable contradiction, the best-paid unpaid hockey goalie in a filthy-rich slum town.

Attila Ambrus ("the Chicky Panther")

Birthplace: Miercurea-Ciuc (aka Csíkszereda), Romania
Date of Birth: October 6, 1967   **Age: 25**
Years in Hungary: 5   **Years with UTE: 5***
Position: Goalie, Superintendent**
Net earnings from hockey: 0†
Total earnings: 9,000,000 Forints ($95,000)‡
Earnings not counting the following days in 1993: January 22, March 12, May 3, June 18, August 3 and 27: 0.

*1988–89, Zamboni driver; '89–90, janitor, no Zamboni privileges; '91–92, active; second half of '92–93 season, removed from active roster to accommodate Sergei Milnikov
**1988, converted from church painter to Zamboni driver; '89, janitor/grave-digger; '90, converted from custodian to goalie, also activated as a pen salesman, chandelier artist, security guard; '90–93, pelt smuggler (unsanctioned); '93–present, also working as post office, travel agency, and bank robber (unsanctioned)
†Richest player in the league
‡1.67 million forints ($18,000) of this sum was immediately paid to UTE forward Károly "Karcsi" Antal; 1.65 million forints ($18,000) was paid to László "Laczika" Veres (unaffiliated)

Attila was also a mystery man at police HQ, which was becoming a worsening headache for Lajos, given the very public verdict on the new alarm systems Lajos's bosses had encouraged the post offices to install. As the *Kurír* wrote two days after the Lone Wolf's most recent post office robbery, the systems were "worthless.... Today's criminals couldn't care less, because in the majority of cases, the police will arrive long after the robbers have escaped."

Lajos was feeling the pressure. Aside from ascertaining that he needed a police car, he'd made little progress on the Lone Wolf case since the Lone Wolf had stopped working alone. He asked Dance Instructor and the Fat to prepare a special report analyzing the information the police did have. A few weeks later the pair rematerialized from a paper foothill with the thirteen-page dossier that would guide the robbery department's renewed investigative efforts:

His actions and behavior indicate that he is afraid of his own gun, potentially because the likelihood of his capture would increase exponentially if he were to fire a shot. . . .

His clothes suggest a secure financial background and a desire to dress well. He may work at a place where presentability is required, and taking into account the gun, he may be a security guard on a van or in some financial institution. This would explain familiarity with the location as well as client service and valuables-protection practices. . . .

The person's energetic and flexible movements seem to indicate that he is an active sportsman, attends a bodybuilding club, or practices regularly on his own, which may be a requirement of his job.

Lajos's team would start with security companies and weight-lifting facilities and go from there.

Attila's physical conditioning was indeed once again an essential part of his day job. Now that Milnikov had returned to Moscow, Attila was placed back on UTE's active roster. And for the first time, it was likely that this season he would get to play. His friend George Pék had taken over as coach — which was both a good and bad portent. Pék had gotten the coaching job only when the previous year's coach walked out after refusing General Bereczky's final offer of a 100 percent pay cut. The Interior Ministry budget cuts were so deep that the team doctor stopped receiving the "antifatigue" pills. When Bóta found out that UTE's rival FTC had bailed itself out of near financial ruin by landing a sponsorship deal with Whirlpool hot tubs, he began devoting much of his time to what he said was an expanded search for sponsors at the city's bars and brothels.

But while Attila's colleagues fretted about their future, for the first time in Attila's life, he had the luxury of knowing that his foreseeable future (say, half a year) was funded. It didn't matter to him if pay cuts were again coming to UTE; he'd never been paid in the first place. Instead, he worried about making himself indispensable to the team. He wasn't yet a great player and he certainly held no sway with the older guys who had known him when he lived in the closet. But there was a whole crop of new players to whom Attila was a wealthy and, thus, respected veteran. If Attila spotted any of the youngsters showing up to practice late or slacking off during drills, he made them run laps and/or carry the equipment bags to the next game. The Panther would never again be a laughingstock. He was dead serious, fast as hell, halfway decent, and completely mad. Pék and Bóta marveled at their Panther, and with their tacit support, Attila anointed himself UTE's unofficial assistant coach for discipline and flagellation.

At the Thirsty Camel pub after the games, some of Attila's teammates liked to get him drunk and find a nuanced way to ask how he had so much free time to berate delinquent Hungarian hockey slobs and still drive a Mitsubishi. Attila, the perennial sponsor of such outings, furnished a variety of responses, including that he was "a bodyguard for some very important people." In a pinch, usually by then so plowed that his tone-deaf delivery halted further discussion, he leaned in and said, "Okay, listen, I'm fucking rich old ladies."

In fact, he was two years into his relationship with the young and sophisticated Judit, whose apartment he'd just paid to have repainted. And despite his compartmentalized existence, he seemed to be considering tearing down the walls behind which he'd always hidden and better integrating Judit into his life. His bad memories of Katalin had all but faded, and Judit had never given him reason to doubt her loyalty. There were times he could even picture having a family with her. In October Attila decided to invite Judit to one of his games, which he'd never done when he was merely a practice-session target and she another potential heartbreaker. Recognizing the significance of Attila's gesture, Judit brought along her parents, and they sat together in the front row of the UTE rink's cold metal bleachers. UTE was playing MAC, the worst of the city's teams, meaning Attila would be subbed in for the starting goalie as soon as Coach Pék deemed it safe. When the score reached 14–0, Pék felt comfortable making the switch, and Attila skated onto the ice to a round of applause from the front row. He maintained UTE's lead but, thanks to his penchant for skating halfway across the ice to poke away pucks, gave up three goals, for a final score of 14–3. Afterward Judit and her parents waited for him outside the locker room, but Attila never emerged from the building. He was so upset by his performance that he sat alone at his stall for hours, head in hands, breathing the stench of failure.

Attila had never had the luxury of self-reflection. He operated, he'd always thought, purely by instinct — instincts that had kept him alive through times he wasn't sure he'd survive and delivered him from a country that seemed intent upon his destruction. He knew there were a lot of things he couldn't explain about himself, and his reaction that night was one of them. He wasn't sure if he was capable of changing his ways, but he was at least willing to apologize for them. One day the following week, Attila got out of practice earlier than usual, bought a bottle of Cinzano like the one he and Judit had drunk together on their first date, and headed to his girlfriend's freshly painted apartment to surprise her.

He dropped his wheels off at the car wash around the corner from the hulking 134-year-old synagogue in Budapest's former Jewish ghetto and walked to Judit's building on Dob Street. When he got to her fifth-floor apartment, there was no answer. He was about to leave when he heard a noise from inside. He bent down and opened the door's mail slot. In the far left corner of his view, he could see a light in the bedroom. Then he saw Judit, running right to left, waving her hands the way Karcsi had during the last robbery. She was also naked.

"Judit!" Attila yelled, beating on the door. "I can see you in there." Pound, pound, pound. "Open this door." No answer. "Judit!" Nothing. Finally, Attila backed up against the hallway's opposite wall and began ramming his shoulder into the door until he was inside. The apartment was search-warrant quiet. He checked the bedroom, kitchen, bathroom: all empty. . . . The closets! Attila raced back to the bedroom and flung open the wardrobe. There it was, his future, huddled behind a rack of hanging clothes with another man.

Attila obeyed his instincts. He lunged at the fornicator's throat with a ferocity that made the man spring froglike from the closet, hurdle the mangled front door, and bound naked from the apartment, clutching only a bedsheet. Judit stopped screaming and started crying. Attila took a seat, started drinking the Cinzano, and by nightfall decided that he was ready to marry Judit. So sloshed that he could barely walk, he proposed to Judit, who, terrified by her questioner's stare, instantly accepted. The next morning, however, Judit's new fiancé awoke with a clearer head and told her he hoped never to see her face again.

A few days later — two hours before the six o'clock practice on Friday, November 3, to be exact — Attila appeared on the concourse level of Budapest's Nyugati train station in a wig and a mascara mustache. If he was thinking of leaving town, he had plenty of good choices. Nyugati station, adjacent to the McDonald's in which the ballroom chandelier he'd assembled with Egri's wife hung from the ceiling, was one of the city's biggest transportation centers.

Attila walked along the line of shops toward a branch of his favorite travel agency, Budapest Tours. But he wasn't there to buy a holiday package. He'd been drinking since he left Judit's apartment and had become set on the idea of an afternoon robbery. He didn't need an accomplice. Nor could he give a crap if it was rush hour.

Situated in a row of similar travel-related businesses, impulse-buy shops, and newsstands, Budapest Tours was separated from the busy concourse by only a wall of clear Plexiglas. As Attila approached, he could see there were no other customers inside and only one female employee, seated behind a long counter. He stepped inside and commenced an inquiry about island excursions. As soon as the travel agent swiveled in search of a pamphlet, Attila pulled his pistol from his jacket pocket and held it close to his body. "Hand over the money and there won't be any trouble," he said with the impatient smile of someone explaining, for the last time, that he wanted a king-size bed and an ocean view. The agent's response resembled that of a woman being robbed at gunpoint: she screamed. Attila grabbed her by the hair. She screamed louder.

Attila looked over his shoulder at the concourse. A crowd of people was already gathering around the entrance. Right, here he was, then, in a bad wig and a spot of trouble. The only way out was through the door he'd entered. He let go of the woman's hair and, without having collected a forint of the agency's cash, charged the exit. Two men moved quickly to block him, and several others piled on, wrestling him to the ground just in front of the store. Someone kicked the gun out of his hand. Attila lay pinned on his back while all around him voices were yelling, "Police, police! Robbery, robbery!"

Attila bucked his legs and twisted his torso, freeing his arms and allowing him to pop up like a break-dancer in the center of a captive concourse crowd. He couldn't allow it to end there, steps from a bungled robbery, hostile faces leering. As hungry arms began swiping at him, he picked the spot where the smallest bodies stood, ducked his head, and barreled into them, making a few spins with his pointed elbows until there was space to run.

A group gave chase, they would tell Major Lajos Varjú several minutes later, but the man had disappeared, up a stairway and into the dimming bustle of the oncoming night. There, on the ground in front of the travel agency, lay his Tokarev pistol. Lajos picked it up as if it were a dead fish and carried it back to headquarters to be traced and fingerprinted.

For the next several weeks, the UTE players noticed yet another oddity about their Panther. Normally he wouldn't shut up. Now he wouldn't say anything. Even to Bubu, he uttered only, "Never trust a woman."

There were three images Attila couldn't get out of his head: Katalin giving his grandmother's ring back to him in Csíkszereda; Judit's mother's pursed mug saying, "What do you know from meat?"; and one he had been trying to avoid for a long time: his mother's naked body on the other side of that window back in Transylvania. On bad days there was his father, too — not the wrinkled version of the man who had offered him the Dacia but the one who was so sure he would "die a gray nobody."

If they didn't think he was good enough, he would show them. It had always been just him against the world. No matter how far he traveled or which government was manipulating the truth, that much had never changed. So he wasn't a socialite, maybe he'd never finished high

school, perhaps he'd spent a year living in a horse paddock. But he was
going to be a success. He had found something he was good at, and
unlike hockey, it paid and paid well. Friday at the train station was an
aberration; his head hadn't been straight. Truth was, robbery was a job
that played to all his strengths: strength, for one; agility; self-reliance;
and the combination of perceptive facilities he'd been honing since
childhood — the uncanny ability to assess his enemies, intuit their
movements, and exploit their weaknesses. On top of that, as with everything he did, he held one very important wild card: he was going to
work harder than anyone else would think possible.

Attila bought a book about England's infamous 1963 Great Train
Robbery. Ronnie Biggs — one of the perpetrators, who'd made a jailbreak after his arrest and was now living like a demigod in Brazil —
became Attila's new role model: defiant, unconquerable; a master of his
craft. As a result, the super's apartment at Villányi Street 112 underwent
a major transformation. It was no longer the ramshackle home of an
unpaid Transylvanian hockey goalie. It was now a secret headquarters
and training center for a world-class criminal business enterprise. As
such, it had to be kept spotlessly clean of any possible evidence linking
its occupant to what he envisioned would be a long and brilliant career.

The wads of money that had been piling up — so many small
bills — inside Attila's otherwise empty silverware drawer were rede-
posited, though certainly not at one of the local banks, forty of which
were then under investigation for embezzlement and fraud. And since
Attila surmised that countless other Budapest financial institutions
would soon have their contents emptied onto his floor anyway, he created his own safe-deposit box, right in the kitchen: his oven. He pulled
out the blackened grate and tucked in the stacks of bills and the gun he'd
fleeced from the guard on whose foot his cousin László had collapsed.
Then he returned the grate and placed a heavy goulash pot over it.

Now that he'd turned pro, the 4 Tigers discount wig bin wasn't
going to cut it as his hair supplier. Attila visited a fashionable downtown
boutique for some imported horsehair. "For my grandmother," he told
the saleswoman. He carefully taped each new wig, turned inside out, to
the lining on the bottom of his mattress.

He pared down his social life to occasional flirting with Éva, a red-
haired woman who owned the car wash he frequented, or honking
his horn at women at stoplights, with varied results. One morning a

woman he'd plucked from an intersection woke up and went into his kitchen with a notion of baking a bread. "Don't touch that," Attila said, leaping from the pullout sofa just as she started preheating the oven. "The last time I used this," he told her, pointing to his well-disguised safe, "the apartment almost blew up." After she left, he unscrewed all of the oven's knobs, hid them in the closet, and concocted the durable rejoinder that the damn flat had come like that but he didn't cook much anyway.

What did he care what they thought? He couldn't expose himself to the hazards of having a woman around, and after his past experiences, he certainly wasn't going to miss having a relationship. If he wanted sex, he could pay for it. And no more accomplices; that's how the best were caught. He told Karcsi he was through with robbery.

Several nights a week Attila donned one of his new Italian suits and silk ties, pulled on his favorite dark leather three-quarter-length jacket, and ventured out on the town. But whatever his destination, the purpose was only to kill time until the rest of the city went to sleep. Early in the morning, usually about two o'clock, he would throw a chip at the Las Vegas croupier or collect his clothes from a brothel floor and say he was finished for the night. In fact, his day was only beginning.

When he got back out to his car, he fished a map and a phone book out of the trunk, and a half-size loose-leaf binder, like the one he used to count roulette numbers, from inside his coat pocket. Here was the mission: proceeding counterclockwise from southern Pest's crime-ridden IX District, known as Little Chicago, he was going to scour every inch of the city's twenty-three districts until his steno pad turned into an encyclopedia of Budapest's financial institutions and their inherent weaknesses.

Knuckles curled around the wheel of his new red Audi, Attila crawled along Budapest's streets in concentrated silence. Beams of white light from nightclub spotlights tunneled through the misty air. Along the Pest side of the Danube riverbank, a huge green and white neon sign atop a hundred-year-old neoclassical building flashed like a distress call the letters of the national bank. OTP . . . OTP . . . OTP. He was inside the gates of an amusement park shut down for the night.

The first task was to locate each district's police precinct. Then he tracked down every post office, travel agency, and bank he could find in the area, checking them off against the phone book. Next: the time trial.

He pulled his car up as close as possible to the precinct station, hit the stopwatch on his Seiko wristwatch, and raced to the projected financial target as fast as he could, ignoring stoplights whenever possible. If it took less than two minutes to cover the distance, the site wasn't likely to enter his catalog and did not merit more than a line. Most of the routes, however, took longer than that, and it was these worthy institutions that were allotted two full pages, front and back. On the left side of the entry's first page, he drew a map of the streets and buildings in the immediate vicinity, noting the types of businesses that were on the street and their likely hours of operation. Then he got out of the car and wandered around the deserted streets, checking out back for an alternative exit or unapparent escape channel.

The rest of the data had to be gathered during business hours. After the morning hockey practice and before a nap, Attila tried to visit at least two sites per day. He went inside, inquiring about a loan or buying stamps. Then while the information was fresh, he hurried out to a bench or back to the car to scribble everything down. Stars collided, snowstorms descended, world leaders clashed, and Attila Ambrus drew up his diagrams of bank interiors. Then he turned the page. On the back side of his blueprint, he listed the following data: number of doors and windows and their locations, same for the phones; whether or not there was a security camera or a security guard, and if the guard was armed; number of employees and the breakdown by gender; the time of his visit and the amount of customer traffic. He also wrote down the date so that he could allow at least six months between his scouting trip and his follow-up visit to ensure he would not be remembered. He stored the notebook in the oven with the cash and guns.

On December 27, a week after Coach Pék's UTE team hit the holiday break at 7–3–3 and just six weeks since Attila had doubled down on felonious living, he knocked off the travel agency down the street from his apartment that had conned him on the Tunisia package in March. He used one of his new wigs and added a pair of fake glasses to his disguise. Two minutes and forty seconds after yelling, "Robbery!" — twenty seconds under his new three-minute time limit — he was done.

It was a small take, 407,000 forints ($4,400), and only the *Kurír* covered the robbery the following day (HALF A MILLION WORTH OF BOOTY). But he was in for the long haul now and was satisfied just to be back in the game. He clipped the *Kurír* story and added it to a plastic bag archive in the bathroom that included stories of other notable crimes. One piece in his collection detailed the downfall of a Chinese bank robber who was caught after having dropped his wallet inside the bank. Every couple of weeks, Attila reviewed his material and the wisdom it offered (e.g., don't ever bring ID to a gig).

Attila's two careers complemented each other nicely. Both physically and psychologically, he was in top condition. He could run for miles without tiring. He could do five hundred push-ups, a thousand leg-sits. His reflexes were worthy of his nickname, and his primary goal both as a goalie and a thief was the same: always be prepared for, or at least in the act of preparing for, anything. This made sleeping unlikely and even unauthorized. If only the building's tenants could see their super at night, marching trancelike around his apartment to ingrain bank layouts into his head, then diving around the floor, role-playing heist scenarios.

Attila's steely cranium was deep in study mode for his first solo bank job on January 31, 1994, when UTE had a crucial, nationally televised game against FTC. The game took place on neutral ice in the hockey-obsessed town of Székesfehérvár, in the country's central-western hills, halfway between Lake Balaton and Budapest. It was a classic Hungarian affair, so Attila had only himself to blame for not considering the possibility that in the second period Bubu would clobber an FTC star so fantastically that the player would remain unconscious even as he was put into an ambulance; a bench-clearing brawl would ensue; fans and players alike would begin tearing down the stadium boards and winging them at one another like gigantic Chinese throwing stars; another ambulance would be called to cart off a twelve-year-old boy, injured in the battle; and when the teams were ready to resume play again, Attila would be one of the few players left who had not been ejected or disabled. Thus, with few other options, Coach Pék presented his second-string goalie with a scenario for which Attila hadn't prepared at all: he put Attila in the game.

Under the circumstances, Attila performed admirably. He saved some good shots, just not enough of them. FTC scored the game's two deciding goals against him, and UTE lost, 5–3. After the game, Coach Pék was livid. "I'm not saying I wasn't throwing anything," he told the daily newspaper *Népszava* regarding the hostilities that had broken out in the second period, "but I wasn't the one who hit the boy."

Two days later Attila went through with his maiden solo bank robbery, but not before redoubling his preparatory efforts. He had been
tweaked by the realization at the hockey game that he was not as omnis-
cient as he'd presumed, and to augment his routine, he decided to revisit
the particularly crucial process of site selection. The only way to know
he was optimizing his chances was if he had a standardized method by
which to compare the feasibility of his potential targets. Thus, he implemented a degree of difficulty rating system. Every financial institution
in his book was assigned a score from 1 to 5: 1 being vegetable-field-
pillaging simple; 5, Great Train Robbery difficult. The scores were
weighted heavily toward the number and accessibility of escape routes,
which Attila delineated on each of his street schematics with a dotted
line, noting their order of preference with a circled number. To score a 1
for difficulty, there had to be at least three flight options, a rarity. Aside
from the odd post office, no bank in his book scored better than a 2,
which was the rating of his inaugural solo effort — the Mór and Vidéke
savings bank on a square in the central business district of Buda, just
across the river from the Gothic-spired Parliament. It was a simple,
medium-size bank; six or seven female employees; no guard; two
equally opportune escape routes leading to public transportation; and a
location blissfully situated on a traffic-snarled road far from the police
precinct. Attila figured a businessman's appearance was least likely to
raise alarm and chose a pair of tortoiseshell glasses, a green sports coat
over light shirt and black tie, and a pair of brown linen dress pants. He
clipped one of his brown wigs into a conservative corporate-style cut.

To make up for the absence of a door watcher, he had bought a sheet
of cardboard and meticulously drawn in large shadowed block lettering
CLOSED FOR TECHNICAL REASONS, and below in smaller print, PLEASE
EXCUSE THE INCONVENIENCE. He taped it to the door as he went in and
pulled it back down when he left with a respectable 1.39 million forints
($12,900). Preparation was everything.

Six weeks later, after another championshipless hockey season
ended with his purchase of a black Mercedes coupe, Attila did a 3: the
Bakonyvidéke Savings and Loan in southern Pest's Little Chicago,
where there was no guard but one male employee. Again, he went as
a businessman, donning (along with a straight dark wig parted in the
middle) a cream-colored blazer over a knit V-necked pullover and dark
pants. But his appearance hardly mattered. It was about lunchtime

when he arrived to find the bank's chain-link front grating pulled halfway down. He ducked underneath it and got all the way behind the counter before encountering the staff, who were sitting around a back table, eating. The one male employee who'd caused the place to score a 3 was so frightened by the word *rablás!* ("robbery") that he knocked his bowl of soup onto his head trying to dive under the table. And for this Attila had been so nervous, he'd drunk himself silly at a pub across the street before feeling emboldened enough to strike. He'd forgotten to take his CLOSED FOR TECHNICAL REASONS sign with him when he left, but the booty was a new personal record, 4.56 million forints ($42,600), enough to live on for at least a year. (HE'S GONE WITH 4 MILLION, read the headline in *Esti Hírlap*.)

By July, he was ready to do a 5.

Eleven

The Old Street Pub was a basement dive with a small bar and three tables, situated on the corner of Ó Street and Hajós Street, five blocks from the city's police headquarters at Deák Square. A little past noon on Thursday, July 21, Attila stepped in wearing a pasta-colored double-breasted suit, a short, curly brown wig, and a thick mascara mustache. He carried a hard dark leather briefcase. "Off work early," he told the pub's waitress, who took his order for a beer and a whiskey. On her way back with his drinks, the waitress noted that if she'd thought it odd that her only customer was wearing Ray-Bans inside her dark cellar, it was odder still that he was reading a newspaper upside down and had a wig hanging halfway off his head.

On his first of many trips to the bathroom with stomach cramps, Attila ruefully fixed his hair and removed his sunglasses. Halfway through his fourth shot of Johnnie Walker, three uneventful hours later, he plunked down some banknotes and headed for the door, clutching his stomach with one hand and his briefcase in the other. *"Halló,"* his waitress called after him, meaning "good-bye" in Hungarian. *"Szia,"* he responded, meaning usually "hello" but also "good-bye" and, since he had mislaid his bearings, a safer choice.

He ambled down the thin, shaded one-way street. The outer part of the sidewalk was lined with parked compact cars whose owners had nowhere else to put them; the inner half was lumped with people trying to squeeze past one another against the paint-chipped buildings. In the road, delivery trucks stopped where they liked; horns blared. Above, the hazy blue sky yawned.

As he walked, Attila felt his blood begin to circulate. He passed the electronics store and then the private security guard company and finally arrived at an arched portico with a big blue cube hanging over the entrance. EUROTOURS, read the sign. HAVE A HOLIDAY ON THE BEACH; LUXURY TRIPS AND AIR TICKETS.

Attila pushed open the brass-framed door and was comforted by the sight of two young women behind a long white counter, as the entry in his robbery playbook had described.

"Yes, hello," Attila said, putting his briefcase on the counter in front of the cute one. "I'm the marketing director of Malév Airlines."

"Oh," the woman said.

"I would like to look into a vacation for my flight attendants," he said. "They work so hard, and I'd like to reward them."

He was slurring his words.

"Couldn't you book this directly through Malév?" the woman asked.

"Maybe to the Canary Islands, somewhere nice."

"Just a minute," the woman said, reaching down beneath the counter, "while I get our information on that. . . ." When she looked up again, the Malév marketing director's feet were on her desk. "Robbery," Attila said, looking down at her through his Ray-Bans.

He hopped down onto the floor on the other side of the counter. "On the floor," he said, pointing his gun at the other employee. "Everything will be fine." He began grabbing the bills from the open counter drawers, when a terrible clanking interrupted his routine. The front door was opening. He had forgotten to hang the CLOSED sign he'd brought with him in his briefcase.

An old woman carrying a basket sauntered in as if she were returning from a picnic. "Hello," she said, approaching the counter.

Attila thrust his right arm — the one holding the gun — down below counter level and flashed a stare at the women on the floor, quickly floating his left index finger close enough past his mouth to be understood.

"I'm looking for information about trips to Italy," the old woman said.

"That's very interesting," Attila replied, sweating whiskey, "because we have an expert on Italy here. But, unfortunately, she's just stepped out for lunch. Could you come back in half an hour?"

"Yes, thank you," the woman said, and she turned and walked out.

Attila had lost nearly a minute and knew he couldn't count on getting so lucky with another customer. He yanked open the drawer in front of him. There was a key inside it. He held it up to the employee beneath him. "Let's go," he said.

She got up and walked slowly to a large wooden bureau in the back of the office. Inside, on the bottom shelf was a small black safe. "Give me the key," Attila said. Then he asked, "Where's the bathroom?"

The woman pointed down the hall. Attila waved over the other employee and herded them both into the water closet. Once they were inside, he said, "Now give me the key around your neck," to the one with a string necklace. She looked surprised. He was drunk but he wasn't stupid. He knew the key he'd picked out of the drawer, a skeleton, was for the toilet, not the safe. He locked the women inside, then headed back to the money box with the string necklace.

He was close to getting it open when sirens rang out on the street. Attila looked at the floor under the counter and saw what he faced: it was a foot pedal. The place was equipped with a silent alarm system. As if it needed another reason to score a 5. There was only one exit, out onto a busy street that could be sealed by police with, for instance, training. He grabbed his suitcase and bounded back over the counter. Police HQ was only five blocks away, but the sirens didn't necessarily mean the police were anywhere close. Cars were virtually useless on such a narrow, congested street. If they were going to have any chance against him, they would have to come on foot — and in that scenario, he liked his odds.

He pulled the door open and stepped out onto the front stair. To his right, two cops not twenty feet away were barreling toward him. Before he had time to think, the first one ran past and turned into the shopping atrium next door that bore the same address as the travel agency. The other followed. A third came puffing up behind.

"What's the problem, Officer?" Attila asked.

"Robbery," the cop said, hurrying by.

Attila wanted to laugh but he was shaking so badly that he felt as if he'd forgotten how to walk. The police would realize their mistake any second.

He started heading in the opposite direction from where the police had come, brushing by the rubberneckers. As soon as he passed anyone, he tried to weave behind his figure so as to shield himself from view from the other end of the street. But when he got about a quarter of a block from the corner, two police cars screeched up to seal the road. It was the improbable doomsday scenario for which he had no provision.

Just then, on his left, a man came out of an apartment building. Attila lunged around him and caught the door as it closed.

He ran to the stairs and up five flights to the top. There was a small door in the corner of the hall leading up another flight. Attila proceeded up the steep narrow stairs to a low-angled attic, which had a small hatch in the ceiling. He shed his suit jacket and pants and stuffed them, along with his suitcase, behind a pile of storage wood and tiles. Then he pushed open the hatch and pulled himself out onto the building's sloping black tile mansard roof.

He had stepped into a postcard. The oversize pool-green dome of St. Stephen's Basilica burst out of the skyline to the west. In the distant north, he could see the Danube River winding its way out of the pollution-ringed city, which, in his immediate vicinity, resembled a multilayered checkerboard of Tuscany red and black roofs. But somewhere below him, the police were scurrying around like blind mice; he could still hear the sirens. At least one of the cops had seen him come out of the plundered travel agency, and at least one other witness — the man who'd eyeballed him as he dove for the apartment building's door — had seen a similarly dressed man enter the dwelling on which he was now perched. For all he knew, the police were already in the building. His feet slipping on the roof tiles, Attila scrambled toward the closest of several short rectangular brick chimneys. Once there, he wrapped his arms around it and pulled himself upright so that he could shuffle around to the opposite side, where, with some luck, he might remain unseen by a cursory check from the attic hatch.

Day turned to dusk and still Attila clung to the chimney. The muscles in his chest and arms went numb. There were shooting pains in his back. Around ten o'clock the city grew quiet. Then darkness settled in, leaving only a twinkling of lights from the Buda hills to accompany him until morning.

The next day
8:00 A.M.

Attila sat amid of a pile of newspapers in the waiting area at the Interior
Ministry's Korvin Hospital. After retrieving his car from a subway station parking lot, he had driven himself to this familiar spot in lieu of
attending the morning workout session at UTE since he was having a
few problems moving his left shoulder. Considering that two hours earlier he had been plastered to a chimney, where he had been unable to
move either arm, or wrist, and had only minimal use of his back, he
wasn't overly concerned. He was already able to turn the pages of seven
newspapers like a one-armed blackjack dealer. He'd also managed to
count the money in the car. That was the greatest agony. Thanks to the
fact that he hadn't had time to funnel anything from the travel agency's
safe, all he'd gained for his rooftop misadventure was 955,000 forints
($8,900).

"Panther," said the young bespectacled UTE team doctor, Attila
Tóth, appearing in the waiting room doorway. "What is it this time?"

"Tennis elbow," Attila said. "I can't move my arm."

"I'm sure it's nothing," Tóth said. "You're —"

"I know," Attila interjected, *"I'm a kid with balls."*

They went to Tóth's examination room, and Attila hopped onto the
table.

"Out late?" Tóth asked, pulling out his stethoscope as Attila unbuttoned his mangled dress shirt.

"Igen," Attila said, managing a smile. *Yes.*

After a few pokes and prods, Tóth put away his equipment and sat
down. "You have an inflammation," he told Attila. He gave Panther a
shot in his arm and suggested his patient go home and go to bed, which
sounded just fine to Attila, who rebuttoned his shirt, went back to his
car, and drove off, swearing never to do a 5 again. As soon as he got
home, he was going to take his encyclopedia out of the oven and draw
an X through Ó Street, he'd just decided when he noticed that a police
car was parked on the street in front of his building. He hit the brakes
and skidded to a stop. *Your nerves are shot,* he thought, trying to calm
down. There were any number of reasons the cops could be on his
block; there were dozens of buildings and hundreds of apartments. He
continued around a corner to the super's spot in the back. He parked

and headed through his building's back doorway, like always. As soon as he stepped inside, he was standing next to two of his neighbors, who were peering down the half flight of stairs leading to Attila's basement apartment, where his door stood open. Curiosity pulled him down toward his flat — just as a policeman was coming out.

"Do you live here?" the officer asked.

"Is there a problem?" Attila responded.

Igen, the man said. "There's been a robbery."

Attila looked into his apartment. Another cop was standing in his living room. "I'm sorry to say it," the second cop said as Attila glanced around at the torn-up space, "but they've taken everything." The officer pointed to Attila's kitchen. "Even the knobs on your oven."

Twelve

It was Lajos's lucky day. Make that his lucky summer. His experience in the furniture warehouse business back home was finally paying dividends. Several times a day he gritted his teeth and arranged and rearranged boxes of unsolved case files as swiftly as if they were duplicate end tables in his feng shuied showroom. He didn't need them and he was running out of places to put them.

Budapest's once-sleepy robbery division was deluged with more than a thousand cases from January of 1993 through the summer of 1994. The thieves were so intoxicated by their success that they were robbing each other. As a result, Lajos was working seven days a week, sometimes under duress, sometimes under his desk, and frequently delusional.

He and his men were making plenty of headway, sure. They caught the infamous One Eye, the Cyclops-like gas station robber who knocked off the same filling station seven too many times. And they were hot on the trail of the priest who stormed a money van with an ex–judo champion and made off with more than 50 million forints ($470,000). (The martial artist, found bleeding from a gunshot wound in an apartment hideaway, had divulged to Lajos before dying that his self-righteous accomplice was almost definitely in Romania, Slovakia, Austria, or Ukraine.) As for the Lone Wolf, please. So he'd robbed ten times. Lajos had a handful of cases of guys who took more than the Lone Wolf's meager 16.3 million forint ($150,000) total with one strike. Plus, the police had already come *this close* to catching him twice now: at the Nyugati train station last November, and stepping out of the travel agency the previous afternoon. A mere mention of the Lone Wolf in the robbery office would invariably provoke someone to sing out, "*Szerencsés csillagzat alatt született,*" meaning, of course, that the thief "was born under the star of luck." And luck, any Hungarian could tell you, never lasted.

Lajos's good spirits this day were due to two things. He was blissfully ignorant of the fact that earlier that morning two Budapest cops had stood in the Lone Wolf's living room, consoling him for being a robbery victim. And he was fully and blessedly cognizant that VI District, in which Ó Street and Eurotours International were located, was not under his jurisdiction, and therefore not his problem. That honor fell to Major János Vigh, who ran the smaller piece of the city's robbery department that handled just seven districts. And, no doubt, Vigh was being asked to field some questions from his superiors that had no good answers. For instance, What the hell happened on Ó Street?

The coverage in the daily newspaper *Népszava* (MILLIONS ROBBED ON Ó STREET) was not flattering. The story noted that witnesses saw the police "pass right by" the thief as they stormed into the wrong building. And the large photograph accompanying the article, taken after Vigh's detectives eventually stumbled upon the crime scene, looked like an advertisement for a new Pink Panther sequel. It depicted one of Vigh's men holding an oversize magnifying glass up to his face on the travel agency floor. The detective had apparently discovered an almost innocuous-looking array of pencils scattered across the ground and was attempting to decode the message. It was indeed a toughie:

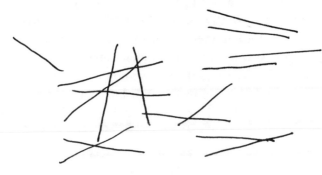

was unintelligible even in Hungarian.

Vigh's team interviewed every eyewitness to the robbery it could find, including Csilla Serbán, the waitress at the Old Street Pub, who said she had served a man in a double-breasted suit and bad wig four whiskeys plus a beer, which he drank in one gulp. Several wig stores in the area were checked, as was the Ray-Ban shop on nearby Szent István Street.

At the end of the following day, Vigh compiled everything he'd uncovered and faxed the revelations to every newspaper and the only television station, Magyar Televizsió (MTV).

SAJTÓNYILATKOZAT (PRESS ALERT)

The perpetrator of a robbery yesterday at Ó Street is described as about 170–175 cm tall. Brown face but not Gypsy. A little stubble. A thick dark mustache.

He had a black wig on his head that was bushy and uncombed, under which you could see his straight brown hair.

If you know anything about the perpetrator, please call the Robbery Unit at 22-550, and after hours the central phone number for the police.

None of the papers ran a follow-up. On Monday, with new appreciation for Lajos's plight, Vigh gave up and turned the file over to his colleague to be folded into the larger ongoing investigation. Though it wasn't easy to admit, Lajos agreed that the Ó Street job sounded like another Lone Wolf special.

To be fair, it was a perfectly maddening time. In May, Hungary had become the second former Soviet bloc country (after Poland) to vote a former communist back into office. Gyula Horn, a sixty-two-year-old ex–Communist Party bigwig who had reportedly helped crush the 1956 uprising, led the newfangled Socialist Party to victory despite campaigning in a head-and-neck brace (the temporary result of a car wreck). But Horn's new old-style government was possibly even less capable than that of the former medical museum curator who preceded him. Promised renewed funding for social programs such as unemployment, welfare, and police protection never materialized, and instead, foreign troops did. This time it wasn't the Soviets but the Americans: the U.S. deployment in 1995 and 1996 of twenty thousand soldiers in Hungary, a staging area for the Bosnian peacekeeping mission, was the largest American military installation in Europe since World War II. And there was one more American invasion on the way. Two months after Horn's election, the American FBI declared that Budapest would soon be home to its first foreign office, which it was calling an international training center for law enforcement from the allied forces of Eastern Europe. Hungary seemed a logical choice. After all, according to the press release issued by the Hungarian information service, Hungary's relationship with the FBI dated back to 1937, since which time the FBI had "trained some 27,000 officers, including one Hungarian."

Unfortunately, it showed. During communism, investigative police work in Hungary generally meant digging through an underemployed family's sock drawers for *szamizdat,* or self-published, materials. The amount of unsanctioned crime that existed in a country where few had anything worth taking was negligible and of scant interest, as a traditional communist-era Hungarian cop joke depicts: Police find a mugging victim lying in his own blood along the Danube walking path, and ask, "Why were you screaming, 'Down with Kádár! Down with the regime!'" Man replies, "If I yelled that I'd been stabbed, you wouldn't have come."

So the fact that the FBI was heading to town was exhilarating news for cops such as Lajos, whose prior training regimen had consisted of divulging his hat size and withstanding a handshake. But FBI director Louis Freeh, who flew to Budapest with President Clinton's blessing for the announcement, was quick to manage expectations. "The best internal mechanism [against crime] in the world isn't going to help if police can't feed their families," he said.

It may have been slim pickings down at Budapest police headquarters, but the summer of 1994 was bountiful for UTE. The team, finally tapping some of the Western investment in the country, signed up a sponsor. After forty-four years of going by the nickname Dózsa, for the Hungarian revolutionary figure György Dózsa (a Székely who led a peasant revolt in the sixteenth century), UTE would now be known as

Office and Home — the English-language name of an office-supply chain funded by Western investors. "Brothel and Pub" might have been more apropos, but as Bóta could now confirm, those institutions did not subscribe to the philosophy of investing for the future.

The financial agreement between the desk purveyor and UTE precipitated a major reshuffling of team personnel. For one, longtime player and coach George Pék, now forty, retired to focus on his more lucrative convenience-store job. Office and Home wasn't exactly shelling out dough. Other notable transactions included the departure of the two Transylvanian stars — Bubu, regrettably to FTC, where he'd been offered a contract that would enable him to eat several days a week, and Karcsi, midway through the season, back to the fabled Csíkszereda team, where he could be closer to his family. Arriving to take their place were the fighting Szatmári brothers of Canada (Hungarian émigrés who together would hopefully make up for the loss of one Bubu), and a pair of Orbáns, George and Gábor.

The Orbáns were the Kennedys of Hungarian hockey, such as it was, and they would soon get their Chappaquiddick. Father George, the new UTE coach, was the Hungarian national team goalie in the 1950s and had since become a highly successful coach on the European circuit. After a couple of years heading up a top team in France, he'd returned to Budapest and turned UTE's rival FTC into Hungary's new hockey dynasty. George's elder son, George Jr., still played for FTC, where he was Hungary's "Goal King," possessor of an even better slapshot than Karcsi's. And George's younger son, Gábor, had also played under him at FTC and was about to join him at UTE after spending the past year in America failing to make the NHL.

"Gabi," as Gábor was known, was a handsome, well-spoken twenty-year-old whose anxious laugh suggested the introspection of someone aware that if his father weren't the coach, he would be receiving four or five wedgies a week. Aside from two years in democratic France's countryside when his father was coaching in Annecy on the Swiss border, Gabi had grown up in Budapest. The family lived in its own two-bedroom apartment in a cluster of brown brick and asphalt buildings built by the state bank, OTP. Mother Klára was an internationally acclaimed folk dancer. They owned an East German Trabant. By Hungarian standards, it was a privileged life, which is to say that aside from some monitored travel, it was not much different from anyone else's. Like any kid who grew up in Hungary in the seventies or eighties, Gabi had studied Russian since grade school and still couldn't speak it, had an appreciation of classical music, and had read most of Schopenhauer. But he never felt that he could live up to the accomplishments of his famous athlete brother.

After graduating from high school in 1992, three years after the end of the communist regime, a family friend got Gabi a medical exemption from the army and he joined FTC, where his father was coaching and his brother playing. While brother George drew a livable paycheck as the league's star, Gabi's scrub salary was 8,000 forints ($100) a month, about the price of two pairs of Levis. He found a second job as a coroner's assistant at the city morgue. In his free time, he pondered what he was going to do with his life now that capitalism had created so many opportunities. He soon decided to leave for the United States.

Leaning on his father's hockey connections, Gabi crash-landed first in southern New Jersey, hoping to latch on with the Philadelphia Flyers, whose practice facility was nearby. But unable to finagle a tryout, he headed to Florida, where an ex-Hungarian player had been appointed to coach the West Palm Beach Blaze, a minor league hockey franchise in the low-paying, lower-profile eight-team Sunshine League. The club's Hungarian coach, however, died of a heart attack just as the season was about to begin, and Gabi was deleted from the Blaze's final roster. In October he returned to his parents' apartment and got into a Budapest state of mind. He went on the dole.

Gabi's father had promised Gabi a spot at UTE that year, which Gabi accepted, despite having come to the understanding that, in Hungary, professional hockey wasn't a career and was possibly an oxymoron. But if the point of capitalism was to make as much loot as possible, he didn't know what a Hungarian career was. Gabi was adrift — until a few weeks into practice with UTE. That's when he started to notice the free-spending Mercedes-driving rookie-berating goaltender. Gabi's life ambition suddenly presented itself. He wanted to do what the Chicky Panther did, whatever it was.

Gabi began following Attila around everywhere. He enthusiastically did all of the push-ups and ran all of the laps Panther ordered when he made a bad play. He asked Attila to play tennis, to go out to eat; he laughed at his jokes. And before practice, after practice, and during practice, he waited for the right moment when no one else was listening to blurt out, "Just tell me what you do, I won't tell anyone, I can be your partner, I'll do anything."

For Attila, it was flattering to have an Orbán fawning all over him. But Gabi was more like a pet than an accomplice. There was no way Attila was letting him in. "I don't do anything," Attila told him. "I'm an *életművész*," a Hungarian term that translated as "life artist," someone to whom working was itself déclassé.

Attila was in fact in a sort of semiretirement even from his unofficial other career. The near disaster at Ó Street had provided enough thrills for a while. He'd pulled ten successful heists over the past year and a half; he didn't need to keep up that kind of pace to make the history books. He was only twenty-six. And when he'd stopped to think about it, he realized he was rich. Or at least, he was far from broke. He planned to enjoy himself, relax for a change.

During the day, when he wasn't out at the hockey grounds, Attila was usually attempting to rustle up a tennis game, leisurely affairs for which he applied the same mellow enthusiasm he had for hockey. For some reason, it wasn't always easy for him to find a partner. Once, restless after a snowstorm, he scooped up an unsuspecting Bóta from his home, saying, "I'm sick of couch potatoes." He then negotiated himself and his friend through thigh-deep uncleared streets to the Interior Ministry facility, where he used a shovel to tunnel a path to the court. He'd become friendly enough with club officials that even on days when he couldn't find a member interested in being pasted, Attila could purchase ten cans of balls and be allotted a court on which to practice his serve, which clocked at a pro-level 110 mph.

Attila had also found a smaller, homier new casino, the Globe Royale, which offered complimentary drinks and had a bearskin hanging on the wall and a pool table in back. Of course, he could rarely get himself to leave when he still had money in his pocket, even if it meant buying everyone, including the security guards, a round of drinks. And his nights didn't always end there. One of his Interior Ministry chums had gotten him on the list at the Cats Club, the new high-class brothel in the ninth-century, cobblestoned artist colony town of Szentendre, an hour north of Budapest. Located in a refurbished mansion on a hill, Cats was as exclusive as a Hungarian whorehouse could be. Though the

Russians had all but taken over Hungary's underworld since the infamous 1991 Magyar Mob Toss (in which a group of Russian mobsters had flung one of their Hungarian counterparts over Budapest's Margit Bridge), Cats was still Hungarian-owned by Gyula Zubovics, an original Hungarian wiseguy who had cut his teeth in the 1980s in Los Angeles, the Hungarian mafia's home away from home. Dimly lit and sleekly appointed, Cats was one of Hungary's premier see-and-be-seen spots for those who didn't want to be seen: cops, members of Parliament, "used car" salesmen, television personalities, serial bandits.

"The Chicky Panther!" the goateed, Armani-attired Zubovics loved to shout when Attila walked in.

"Zubovics!" Attila called back, since he never knew the owner's first name. "Where did you get that suit?"

"You couldn't afford it, my little goalie," Zubovics would respond. Gangster cred unknown, the Transylvanian goaltender was something of a novelty at Cats, the congenial pauper in the proverbial palace. But it was an equal opportunity palace, and while there, Attila lived like a king. His favorite item on the Cats menu was two girls, any style, in the private room (hot tub and sauna included), where he could do as he pleased while watching the table dancers at the bar through a one-way mirror. For an hour, the prix fixe was 100,000 forints ($900) — a little more than the average Hungarian monthly wage, and at least as much as Zubovics's designer threads.

One night while Attila was waiting on the gun-and-coat-check line outside Cats, he discovered another way to spend his hard-earned money. Next to him was one of the principals of the Conti-Car auto dealership, one of the biggest mob-run rackets in Europe, who invited him to visit the group's lot on the outskirts of Budapest. He headed out a few weeks later and liked what he saw: barely used Lamborghinis, Ferraris, Porsches, Audis, and a full bar crowded with backslapping Cats Club regulars inside the ten-car showroom. Every several months from then on, Attila went back to Conti-Car and traded his wheels for another slightly used, and undoubtedly untraceable, model.

That fall, after swapping his Mercedes for a red convertible Audi Cabrio, Attila stocked his new ride full of coffee, rice, sugar, candies, and household appliances and headed over the border into Romania like Santa Claus. He hadn't been home since the end of his frenzied pelt-smuggling days, and feeling accomplished for the first time in his life, he was ready. Regrettably, little had changed in Romania. Though the country was governed by the democratically elected president Ion Iliescu, equal rights for Romania's citizens was evidently not on the agenda. Romania's parliament passed a law banning the display of the Hungarian flag, prompting a letter of disapproval from U.S. president Bill Clinton. In Cluj Napoca (or in Hungarian, Kolozsvár) — the western Transylvanian capital that Hungarians venerate the way Americans do Williamsburg, Virginia — the Romanian mayor was tearing down Hungarian statues and even painting dogs with stripes of red, yellow, and blue, Romania's flag colors. Meanwhile, Transylvania remained best known to the rest of the world for two buildings — one, the soaring medieval Bran Castle on a rural milkweed-strewn lookout; the other a modest two-story home in the colorful sixteenth-century village of Sighisoara that has been renamed Dracula House Restaurant — both of which are believed to be connected to a vampire who never lived anywhere at any time. (The source of the confusion stems from the worldwide popularity of Irish writer Bram Stoker's 1897 book *Dracula,* whose vampire was named after a vindictive spear-wielding fifteenth-century Romanian prince, Vlad "the Impaler" Dracul. The Impaler may once have attacked the castle and was most likely born in the Sighisoara eatery.)

On Attila's way over the Hargita Mountains, he stopped at the tiny wooden fifteenth-century Franciscan monastery on a bluff in Csíksomlyó, site of the annual Whit Saturday festival to which more than a hundred thousand Hungarians travel each June. He dropped some coins into the well and wished for his continued good fortune, a custom he would follow on each subsequent visit home. It was just a little farther, through the final sweeping turns into the valley, until the white road sign announced Miercurea-Ciuc, and beneath it in smaller letters, the city's Hungarian name, Csíkszereda. Other indications of communism's collapse were soon apparent. The streets and parks, once kept clean by city workers, were strewn with garbage. And in the town's old cobblestoned center across from the Hockey Klub restaurant and bar was a new café, New York Pizza.

Attila stayed on the couch at his aunt and uncle's apartment, as in the old days. No one mentioned Károly Ambrus, Attila's dad (and his aunt's brother), whom Attila's relatives occasionally saw pedaling around town on a battered bike. The Dacia had apparently died.

According to the local grapevine, Attila's mother was now a Jehovah's Witness, living in a nearby village with her seventh husband.

Attila presented his aunt and uncle with the food staples he'd brought, as well as a new toaster and a color television, explaining his generosity by saying, "Hockey pays well." And he had the newspaper article to prove it. In the season opener that October (technically, just an exhibition against the junior national team), Attila had played well enough to make the news for the first time, at least as a sportsman. The neatly clipped story he had preserved between the pages of a book was from Hungary's national sports newspaper, *Népsport,* and credited Attila with maintaining UTE's 12–1 victory. "Another goal would have been scored," *Népsport* wrote, "but UTE backup goalie Attila Ambrus defended the net with élan."

Ninny and Uncle László, who remembered when their nephew's life dream was to be a professional hockey player, teared up when they saw the paper. Later Attila pulled Uncle László into the kitchen. He knew László hadn't been able to find work for almost a year. "I could help out, you know," Attila said, reaching for his wallet.

"No," said László, grabbing Attila's arm. "I couldn't accept it." Though he didn't say it, neither did László accept Attila's explanation for where the money was coming from. He'd seen cousin Laczika's Jeep (though no one in town had had the gumption to question how the timorous carpenter had claimed its possession). "But maybe I could come stay with you in Budapest for a while," László suggested. "Find some real work?"

Attila tried to dissuade László. "Budapest isn't so ripe these days," he said, but László heard only what he wanted: ripe. Unable to turn down the man who had practically raised him, Attila reluctantly agreed to accept a new roommate and hazard the discovery of his oven's inedible contents. But he wasn't taking on another accomplice. He'd figure something out for László, and the living-space issue wouldn't be so bad. He wasn't around that much anyway.

Attila had begun spending more time than he'd anticipated with Éva Fodor, the feisty thirty-four-year-old woman with the coquettish smile, who owned the car wash near Judit's place downtown. For both personal and professional reasons, Attila knew he could never let a woman get too close again. But Éva was always surprising him. In November of 1993, after Attila's breakup with Judit, he'd stayed at the wash late one night and offered Éva a rare insight into his rejection complex — "Why are you even listening to me? I'm just a hairy-soled Transylvanian" — which was compounded by his inability to get Hungarian citizenship.

The next time Attila showed up at the wash, Éva told him to buy her four bottles of premium liquor and perfume. "And then what?" Attila asked. "I'll cheer you up," Éva said. It sounded worth pursuing to Attila, who never imagined what Éva had in mind: in January 1994, about two months after he'd decided to dedicate his life to robbery, his name was called in a municipal chamber and he was asked to swear to uphold the laws of the land. He lied and was pronounced, at twenty-six, a Hungarian citizen. After trying to get his citizenship for six years, the car wash girl had gotten it for him in two months. Clearly, Éva Fodor was a woman to be reckoned with. Attila was intrigued.

Wax by wax, Attila was growing on Éva, too. Except for that late night after his breakup with Judit, Attila was cagey about everything. When he told Éva he was a professional hockey player, she just nodded. "I'm also a silent partner in a car dealership," he said. "Oh," she said, and let it rest. She knew the deal. She saw forty customers a day who were silent partners and business consultants, and all of them paid in stacks of small notes. They were probably all crooks, but Attila was different. The fact that he wouldn't talk much about himself spoke volumes. All she needed to know was Transylvania; to her, his birthplace explained everything. She, too, had grown up in a place that she regularly avoided mentioning, a mostly Roma village called Gergely in the eastern Hungarian plains near the Romanian border. She wasn't poverty-stricken as a child, nor was her family Gypsy. The Fodors lived on a small farm with pigs and chickens; her father owned two general stores. But she knew too well that to be mistaken for or associated with Gypsies could destroy your hope for a better life. It had taken all of Éva's strength to leave home at seventeen and, against her father's wishes, head to Budapest. She put herself through night school to become a teacher while working days as a teaching assistant, barmaid, and clothing-store saleswoman. She was briefly married and bore a son, and when the divorce was finalized, she found a contact willing to sponsor her passage to America. She lived for eight months in a Brooklyn studio apartment, working in a Hungarian-owned wig factory that produced hairpieces mostly for Hasidic Jewish women. But after it became clear that she wasn't going to be able to stay permanently, she moved back to Budapest and cobbled together enough money to buy the two-car stall on Dob Street and turn it into the Quick Wash. Thanks to the growing population of people in Budapest like Attila, she found that she could make a decent living wiping down pleather. With the money from the wash, she also opened a little clothing boutique in the Budapest suburb where she lived with her son in a small apartment.

When Attila found out that Éva also had a clothing store, he asked if she would help him pick out some clothes. He showed up at the appointed time with Bubu and Karcsi in tow, wanting to know if she might be able to give them a discount. "You know, Bunny," he whispered, using his new nickname for her, "they have nothing." That, Éva believed, was the real Attila Ambrus. Not the guy who used to screech up to her curb and yell, "I need it done in an hour. I don't care what it costs."

Eventually, Attila's flirtation with Éva turned into a casual romance. He never let her stay at his place, but he spent a few nights a week in her two-story apartment building in the quiet, undeveloped Budapest suburbs. He taught her how to play tennis. She cooked him what he professed were among the best bean soups and pig's feet he'd ever tasted. And when Attila's uncle László arrived from Transylvania, Éva agreed to give him a job as the night watchman for her car wash. Sometimes Attila had to remind himself to keep Éva at a safe distance.

For the first time in his life, Attila had a whole crew of admirers. Aside from Éva and the ankle-nipping Gabi, there was also Gabi's father, UTE coach George Orbán, who was utterly enthralled by his backup goaltender. Coach Orbán had been around hockey a long time and he'd never seen someone as dedicated as Attila. Even though Attila had almost never seen game action, Orbán could see he was a gifted athlete who kept himself in top physical condition. Plus, despite the fact that Attila didn't even request a paycheck, he was the only member of Office and Home who never skipped a practice. As a former goalie himself, Orbán took an interest in helping Attila develop his skills: playing the angles, staying in the net. He even contemplated appointing Attila team captain, but it just wouldn't have made sense. Goalies weren't usually captains, and Attila wasn't even the starter. But Orbán enthusiastically supported Attila in his unofficial role as the Office and Home disciplinarian, and he got Attila into the games whenever he could.

Despite Attila's and Coach Orbán's efforts, however, UTE's promising season quickly fell apart. The highlight of the year turned out to be the new brand of fighting that the steel-skulled Szatmári brothers had brought over from Canada. Previously in Hungary when players fought, they hacked at each other with their sticks as if participating in a medieval jousting competition. The Szatmáris, to the astonishment of Hungary's regular brawlers such as Bubu, actually took off their gloves and attempted to beat on their opponents like gentlemen. It may have worked in North America, but in Hungary it was an easy way to get your ass whupped. UTE finished the 1994–95 season with a miserly 7–13–2 record, the club's first losing season in its history. It was almost as if they didn't know who they were anymore. On the bus home from the last game, one of guys pointed to the cursive words *Office and Home* that had been emblazoned across their jerseys all season and asked, "What does this say?" No one knew. Their minds had been focused on other things, such as trying to figure out how to come up with the rent. Attila's mind had necessarily begun to drift as well. All that losing was getting to him. During one game he was so aggrieved by his teammates' performance that he smacked the net over and skated off the ice in the middle of play. For hours after losses he was inconsolable. If he wanted to remember the feeling of winning, he was going to have to look elsewhere.

Thirteen

The FBI's first foreign training academy opened in Budapest on April 25 in an unmarked suburban housing block donated by the grateful Hungarian government. The inauguration ceremony went swimmingly, save for the last-minute cancellations of FBI director Louis Freeh and U.S. Attorney General Janet Reno, who sent promises that they would visit Hungary sometime after the dust cleared in Oklahoma City, where the largest domestic act of terrorism in U.S. history had just claimed that city's federal building, along with 168 American lives.

Eastern Europe's disillusionment with its governments may have been pronounced, but it hadn't yet blossomed into civilian plots to bomb its people and institutions. Nor had the region's burgeoning crime wave reached American proportions. Statistically, violent crime and robbery were actually worse in the United States than in Hungary in every category but auto theft. The concern of the FBI, however, was the less obvious dangers of postcommunist capitalism. It wasn't just animal-pelt smugglers and post office bandits who were exploiting the weaknesses in the fledgling system. There were also a host of others — among them, cops and former KGB agents — who now had access to former Soviet Red Army weapons caches, and a world of potential buyers. Unsuspecting men and women seated in first class on regional Eastern European flights found themselves being solicited over soft drinks about their interest in acquiring nuclear arms. In the first few years of the 1990s, the

FBI tracked thirty-seven cases of illicit shipments of radioactive material from Eastern Europe; no one could be sure how many deals went undetected. The end of the Cold War had buried one American enemy but possibly created thousands of even more dangerous ones.

Overnight, the budget of the U.S. law enforcement service in Hungary leapfrogged that of the country's own national police. The FBI's International Law Enforcement Academy (ILEA) flew police officials to Budapest from all over Eastern Europe to train them to be better crime-stoppers. The two-month course it offered was said to be modeled on the same one given to recruits at FBI headquarters in Quantico, Virginia, *modeled* being the operative word. ILEA sessions began with an explanation of what a credit card was. Another session included a film clip of Clint Eastwood playing Dirty Harry, in which Harry kicks a suspect in the same leg that has just taken a bullet. It was an example, the FBI trainers told their trainees, of what *not* to do when apprehending a suspect. There was a lot of ground to cover; attendees were asked not to leave the premises until the two-month program was over.

Lajos Varjú was among the Hungarian officials offered a chance to attend the academy, but he no longer felt comfortable leaving his post for eight minutes, much less eight weeks. However, he did become friendly with three FBI agents who made regular visits to the Budapest police headquarters during which Lajos learned to sing "Yankee Doodle," even if he had no idea what it meant. In the course of one of the FBI flybys, Lajos managed to win the attention of the FBI interpreter long enough to ask his American counterparts a question about crime fighting. After a six-month break following the debacle the previous summer at the Ó Street travel agency — the longest hiatus since the Lone Wolf's streak began in January 1993 — the Budapest serial robber had pulled what was at least his eleventh successful job on January 12, 1995. The latest target was the same bank the robber had pillaged ten months earlier, where he'd so frightened the only male teller that the man had taken a soup shower under the table. This time the Lone Wolf had waltzed in, announced himself as "the guy from last time," and waltzed out three minutes later with 2.8 million forints ($22,400). ("Sir robber is smart, tricky, and daring," wrote *Blikk*.)

The crack FBI team had a recommendation for Lajos: profiling. First, Lajos was told, he should begin gathering forensic evidence at crime scenes. Then he should start up a database of the findings.

Brilliant, Lajos told them. And slightly presumptuous, he didn't bother mentioning. Where to start? His forensics unit was largely composed of former secretaries and interns, since few Hungarians no longer receiving a weekly allowance from their parents saw the rationale in working full-time for $150 a month. There were twelve hundred openings at the Hungarian police. Adjusted for inflation, police salaries were now worse than they had been at the end of communism. Resources were so scarce that the Budapest police chief had recently admitted publicly that because of an ammunition shortage, the city's cops were no longer allowed to take target practice. There were no state secrets anymore.

As for compiling a witness interview database, it hardly seemed worth the hassle. The only computer in Lajos's filing cabinet of an office was a hand-me-down from the fourth-floor administrative offices, made from mismatched parts and connected to an outlet whose current was occasionally shut down because of the delinquency status of the building's electric bill.

If the FBI really wanted to help, Lajos thought, they'd start cutting checks.

That spring, however, Lajos did fish out all of the Lone Wolf's files and asked Dance Instructor to browse through them again. Instructor quickly discovered what he believed was a trend. Just when the Lone Wolf appeared on the verge of becoming the country's most prolific criminal, he had apparently begun to lose his appetite for robbing, at least in Budapest. In 1993 Dance Instructor had the Lone Wolf down for seven jobs (or eight, counting the unsuccessful attempt at Nyugati train station); in 1994 just three; and so far through the first several months of 1995, only one. Dance Instructor also postulated that the reason the thief never wore gloves while committing his crimes was that he probably had no police record and knew that his prints — even if recorded — were not on file. It was almost as if the thief *wanted* the police to know who he was.

Lajos agreed with Dance Instructor. He didn't think the Lone Wolf was your standard Planet of the Zorg–type felon. In fact, given the sporadic timing of the crimes, Lajos was pretty sure he was a sailor. That's right: he goes out to sea, he comes back, he robs. The robberies were the sailor's way of getting his thrills while on leave back home, high-flying stints that included big spending and, odds were, gambling.

Lajos sent Keszthelyi and Dance Instructor across town to the headquarters of Mahart, the Hungarian state shipping company, where they misspent the next two months digging through thousands of employee files and investigating the mariners who were on leave during the time of the robberies. Meanwhile, Lajos and Mound made the rounds to the city's gambling halls, to which they brought about ten different police sketches of the Lone Wolf, each from a different robbery and each portraying a different face and hairstyle. The casino managers agreed to call if the unrecognizable individual entered their midst.

By the time summer arrived, no one had called, none of the sailors had checked out, and there were no new robberies. Once again Lajos asked the FBI for assistance and was counseled to try approaching the case in reverse, predicting the financial target where the thief would show up next. Lajos liked the idea and began compiling a list of the city's banks and post offices. He also recalled from the field his four main detectives on the case — Keszthelyi, Mound, Dance Instructor, and the Fat — and assigned them each a group of institutions to visit. Appointments were made, and the detectives fanned out across the city with the sketches and instructions. They taught the employees how to use stalling techniques should the Lone Wolf — or anyone else, for that matter — attempt to deflower their business. And most important, they beseeched the bank's management to invest in security systems, particularly cameras and guards. They couldn't be too careful.

Sure enough, on the afternoon of July 24, 1995, a call came in from a bank whose staff Lajos had briefed only a month earlier. The Lone Wolf had just walked out the door with 2.5 million forints ($20,000). He was long gone by the time the police arrived at the scene, but not all was lost. The bank had in fact heeded Lajos's advice and invested in a security camera. The entire robbery had been recorded. Lajos couldn't believe it. For the first time, he was going to get a look at his nemesis.

Lajos raced across town to the bank's central security center to get the videotape and then back to HQ and up to the fifth floor, where Mound, Keszthelyi, and the Fat were waiting next to the heretofore unused VCR. He put in the tape and they gathered around a small television.

The choppy, silent black-and-white pictures showed a bird's-eye view of the waiting area, into which a man with a mustache and short dark hair entered, dressed in a shirt and tie and carrying a black briefcase. He stepped up to one of the teller windows and appeared to inquire about something. Then, after about thirty seconds, the tape seemed to jerk into fast-forward mode. Quicker than the stuttering video frames could capture, the man pulled a gun out of his suitcase, jumped up on top of the waist-high counter, and disappeared into the back of the bank. The picture fell motionless for a little more than two minutes. Finally, the Lone Wolf appeared on-screen again, coming through a side door into the customer area with a plastic bag in his hand. He picked his briefcase up off the floor, stuffed the bag inside, and nonchalantly left out the front door.

Lajos rewound the tape and played it back again, this time freezing the picture on the only direct shot of the robber, as he entered. As the detectives leaned in, they noticed something oddly familiar about the man.

"It could be anyone," Lajos said, shaking his head in disappointment.

"Lali," Mound said to his boss. "It could be you."

With his thick shock of black hair; bushy, coarse mustache; and fuzzy dark eyebrows, the Lone Wolf bore an uncanny resemblance to none other than Budapest's robbery chief, Lajos Varjú.

The bank's address, on Lajos Street, no longer seemed incidental.

~

Blikk, July 25, 1995, front page:

2.4 Million Robbed
Big Bucks and Four Double Whiskeys

The criminal with no mask robbed the bank in his usual gentlemanly way. . . . He's getting on the nerves of the police. . . .

Before he entered the bank, he was seen drinking four double whiskeys at a pub fifteen meters away.

"A couple of minutes before noon, this gentleman entered," said one of the tellers, Krisztina Sipos. "He was asking about bank loans and looking through leaflets. Just when we recognized that he was the guy we had the police sketches of, he pulled out a gun and jumped over the counter."

Attila threw the paper down on the ground and stomped out a Székely jig on his latest press. He was furious and, understandably, horrified. Five full frames of his face stared up at him from the tabloid's front page.

How could this have happened? He'd been eyeing the Lajos Street bank for over a year; it was just down the street from his new hideaway, the cozy basement Globe Royale Casino. But the last time he'd been inside the bank, a 3 in his book, there hadn't been any video camera. Of course, he should have updated his data, but he hadn't planned on doing the job until the fall. Then last weekend he met Betty. She wasn't Éva, but she was the singer for the Hungarian rock band the Beasts, and she wanted the Chicky Panther to take her and her two friends to Costa Brava in Spain that weekend. (Éva wasn't really his girlfriend, and anyway, she wouldn't have to know. He could say he had a training camp.) But he hadn't worked a paying job since his last robbery six months earlier, after which he'd taken luxury holidays with Éva to Italy and Thailand. He was running short on cash, especially to be hosting a vacation for a rock star and her posse.

He'd checked around the bank's premises the night before pulling the job and had even taken the time to prepare a surprise for the robbery chief with whom Attila was rather annoyed. He'd seen Lajos quoted in the papers describing Attila as "lucky," when in fact Lajos had no idea what kind of preparation went into Attila's business. As if to set him straight, Attila had cut and styled one of his dark wigs and darkened up his thick mustache to resemble the naive detective. But now who looked naive? Lajos wouldn't be calling Attila lucky anymore, Attila thought; stupid, perhaps, or simply finished. *Blikk*'s national circulation was about 200,000. The Panther was out of the bag.

Fourteen

Tired of the wisecracks about being the serial robber, Lajos called a special meeting of his department and told them he was forming a sub-group to deal exclusively with the Lone Wolf case. They were going to catch a thief whose luck had finally run out, he told his team. "Who wants to take the lead on this?" he asked. "Anyone?" The ambitious young detective József Keszthelyi put up his hand. "Okay," said Lajos. "You start today."

That afternoon the handsome twenty-six-year-old Keszthelyi took the Metro to the Lajos Street bank, where he was greeted as if he were a cockroach. "You're only hindering my employees from working," the bank's manager, Belá Zarka, told Keszthelyi as he ran the young detective off the premises. "In any case, the insurance company is going to pay the damages."

Resilient as a roach, Keszthelyi headed back to HQ, made a copy of the bank's surveillance tape, and then phoned up the portly television personality László Juszt, the host of Hungary's top-rated program, *Kriminális*. Juszt's show was a sort of *Hungary's Most Wanted*, produced with the budget and technical sophistication of a typical American junior high school A/V department. But the show had been a huge hit, an example of how the creation of a free press had resulted in a great flowering of the tabloids. And as a result, the forty-two-year-old Juszt was one of the most important people at the police department and one of Hungary's brightest homegrown stars.

Paunchy and pale, Juszt had vaulted into the television news spotlight just after communism fell, doing short segments he called *Sokkoló* (Shocking), which investigated such contemporary horrors as traffic accidents. Two years later, in 1992, Juszt's instinct for schlock led him to pitch a new idea — *Kriminális* — to his bosses at the nation's only television station. They were skeptical. In communist times, there had been a similar show, called *Blue Light*, which had a loyal following and an even less telegenic host. But in those days, when the station carried little more than *The Flintstones, Columbo,* and cadaverous men reading irrelevant news, it didn't matter how thick your Rolodex was. Reporting a story meant accepting the information with gratitude for the government official who had invented it. Without that luxury, where in the world did Juszt expect to find his news? No worries, Juszt told his station bosses. The son of a former communist minister, Juszt was quite sure his old connections and these egregious times could keep *Kriminális* flush with enough material for a 24-hour news channel.

He was right. Even after the arrival of the ballyhooed new FBI training academy, the number of stories at Juszt's disposal kept multiplying. By 1996 a new crime was committed in Hungary every sixty-three seconds; three to four armed and increasingly violent robberies played out each week on the streets of the capital; each morning thirty-seven drivers awoke to find out that they no longer owned a car; and every Thursday night almost 4 million viewers, or 40 percent of Hungary, tuned in to *Kriminális* to watch their country's dismantling.

The program had started covering the Lone Wolf story after the embarrassing mishap last year at the travel agency at Ó Street, when Major Vigh's men had responded to the wrong address. So Juszt was quite happy to take a call from Lone Wolf lead detective József Keszthelyi over at the robbery department. A bank camera videotape? Send it right over, Juszt said. Nothing like an exclusive. Just a few hours after Attila and the Hungarian rock band boarded an overnight bus for Spain, *Kriminális* broadcast the bank video footage from the Lajos Street robbery, flashing a special police hotline number on the screen for viewers to call if they recognized the perpetrator.

Keszthelyi passed the next two weeks like a secretary. He fielded hundreds of calls, most of which were along the lines of the one from a man who was sure that the robber was the limousine driver for Viktor Orbán (no relation to the hockey Orbáns), then head of the conservative Alliance of Young Democrats and Hungary's next prime minister. One caller swore he'd worked at a glass company with the thief for a brief time in 1988. But Keszthelyi didn't think any of the tips or descriptions fit Dance Instructor's profile, so he turned his attention back to the one unimpeachable piece of evidence he did have: the videotape. All Keszthelyi needed, he believed, was a close-up of the Lone Wolf's face and the game would soon be over. But when the technical department enlarged a frame from the footage, the best image they could come up with revealed the serial robber to be nothing more than a thousand indistinguishable dots on a blank page: a big gray nobody.

There was no other physical evidence to go on, since the forensics team that had just been trained by the FBI hadn't managed to stumble over a single fingerprint suited for identification (again), even though the video showed the Lone Wolf robbing with his bare hands (again). Too embarrassed to ask the FBI for help, Keszthelyi shipped the videotape to England's Scotland Yard in a package marked URGENT. Several weeks later word came back. Scotland Yard had pronounced the discount-bin videotape worthless.

After working the case for four months, including commissioning two psychological profiles ("This person is addicted to robbery," stated one), Keszthelyi not only couldn't produce the Lone Wolf, he couldn't even produce a useful facsimile of him. The young detective did, however, deliver a summary report to his boss that was like no other in the robber's file. "Due to the 'most excellent' expertise of the police department," Keszthelyi wrote in the blistering dossier he hand-delivered to Lajos on November 16, 1995, "it will be very cumbersome to prove that the perpetrator committed this crime. I therefore recommend we terminate the investigation."

The desperation felt by the Budapest police mirrored the mood not only at Villányi Street 112, where the Lone Wolf was convinced he was now living on borrowed time, but also in the entire country, where people felt duped by the capitalist pipe dream. It had been six years since the transition from communism to free market capitalism and democracy, and still the country's infrastructure was so ill-functioning that those without friends in high places couldn't get a telephone line in their homes without being put on a Soviet-era queue 770,000 people long. Meanwhile, the American conglomerates that had swarmed into the city and taken over the downtown office buildings paid no taxes for doing business in Hungary but were happy to offer worse health benefits and less vacation time and expect far higher productivity than the Hungarians' previous employer, the state, had. And while the foreign investment had significantly helped grow the economy, some local politicians pointed out that these new foreign despots deposited their profits back into someone else's pocket, leaving Hungary still too poor to take care of all of its own.

Many Hungarians were beginning to wonder: Why had America been their country's role model? It couldn't care less about them. In Taszár, Hungary, where the U.S. troops were stationed in support of the American effort in Bosnia, Hungarian families had spent their life savings to open stores and restaurants catering to the Americans. Instead, they found themselves serving the American government with lawsuits for damages in connection with eighty-eight automobile injuries or deaths and four hundred incidents of destruction of property. And as with everything else that had been marketed and sold to Hungary as something to improve its lot, the FBI training center was beginning to appear of questionable value to the locals. Whether by plan or neglect, one month after the FBI's arrival, a powerful branch of the Russian mafiya was chased out of Czechoslovakia in an FBI raid and decided to relocate to Budapest, where it was growing and flourishing under the Bureau's nose.

In a country infamous for its gloom, Hungary's national mood in 1995 was estimated to be the worst it had ever been. Prime Minister Horn splurged on his biggest social program to date, a 2-billion-forint ($16 million) "Optimism Campaign," which included retraining teachers to positively spin class lessons. But it appeared that many of the prime minister's own cabinet members had already thrown in the towel. Hungary's tourism minister proposed as his office's new marketing campaign: "The Russians came. The Mongols came. The Turks came. They took everything. Come to Hungary and see what's left." And the city of Budapest, wracked with debt, allocated 95 million forints ($760,000) for a new museum that would take visitors on an underground tour of the municipal sewerage system. Paris had a similar sewerage exhibit, but the

Hungarian capital had long ago lost its resemblance to the City of Light. With the new museum, Hungary's also-ran Paris of the East had finally forged its own identity. At last, Budapest was a showcase for shit.

~

There was an unusual display at the UTE stadium that season as well. The team's sponsor, Office and Home, had bailed out of its deal with the club, presumably underwhelmed by the partnership's impact on brand recognition. Once again, the number of qualified professionals on UTE's roster shrunk by a factor of the reduced odds on getting paid. Among the disgruntled departures were Coach George Orbán and the previous season's regular goaltender, whose unanticipated retirement meant that for the first time in UTE's storied history — and perhaps even professional hockey history — a former team janitor was named the starting goalie.

As a result, the former pelt smuggler and pen salesman whose father said he would be nothing more than a gray nobody was now making news in two sections of the Hungarian newspapers. In the sports section, Attila was unrecognizably depicted in game-action photographs behind a lattice-grille face mask and white helmet. In more prominent parts of the paper, his big round face was plain to see, as the tabloids continued publishing the blurry but troubling frames from the Lajos Street bank video.

Fame, Attila quickly discovered, had consequences, and with both of his lives on public display, he began to look at the world in a way he hadn't done since his arrival in Hungary seven years earlier. No matter where he went or what he was doing, he saw escape routes. Unfortunately for UTE, this proved to be a major distraction from his attempts to sight and stop hockey pucks. On the opening weekend of the 1995–96 season, the cover of *Népsport* featured a photo of Attila in a pose that would become distressingly familiar to UTE fans: lying sideways across the goalmouth with his stick in the air and his feet splayed. "The UTE goalie Attila Ambrus can only search for the puck deep in the back of the net," read the caption next to the story of the team's 10–2 loss to Alba Volán.

To say that Attila had a lackluster season wouldn't be fair. Attila's 1995–96 season as UTE's starting goalie may be the worst performance by a goaltender in the history of hockey. During one six-game stretch, from November 3 to December 15, the Chicky Panther gave up eighty-eight goals, twenty-three of which were deposited in a single outing against Alba Volán in which UTE itself did not score a single goal. Stadiums all over the country, most of which featured scoreboards configured for one-digit tallies, had to make special preparations for Attila's arrival. In one case, that meant making a cardboard sign with a 1 on it and sending a boy over to stick it to the board; another time an arena announcer informed fans they would have to keep track in their heads after the arena's scoreboard hit 9. UTE contests had always been hallowed, and this year there was special cause to invoke the Holy Spirit. Shouts of "Christ Almighty!" and "What in heaven's name?" billowed from the stands as Attila missed shot after shot after shot. At the end of some games, Attila's head was so swollen from being pelted that he could barely remove his helmet.

The Panther had no sanctuary. When Attila stepped off the ice and out of the path of 100 mph flying disks, he stepped straight into the vortex of a citywide manhunt.

Somehow neither Éva nor his uncle László (who was still working nights at Éva's car wash and sleeping days in Attila's bed) seemed to recognize Attila's mustachioed mug in the photos blanketing the city's newsstands. But fearing capture and isolated by his inability to share his troubles, Attila tumbled into a chasm of manic behavior and illogical thinking. Aware that the couple of million forints ($15,000) he had to his name would have to last, he drove each day to the Keleti train station and exchanged a wad of forints into U.S. dollars with the Middle Eastern money changers at the best black market rate. Then he turned around and headed to the Globe Royale Casino, where he lost himself and his fresh American currency playing slot machines and roulette. Sometimes the only sleep he got was a few hours on a table at the Cats Club.

Éva could see that Attila was in a funk. Though he still bunked with her several nights a week, he'd become even more remote than he had been in the early stages of their courtship. He wouldn't show up at her apartment until the middle of the night and would spend an inordinate amount of time in her bathroom, stricken with stomach cramps. He wouldn't say what was bothering him, but she could see from the casino chips on his car seat where he was going after hockey. One night when she tried to stop him from going gambling, he told her she was his "lucky charm" and dragged her along. She watched him finish two bottles of whiskey on his own and then refuse to leave until the 3:00 A.M. closing, by which time he was both completely blitzed and thoroughly forintless. Éva liked Attila, but trying to rationalize with him was like performing a Skinner experiment on a rat. All she had to do was mention the words *szerencse játék* (gambling) and he would robotically pack up the little suitcase he kept at her apartment, mutter, "Nothing is ever good enough for you," and disappear for a week.

Noticing his increasingly irritable moods, Bubu, then playing for FTC, asked Attila what was wrong during one of their less frequent get-togethers. But all Attila would offer was "At least you can sleep at night" as he downed another *pálinka*. Since Attila and his uncle's work schedules were diametrically opposite, he could practically avoid László altogether.

But avoiding people didn't help Attila feel better. In fact, he was beginning to hate himself. He was in an excruciating limbo, always wondering if and when and how the hammer would fall. If he could just get away with this one, he swore, he would give up the robbery game. It was too much. If the Lajos Street bank had gotten a camera that quickly without his knowing, how could he ever keep up? The security improvements were coming too quickly.

About this time, Gustáv Bóta approached his Panther with an enticing business opportunity. Bóta had heard through his contacts that the infamous Black and White Club downtown on Klauzál Square was up for sale. Owned by Semion Mogilevich, the reputed head of the Russian mafiya, the Black and White was a sleek, exclusive "businessman's" paradise, the Russian-owned in-town version of the Cats Club. It was a Budapest landmark. Perhaps, Bóta suggested, Attila would like to take it off Mogilevich's hands, settle down. Attila imagined himself, Zubovics-like, surrounded by velvet ropes and security guards, chatting up the country's finest crooks. "Let me think about it," he told Bóta. He was also thinking about something else: Éva.

Before he'd gone and blown his life to smithereens at Lajos Street, they had had so many effortless good times together. Scuba diving in Bali, skiing in the Italian Dolomites, sightseeing in Paris. He genuinely liked her and, to his surprise and consternation, even respected her. She probably wouldn't like the idea of his owning a whorehouse, even a well-respected one, but if she only knew how much better that was than his current gig.

He decided to invite Éva home with him to Transylvania for the holidays. Éva accepted, not that she had much choice. A few days before Christmas, Attila showed up at her apartment and said, "Pack your bags." He felt like an animal-pelt smuggler again.

Éva loved Attila's spontaneity. Half the way to Csíkszereda she kept the car window down just to feel more alive. She knew she was the first woman Attila was taking home.

As soon as he tasted the chilled Hargita Mountains air, Attila felt a calmness come over him. He drove Éva out through the hills of Székelyföld to St. Anne's Lake, where in the summers he used to hike and pick mushrooms. "It's like we're in a time warp," he told her along the way, pointing to horse-drawn carts bumping along the snowy roads. Attila also took her with him as he distributed the usual food staples he'd brought from Hungary up and down the two frozen mud streets of Fitód, his native village that had been too insignificant for Ceaușescu to bother erasing. Éva was charmed. Fitód was a little like her hometown of Gergely; most people were still without plumbing, phones, or cars. Attila knew everyone by name, and they all remembered him. Dénes Ambrus, his father's brother, who still lived a few doors down from Attila's childhood home, recalled little Attila as "a horse always about to bolt." He invited his nephew and Éva to a pig-killing ceremony.

Attila and Éva stayed in Csíkszereda on the couch in Attila's aunt and uncle's apartment. Éva already knew László (who had also returned for the holidays), and she and Ninny hit it off immediately. It was a real family affair: cooking, drinking, dirty underwear strewn about the living-room floor.

One morning Attila and Éva arose before sunrise and drove through darkness to Uncle Dénes's Fitód home, where a group of villagers were dressed in the traditional white riding pants, black vests, and pointed Robin Hood hats. They spent the morning drinking homemade *pálinka* and singing folk songs before chasing, and eventually stabbing and dismembering, a screeching 350-pound animal. Attila had a ball. Éva almost threw up. *Great people,* she thought, but she could do without the pig intestines.

As their stay was nearing its end, Attila told Éva there was one more thing he wanted to do. On their last afternoon in Csíkszereda, they drove to the cemetery on the edge of town, where Attila's grandmother was buried. As they stood at her gravestone, Attila began to talk about his family, and for Éva, the hazy first act of her boyfriend's life finally came into focus.

Anna Ambrus was Attila's paternal grandmother, a Russian Jew who had emigrated in the early 1900s and changed her name from Friedman when the first "Jewish laws" limiting her freedoms were introduced in Transylvania in 1940. Like the rest of the villagers, Anna and her husband were farmers who owned land and livestock that produced goods they sold and traded in nearby Csíkszereda. But when Attila's grandfather died in the 1960s, Attila's father sold all the land but the house with the oversize attic perfect for smoking meats. Károly Ambrus wasn't going to be a farmer. Exceptionally bright, he had become one of the rare Hungarians to be granted a scholarship to a prestigious technical university.

All Attila knew about his mother was that she was several years younger and had met his father in 1964 while he was on leave from the Romanian army. They were married soon afterward. Then inexplicably, a year after Attila was born, Klara Ambrus fled Fitód. And later that same year Károly and Dénes Ambrus's other brother was killed while working on an electrical pole in a storm. Soon afterward, Attila's father slipped into a despairing alcoholic stupor.

Anna Ambrus, who slept on a hay bed on the other side of a curtain from Attila, took on the responsibility of raising her grandson. Attila had run into her arms seeking protection from his father so many times, he could still smell her freckled skin. As far as Attila was concerned, she was the only mother he ever had.

After Anna died in 1976, Attila's aunt and uncle did everything they could for Attila. But they couldn't make Attila behave like the other kids. He didn't have a mother, and his father couldn't care less about seeing him unless he'd gotten into trouble again, in which case Károly would materialize at László and Ninny's apartment to deliver Attila a few slaps. Attila gradually began getting into bigger and bigger trouble, as if it were his way of hitting back at the man who made him feel worthless. Ultimately, Attila's mischief culminated with the episode that literally left him scarred for life, the theft of the musical instruments. When the two friends with whom Attila committed the crime were caught after brainlessly advertising the instruments for sale in the local paper, Attila's accomplices claimed that Attila was the crime's sole culprit — a believable accusation, given Attila's lengthy petty criminal record. After two months in the Csíkszereda jail, Attila accepted full responsibility and, despite his relatives' pleas, was sentenced to two years in a chain-link-fenced juvenile detention facility near the Moldavian border. As one of the institution's only Hungarians — who spoke no Romanian — among thousands of wayward Romanian adolescents, Attila was ridiculed, beaten with rubber sticks by the commanders, and, one night, awakened by the whispers of two of his bunkmates, who were bearing down on him with steak knives. He spun away from their swipes just in time to escape with only the deep, long cut along his left arm. He was too afraid of further retribution to see the doctor, so he bled through his shirts for days and went months before regaining pain-free use of his arm. At seventeen, he went back to Csíkszereda, hemorrhaging hope, only to be called away again two months later for another sixteen months of humiliation in the Romanian army. There was nothing left to say. Éva held Attila as he cried. She had always wondered about the origins of his scars, and now she knew. "When she died," Attila said, pointing to his grandmother's stone, "my life took a fatal turn." If only Éva knew just how far down the wrong path Attila was standing.

The next day Attila and Éva began the long drive home through the snowy central Transylvanian hills and the barren western Romanian plains. Attila felt closer to Éva than to any woman since his grandmother, and he figured he might as well pop the question. "What do you think about my buying the Black and White bar?" he asked. Not a bad idea, Éva told him, but she had a better one. "Why don't we buy a bar together?" she said. There was a smaller, quieter place she knew of for sale in Érd, the suburb west of Budapest where she lived. He could take a management course at night to learn to run the place, and they could go into business together and settle down outside the city. It wasn't what he'd imagined, but by the time they arrived back in Budapest, Attila had agreed.

Fifteen

There were no more hockey nightmares that season. After UTE had gone 0–11 leading up to the holiday break with Attila in the net, it forfeited the remainder of its games. That was fine with Attila. Twice a week he headed to a suburban office building for a business management course in preparation for his gig in the bar on which Éva had made a successful 2-million-forint bid ($13,000). By February they had a closing date that they would never make. The night before they were scheduled to sign the papers and hand over the cash, Éva was awakened by her phone. "Bunny," Attila said, in slurred speech from the Gresham Casino. "You know I love you. Can I borrow two million forints?"

In several hundred spins of the roulette wheel, there went the bar, the family, the quiet suburban life. Of course he was sorry, but as much as he'd legitimately considered settling down with Éva, he couldn't help that it freaked him out. That, or he was simply a schlemiel. But he knew from experience that relationships didn't always work out. And when he'd thought about it, co-owning a bar in the 'burbs didn't seem particularly more secure than his robbery career, which at least he could control on his own. In some ways the prospect of pouring drinks for people was even more frightening to Attila than robbing banks. He wanted to be *somebody*, not *somebody's bartender*. The Black and White Club wasn't for him, either. Attila gambled instead that his best chance of making something of himself was to continue pursuing work as a modern-day bandit.

If there was anything for which Attila had a particularly well honed talent, it was recognizing the forces and tides of his environment. Several years of religiously reading the newspapers and running from the law had made him an expert on the Hungarian People's predilections. In the current milieu, American pop star Madonna's book *Sex* was being translated and marketed for the Hungarian market as *Slut*. The International Bodyguard and Secret Service Association had recently held its first-ever meeting in Budapest and proposed inaugurating a biannual Olympic-style Bodyguard Games. And just in time for the country's millicentennial celebrations — eleven hundred years since Árpád made his famous ride — the mafia was beginning to kill people with car bombs, more than thirty of which would go off like fireworks around the capital that year. People were needy and scared — and there was no one left to believe in.

Broke and single again after Éva promptly dumped him, Attila got to thinking. With a little extra planning, he could easily be a prime-time player. The table was set just right. Most of Hungary would soon be rejoicing in the gentleman bandit's return.

⁓

László Juszt's program began as it always did, with a suspenseful drum-and-bass soundtrack playing over a blue-backgrounded montage of slow-motion images traced from footage of SWAT team–like police shoot-outs and car chases. Then the words INNOCENT UNTIL PROVEN GUILTY appeared in yellow letters across the screen. After the opening sequence, Juszt appeared, bespectacled and bemused, in a double-breasted suit behind a podium in a monitor-filled newsroom. "Good evening. I kiss your hand," he said, using the old-fashioned Hungarian address that was his trademark.

Juszt informed his guests that he had landed a special guest that night whose profile was on the rise: Colonel Lajos Varjú, who had been promoted to chief of all of Budapest's robbery divisions in January. The colonel, Juszt told his viewers, had been busy the past couple of weeks chasing the robber whom *Kriminális* viewers would remember from a

segment the previous summer, when the thief had been caught on camera in a Lajos Varjú getup cleaning out a bank on Lajos Street. After
eight months off, the bandit had re-emerged and knocked off the post
office next to the Gellért Hotel, walking out with nearly 10 million
forints ($65,000), a new personal record.

Of particular note during this robbery, however, was that the thief
had entered the bank carrying a bouquet of red roses, which he'd
handed to one of the tellers before announcing that he was there to rob
the place. He'd then rounded up the six female employees in the back
room and told them, "I don't want to cause anyone trouble, but no
one can leave the room for two minutes. *Viszlát.*" *Bye.* When Lajos's
men arrived, they found the familiar hand-lettered sign on the front
door: CLOSED FOR TECHNICAL DIFFICULTIES. PLEASE EXCUSE THE
INCONVENIENCE.

Before beginning his interview with the robbery chief, Juszt gave
his audience what he called a "robber's-eye view" of the day in question. He rolled a segment that took viewers on a narrated tour of the
heist, beginning at the famous fish restaurant Szeged, where the thief
had been seen drinking whiskey for an hour before the robbery, then on
to the flower stand next to the Gellért Hotel, where he'd bought the
roses, and then to the post office for the main event.

When the piece ended, the camera returned to Juszt, now seated on
a soundstage in a leather armchair. After he welcomed his guest, the shot
jumped to Lajos, smiling uncomfortably in the hot seat, dressed as if he
were there to screen-test for a role in *Miami Vice*. A pair of tinted, gold-
rimmed aviator-style glasses sat on his nose, above which his bushy eyebrows sprouted like alfalfa. A silver clip held his royal blue tie to a lime
green shirt.

"There have been seventeen post office robberies in the country
since January, a total sum of twenty-three million forints [$150,000],"
Juszt began. "Nine of them happened in Budapest on a Thursday. Are
we correct in our hypothesis that if it's a Thursday, it's a post robbery?"

Lajos leaned over his right elbow, awkwardly perching his broad
head on his hand. "If you look at just these eight or nine, probably, but
it's not always the case . . . ," he said, sweating under the set's bright
lights. This wasn't Lajos's thing, television, but if it might help solve the
Lone Wolf case, he'd do anything.

Attila's first Hungarian passport, issued when he finally received citizenship in 1994. He'd begun robbing the previous year. (BALÁZS GÁRDI)

Attila and his grandmother, Anna, who raised him, standing near their home in eastern Transylvania, circa 1975, a year before she died. "When she died, my life took a fatal turn," Attila said. (COURTESY OF ATTILA AMBRUS)

From left to right: Attila's father, Károly Ambrus; Attila in his Romanian army uniform; Attila's cousin Edit; and Attila's uncle László, who raised him after his grandmother died. Standing outside Attila's military barracks in Galati, Romania, in 1987, the year before Attila escaped from the country. (COURTESY OF ATTILA AMBRUS)

Two future Hungarian hockey stars, Karcsi (left) and Bubu, broke and homeless, at the Keleti train station in Budapest on the day they arrived in Hungary from Transylvania in 1990, months after the Romanian revolution.
(COURTESY OF JENO "BUBU" SALAMON)

Attila and Éva, having dinner together on vacation in Thailand, 1995. He almost gave up the life of crime for her.
(COURTESY OF ÉVA FODOR)

UTE goalie Attila Ambrus in 1994, the year the team saved itself from bankruptcy by signing up as a sponsor the Western-funded desk wholesaler Office and Home, which put its logo on the front of the vaunted Hungarian team's jerseys.
(COURTESY OF ATTILA AMBRUS)

The 1994–95 UTE team. Top row, second from right: Gabi Orbán. Middle row, far left: Coach George Orbán; far right: Gustáv Bóta. Bottom row, second and third from left: Karcsi Antal, seated next to his one-time robbery accomplice, Attila. (Bubu had departed for UTE's crosstown rival, FTC.)
(COURTESY OF ATTILA AMBRUS)

Attila (left) and Gabi celebrating their successful robbery partnership with a "luxury, all-inclusive, money-is-no-object two-week trip" to the Dominican Republic, fall 1996.
(COURTESY OF ATTILA AMBRUS)

László Juszt, host of the hit TV program Kriminális, *during his heyday in the mid-1990s as Hungary's most famous journalist and chronicler of the Whiskey Robber. He would be arrested and thrown off the air in 1999.*
(SIPOS ISTVÁN/RED DOT)

The Whiskey Robber, mid-1990s, gets
a Christmas present he likes: a bottle
of his signature drink, Johnnie Walker
Red. (COURTESY OF ATTILA AMBRUS)

The bandit at rest. (COURTESY OF ATTILA AMBRUS)

Police photo from a lineup at
the Gyorskocsi Street jail,
January 21, 1999, six days
after Attila (second from
right) and Gabi (second from
left) were arrested for the first
time. Two of the other three
men pictured are the Szucs
brothers, who had been in jail
for the previous ten months
for several of Attila and
Gabi's robberies. Gabi has to
pucker his lips to keep the fake
mustache on his face. None of
the witnesses fingered Gabi or
Attila as the perpetrators.
(COURTESY OF BUDAPEST
POLICE DEPARTMENT)

Attila and former Budapest robbery chief Lajos Varjú, who unsuccessfully tracked the Whiskey Robber for five years before resigning from the force, meet for the first time at the jail in March 1999. Attila is muscle-bound from a daily exercise regimen developed to aid his impending escape. He is also drunk.
(PÉTER VÁRKONYI)

The view from one floor above the street, looking up at the fourth window of the jail administration building out of which Attila escaped on a rope made of bedsheets, towels, and shoelaces. The rope ended seventeen feet above the ground.
(COURTESY OF BUDAPEST POLICE DEPARTMENT)

Hours after Attila's escape from the Budapest jail on July 10, 1999, the city of Budapest is sealed. Police search every car leaving the city.
(GÁBOR CZERKL)

Attila's lawyer, George Magyar, sits next to a life-size cardboard cutout of his famous client for a press conference in summer 1999. Magyar claimed he had received an offer for a "Hollywood movie deal" and an energy-drink sponsorship for Whiskey Robber beverages. Attila could not attend because he was being hunted by INTERPOL and the entire Hungarian police force. (SIPOS ISTVÁN/RED DOT)

The fugitive Whiskey Robber in action, captured by bank surveillance cameras inside and outside the Ulloi Street OTP Bank three months after Attila's escape from the Budapest jail.

The Whiskey Robber's hockey teammate and robbery accomplice Gabi Orbán, in handcuffs, being led into the courtroom during the trial, which began in the summer of 2000.
(GÁBOR FUSZEK)

Like a final score for the ages, Whiskey Robber fans spray-painted the number of Attila's robberies versus his number of arrests on the wall of the apartment building in which he hid during his escape. Viszkis, in Hungarian, is an informal term meaning "the whiskey guy." BM is the abbreviation for the Belugium Ministerium, or Interior Ministry, the government branch in charge of the police.
(GÁBOR FUSZEK)

Attila in prison-issue garb and behind glass at the maximum-security prison in Sátoraljaújhely, Hungary, June 10, 2003.
(LISA HYMAN)

Juszt turned the discussion to the serial robber, steering Lajos head-on into the question he'd been waiting all week to stick to the robbery chief: "Do you have any idea who this guy is?"

"Yes," Lajos said, "we're not so stupid as to have no idea." He paused as if considering how to sum up the preponderance of nothing he knew. "He's done not only post offices but also banks," he continued. "Over the past several years, he's taken more than twenty million forints [$130,000] himself."

Juszt leaned in toward his guest and, referring to the bouquet of roses and the fact that the thief had previously disguised himself as Lajos, asked, "Is it annoying that he's playing a game with the police?"

Lajos sat back in his chair. How should he put it? "At the beginning it was annoying," he said. "Then it became very annoying. And now," he said, turning his right palm up, bobbing his head and rolling his eyes, "it's *extremely* annoying."

Juszt turned back to the camera. "We would like to offer something to the perpetrator," he said, whom he correctly assumed was watching. "If you're going to do a job next Thursday, we'll have a crew standing by to cover it."

Things were getting interesting again for Attila. One morning he made sure to arrive early for a weight-training session at UTE and pretended to be reading the newspapers at his locker when his teammates arrived. BANK ROBBERY WITH A BOUQUET OF FLOWERS was *Blikk*'s front page headline; YEAR OF THE ROBBERS, announced *Kurír*. "Look at this guy," Attila said, pointing to his heroic portrayal in the papers. "He's making fools of the police." Indeed, his teammates agreed, the city's "gentleman robber" was an outstanding chap. In fact, it was somewhat thrilling just to be able to say so. Under communism, supporting a criminal was just as unthinkable as reading about a likable lawbreaker in the state-controlled media.

Attila's comeback had been perfect — except for one little thing. He couldn't take any credit for it. What a deal. Of all things, his career choice required a commitment to the one he'd spent a lifetime running from: anonymity.

It was 1996, and once again a specter was haunting Hungary — the specter of another UTE hockey season. Attila's old friend George Pék had accepted a plea from an emasculated General Bereczky to come back and coach, but after the previous season's Panther-led debacle, it wasn't going to be an easy assignment. The team was negotiating with the cough drop manufacturer Halls for a new sponsorship, and whatever it was worth would constitute UTE's entire budget. The Interior Ministry, which had continued to offer a minimal level of financial support for UTE up to that point, had severed the cord entirely. If anyone thought the locker room smelled now, wait until the next time the pipes burst.

Needless to say, the players who remained at UTE were running out of reasons for doing so. Among them was Gabi Orbán, who still lived with his parents in an apartment building not far from Attila's place and was just as clueless as to how he would ever be able to afford to move out. Well, he still had one idea.

One summer morning after a workout, Gabi persuaded Attila to give him a ride home. "I'd do anything for a car like this," Gabi suggested as they rocketed through the streets in Attila's new red Alfa Romeo.

"Anything?" Attila asked.

At exactly nine o'clock in the morning two Sundays later, twenty-two-year-old Gabi Orbán was standing outside Attila's building. He'd arisen at 6:00 A.M., told his parents he was going for a run, and run he did — straight to the bus to the no. 61 tram that snaked south through the grass-lined middle-class suburb to the XI District, where his father's favorite goalie lived. Gabi had been standing there at his life's crossroads for over an hour. He knew Attila's position on punctuality, and he was in no mood to run laps.

Before Attila agreed to share his secret with Gabi, Attila asked him to spend two weeks thinking about whether he was really ready to change his life. Gabi spent the fortnight sleeplessly shuffling through images like a school filmstrip on choosing a career: *drug smuggling... maybe... contract killing... he'd prefer not... stealing cars... that could be something.* The common illustration that followed each clip was a smiling Gabi seated behind the wheel of a Mercedes 190E. Gabi was more than ready. He already felt guilty.

He looked at the wall of buzzers outside Attila's building. Panther had said his was the bottom one on the left. Of the six, it was the only one without a name next to it. Gabi rang and was buzzed in. When he got to Attila's door, down a small flight of stairs to the left, Panther's hazel eyes were peering out at him from behind it. Without a word, Attila pulled open the door and Gabi stepped into Panther's secret world — a little too quickly. Attila, wearing an Adidas sweatsuit, put his hand against Gabi's chest like a cop, stopping him in his tracks.

"Shoes," Attila said.

"What?" Gabi asked.

"Take off your shoes."

Once appropriately outfitted, Gabi entered Panther's dwelling, a cool and dark room with only a narrow ray of natural light streaming in from the kitchen. A soccer game flickered on the large television in the corner. The red-and-black-checkered carpet was spotless, and there was no Uncle László to be found. (Éva had been too good-hearted to fire Attila's uncle from her car wash after the pub debacle, but László was also accustomed to Attila's occasional requests to clear out for a day or two so he could "entertain a lady.") On the wall was the black bearskin and Attila's favorite painting, which he had bought in Transylvania with his pelt money in 1992, portraying a peasant farmhouse on the plateau at sunset.

"You want a drink?" Attila asked, pulling out a bottle of Johnnie Walker Red from behind the white flower-patterned cover that draped his antique mahogany study table.

"No," Gabi said, sitting down on a wooden chair. "I don't drink." Not to mention that it was 9:00 A.M.

Attila poured himself a tall glass of whiskey and took a gulp. "So are you ready to hear about this, then?" he said.

"Yes," Gabi said.

"Then there's no going back," Attila said.

"I'm ready," said Gabi.

Attila went into the bathroom, from which Gabi could hear him rummaging around in plastic bags. When Attila returned, he was holding several newspapers in his hand. He opened a copy of the tabloid *Reform* to a centerfold where a double-sided story appeared, illustrated by half a dozen police sketches. He said nothing as he set the paper down on the study table in front of Gabi.

Gabi looked over the photos and the story of the man the newspaper was calling "Budapest's own private bank robber."

"You want to do something like this?" Gabi asked.

"Look again," Attila said.

Gabi turned his eyes back to the paper. "What?" he asked.

"That's me," Attila said, pointing at the sketches. "I'm the one they're talking about."

Gabi couldn't believe it. He looked at the drawings again, but they looked nothing like Panther. He turned back to see Attila bouncing up and down on his toes like a child who's just been told the toy store is about to open. Attila then dropped into a tuck and somersaulted across his living room until he hit the far wall, then reversed his direction and tumbled all the way back. "It's me!" he shouted from his back, kicking his legs in the air. "It's me!"

Sixteen

Having disclosed his secret to the coach's kid, Attila was stricken by his own stupidity. It had been three years since he had let anyone into his shadowy world, and his memories of his two accomplice experiences — with Karcsi and with his cousin László — weren't particularly reassuring. But at least with them, Attila felt relatively comfortable that they wouldn't blab — or that even if they did, they would only sound like another incomprehensible Székely spinning fairy tales. Gabi, on the other hand, knew a lot of people in Budapest. And it wasn't difficult to imagine the little squirt bragging around town about his new career in the limelight.

After mulling it over, Attila decided he needed to come up with a litmus test for Gabi's trustworthiness, even if it was a smidgen late. He invented a new birthday for Bubu and a coming-home party for another teammate and invited Gabi out for a series of boozy nights on the town. He made sure to bring along many hot women, cool teammates, and the city's celebrity hockey fan, Gangsta Zoli — the only Hungarian rapper (who was at work on a soon-to-be-bestselling album, *Helldorado,* about what he called "the wild, wild East"). Then Attila would see to it that Gabi got blitzed and would follow him around to see if he talked. It wouldn't be a scientific assessment, but it would have to do.

On their first evening, at the LeRoy Café, Gabi, intoxicated not only by the attention he was receiving from Attila, picked up a woman whom he thought he could impress by downing several triple shots of pear *pálinka*. After a few rounds he put one of his shot glasses back on the bar and tried to sit back on his barstool but missed, leaving Attila in a familiar predicament: lifting an unconscious partner off the floor. He carried Gabi out to his car and drove him home. But Gabi didn't talk out of turn that night or on any of the others. He'd passed the test.

A few weeks later, in the deadening heat of an August hill sprint, Attila told Gabi he'd pick him up at a bus stop a few blocks from the stadium after practice. When Gabi arrived at the appointed station, Attila collected him and drove them to a busy intersection in southern Buda, where a post office sat in the middle of a diagonal row of corner shops.

Attila nodded ahead. Gabi looked across the street. "You want to do a post office?" he asked with obvious disappointment.

"You're not ready for a bank," Attila said.

"Don't I need a gun?"

"Leave everything to me," Attila said. "Be at my apartment at six A.M. sharp next Thursday. And don't shave between now and then."

When Gabi arrived the following week, Attila's formerly spotless apartment looked like a costume shop on the eve of a masquerade ball. There were wigs, glasses, hats, coats, and ties all over the checkered carpet and the bed, which hadn't been folded up. There was also a big plate of smoked sausages, raw onions, goat cheese, and several rashers of bacon, which Attila paid to have shipped from Uncle Dénes in Fitód. "See this, Gabi," Attila said, sitting down at his small table with a glass of whiskey. "Soon you're going to be eating from the bowl of life with the biggest spoon."

After they ate, Attila went to the kitchen to get his notebook out of the oven. He came back and opened it to the page featuring the post office they had observed from the car the previous week. Gabi looked in amazement at Attila's densely inscribed book.

"This is a serious business, Gabi," Attila said. "Don't forget that."

Attila had rated the Fehérvári Street post office a 2 because of its distance from the police station and its surplus of worthy escape routes. Gabi's job, Attila explained, was to wait in line for a teller until Attila found the right moment to begin, then pull his gun at Attila's word:

rablás (robbery). From then on, Gabi was to guard the door and keep track of the time. Anyone trying to enter was to be allowed in and then immediately made to get on the floor. No one was allowed to leave, for any reason. At three minutes Gabi was to yell out the time — but never was he to use Attila's name or nickname.

"How long do we have?" Attila asked.

"Three minutes."

"How long?"

"Three minutes."

"Say it a hundred times."

While Gabi reiterated his instructions, Attila went into the bathroom. His stomach was bothering him. After a while he returned to the living room and dangled a gun in front of his partner. "No matter what, you don't shoot at anyone," Attila said, yanking it back just as Gabi reached for it. "Understand? If anything, you shoot at the ceiling."

"So the idea is to create a panic, right?" Gabi said, snatching the gun.

"No," Attila said, annoyed. "Listen to me, Gabi. If you create a panic, the situation gets out of your hands. You always have to be in control. This is very important. You have to be strong enough and fast enough to scare them, but they must always believe you are in complete control of the situation. Do you understand?"

"Yes."

"That means you don't use the gun."

"What do I do with it?"

"Point."

At 1:00 P.M. Attila told Gabi to go to the bathroom and shave everything but his mustache. "And shave your sideburns — all the way to the top," Attila said. That way the color of the wig wouldn't clash with Gabi's real hair. While Gabi was in the bathroom, Attila emptied the bullets from his pupil's gun.

When a mustachioed Gabi emerged, Attila handed him a wig and a fedora and told him to put them on. Gabi returned from the bathroom looking like a grade-school thespian. Attila fell off the bed laughing, but it was the cackle of the stupendously doomed. He and this clown he'd handpicked were supposed to knock off a post office in a few hours. Attila took a mascara brush and darkened Gabi's patchy mustache, then it was time to put on their dress shirts and suits over their shorts and T-shirts. "Always keep one eye on me and it will be fine," Attila told Gabi before swallowing his third glass of whiskey. Soon Gabi's stomach was bothering him as well, and he and Attila were fighting for turns in the bathroom.

Around 2:30 Attila got his Camel gym bag out of the closet — which folded and zipped into a coaster-size pad — and stuffed it into his back pocket. They synchronized their watches and prepared to leave separately. Gabi was to take a taxi — one without a CB radio — to a location several blocks from the post office and give the driver 5,000 forints ($32) to wait while he ran an errand. (A what? An errand.) Attila was going to take a separate cab to another corner. They would meet on the opposite side of the intersection from the post office.

Attila was about to send Gabi off when he realized he'd forgotten something. "Wait a second," he said, running back into the kitchen. He was so drunk that he'd almost forgotten his plan. "Watch this," he said, emerging with two empty bottles of wine. He picked up the oversize shoebox in which his Transylvanian meats had come and placed the bottles inside. Then he grabbed a blue Parker pen and a paper napkin, on which he wrote, *Greetings Colonel Lajos Varjú, vice commander, sir!* He thought for another moment but couldn't come up with anything else, so he just signed the note, *XY!!* and stuck it in with the bottles. Attila wrapped the package in brown construction paper and taped it up. Then he picked up the pen again and inscribed another higher-profile name on the top of the box — Sándor Pintér, national police chief — along with a fictional address. He'd show them lucky. Attila handed Gabi the package. It was time to go.

By 3:30 P.M. one-third of UTE's starting lineup was positioned on the pavement at opposite ends of the Fehérvári Street shops. It was a splendid afternoon for robbery: cloudless and August-delirium warm. Gabi was miserable. He was sweating profusely beneath his double-layered clothes, and his scalp was itching under the wig. In his arms he cradled the package for the police chiefs.

Before assuming his post at the corner, Attila had strolled by the glass front door of the post office, taking a quick count of how many customers were inside. Now, when anyone came in or out, he threw his left hand down to his side and, like a baseball catcher, signaled to Gabi with his fingers the number of people left in the building. This went on for twenty minutes. Every time the count got down to one — the number Attila had said they needed in order to start — someone else went in. Thanks to the half hour Attila had wasted having two more whiskeys at the pub across the street, Gabi was becoming convinced that the post office would close before they ever got inside. Then the sign came: one index finger pointing down, followed by a quick thumbs-up. They began walking toward the door from opposite sides.

Gabi entered first, as planned, and got in line to send Attila's package behind the only customer in the place. The interior looked just the way Attila had drawn it in the diagram. It was a rectangular office with a small foyer and four glass-encased teller booths. No security guard, no camera, and all female employees. When the customer in front of Gabi left, the woman working booth number one told him, "Just a moment, please." She stood and walked out into the front, past Attila, who was filling out a lottery ticket at a counter; pulled a key out of her pocket; and locked the front door. "We're about to close," she told Gabi upon returning to the booth. Gabi handed her the package, and just as the teller turned her head to pull the mailing forms from her desk, Attila's voice pierced the stillness. "Robbery!" he shouted. "Hands up and two steps back!" (No more "Down on the floor!"s for Attila. He'd learned after the calamity at Ó Street that if he got the employees down there, they were liable to hit an alarm.)

Attila's command was so jarring that even Gabi almost put up his hands, but he regained his composure and instead reached for the gun in his raincoat pocket. He pointed it at the teller in front of him, who already had her hands in the air, and said unconvincingly, "If you do what he says, everything's going to be fine." One of the other employees was already on the phone with the police when Attila bounded onto the chest-high counter and vaulted his body and legs over the tall glass divider.

Impressed, Gabi backed up toward the door to assume his post. Within a minute he began to hear what would become a familiar sound: the *shoosh, shoosh, shoosh* of the packs of bills hitting the bottom of the plastic grocery bags Attila used to collect the money before transferring it during the getaway to his Camel duffel, which he never allowed to be seen during the robberies' commission. Gabi also could hear the post office phone ringing off the hook, but he was only supposed to keep track of the time. *Two and a half minutes. Two-forty-five . . .*

Just as Gabi was about to yell three minutes, Attila came back through the side door and walked quickly toward him. With the key that was already in the lock, Attila let them out into the sun, then turned and, with the same key, closed up the office for the day.

Lajos Varjú pulled up to the post office in his newly issued white Volkswagen Golf, sirens and blue lights blazing, to find the building secured. No one, including the police, could get in — or out. This hitch was a little tough for Lajos to take, since the post office was one of three Lajos had preselected as a probable Lone Wolf target due to its distance from the local police precinct and its location in Buda, where most of the robberies had occurred. As instructed, one of the employees had called the police hotline as soon as two suspicious men sauntered in wearing raincoats on a sunny August afternoon. But the operator at police headquarters was so incredulous that one of the places the robbery department had prepped was actually in play that she asked the employee to call back if she was serious. When no callback came, the operator phoned the post office but got no answer.

It was Thursday, and as Lajos stepped up to the curb in front of the locked post office, József Jónás, the on-scene reporter for *Kriminális,* was already taping his stand-up piece for that evening's show. "Here come the police now" were the words Lajos caught from the *Kriminális* reporter's mouth as he approached the crime scene, followed by "Colonel Lajos, what do you have to say?"

Lajos staggered through an interview in which it became apparent that the media had surmised the same thing he had from the scant information already available. The nonviolent post office robbery was the latest effort by the Lone Wolf, who once again had taken on what one newspaper would call "a servant." When Lajos finally got inside, he was handed the evidence the dispatcher had warned him about, a wrapped shoebox addressed to Sándor Pintér, the highest-ranking police officer in the country. Lajos had little choice but to call in the bomb squad to open it. His next call was to his wife, informing her not to wait for him for dinner. He couldn't bear to sit with her through another episode of *Kriminális.*

Fortunately, all the reporters were gone by the time the captain of the bomb squad handed Lajos the empty Boglari merlot and Kiskőrösi Kékfránkos (both 1994 vintages) and the napkin offering him greetings.

Lajos then stomped over to the two *sörozős*, or pubs, across the street, where he'd also prepped the staffs with sketches and asked them to be on the lookout for a man in a wig ordering whiskey. At the Jáger Pub, the owner slapped himself on the forehead with his open hand. "I knew I was supposed to remember something," the bar owner said, pulling a folded-up Lone Wolf police sketch from his breast pocket. "This guy was here earlier with another guy," he said, nodding at the small green benches surrounding a row of wooden tables with red-and-white-checkered tablecloths. "You were right, Detective. He drinks whiskey. Had two Johnnies and left a great tip."

That night, back at police headquarters, the empty halls of the police building echoed with Lajos's screams while his wife and 4 million others tuned in to a memorable *Kriminális*. The show's on-scene report featured a tongue-tied Lajos stepping onto the sidewalk in front of the post office in a white Puma T-shirt and ruefully admitting that the job indeed appeared to have been done by the city's increasingly famous robber who was "asking for the money — because that's how he does it: he asks." Noting the thief's penchant for downing whiskey before the heists, *Kriminális* host László Juszt christened the thief the *Viszkis Rabló*, or the Whiskey Robber. The nickname not only stuck but, to the apparent delight of everyone, as *Blikk* wrote the next day, the Whiskey Robber was "making the life of the police an absolute misery."

The following week that misery grew with the publication of a story in the daily newspaper *Népszava* that Lajos had done his best to suppress. The article, headlined THE GENTLEMAN ROBBER SENT A MESSAGE TO THE DETECTIVES, described the Whiskey Robber as a *korszerű betyár*, or a modern bandit. It was a clear reference to the nineteenth-century Hungarian folk legend Sándor Rózsa, known as the Hungarian Robin Hood, who stole from the elite as they crossed the Hungarian plain on horseback and who fought as a freedom fighter against the Hapsburgs in the 1848 revolution. "It isn't impossible that he [the Whiskey Robber] is giving his money to the poor," *Népszava* wrote.

With sixty thousand homeless on the streets of Budapest, and two-thirds of the country living around or below the poverty line, who didn't want to believe it?

Seventeen

Except for the fact that the old shoes in his closet now held 2.5 million forints ($16,500) instead of his allowance, nothing about Gabi's life changed for three weeks after the robbery. Amid the *Star Wars* movie posters and Bobby Orr hockey manuals that decorated the childhood bedroom in which he still slept, the Whiskey Robber's accomplice impatiently waited out his boss's mandatory spending freeze. The only benefit Gabi could see in Attila's agonizing austerity program was that it bought him some time to devise an explanation for how [blank] had suddenly made him rich. What had transpired, he decided, was that he'd started a company selling tourist trinkets and spoof gift items such as signs reading, THE MORE PEOPLE I MEET, THE MORE I LIKE MY DOG. Sales were surprisingly brisk, he told his parents, who were fighting with each other too much to notice that their son had no merchandise to speak of, much less an office or a clue as to how to run a business. Twenty-two days after the robbery, Gabi fished 2 million forints ($13,000) out of a penny loafer and bought himself a charcoal gray Mercedes 190E.

Not coincidentally, that was about the same time that Attila told Gabi they were going to celebrate their new partnership with a trip. After practice one day, so as not to raise the suspicion of their teammates, Attila and Gabi split up and sped separately through the streets in their luxury vehicles to a travel agency Attila had picked out. Attila was twenty-eight years old now and had been to Austria, Egypt, France, Spain, Italy, Thailand, and Tunisia — enough to know what he wanted in a vacation. When they got to the counter, Attila asked for a "luxury, all-inclusive, money-is-no-object two-week trip for two to the Dominican Republic."

"And make it sing," he added.

The total cost was 750,000 forints ($5,000). They were handed the paperwork, and Gabi watched to see what Attila would do. Attila picked up a pen and wrote down his name and address on the forms; Gabi followed. Then they piled up what remained of their stolen money on the counter and left with their plane tickets and itinerary in hand. Outside, Attila launched into one of his many lectures, this one inspired by the pseudonym Gabi had used on the travel documents they'd just filled out. "Everyone slips on a banana peel," he said to Gabi. "Your car, your television, your vacations, anything you buy has to be legitimate. Are you listening, Gabi? You have to pay attention to everything. Your parents aren't going to find the money, are they? Remember, there's no perfect crime. Keep that in mind. That's why the details are the most important thing. It's easy to take the cash, but before and after you have to pay attention."

The visit to the travel agency had also illustrated for Gabi another of Attila's familiar tutorials: less than a month ago Gabi was rich, and now he was once again forintless. "It's incredible," Gabi said. Attila, who had already broken his own three-week rule and lost the bulk of his remaining cash gambling, laughed. "You see, Gringo," he said, employing his new nickname for his accomplice, "it's a vicious cycle. Journeys, casinos, girls, high life."

They weren't the only ones living above their official tax bracket. The previous morning — September 20, 1996 — the biggest scandal since the fall of communism exploded across the pages of the nation's newspapers. Márta Tocsik, a well-connected Hungarian politico, had been hired as a lawyer by the Horn government to do a privatization deal involving the transfer of public lands. For her few weeks of work, the Hungarian media reported, Tocsik, who had never even passed the bar exam, was paid 800 million forints ($5.2 million), much of which was allegedly promised to be funneled back into the pockets of government officials. The Tocsik story, soon dubbed by the Hungarian media "the Scandal of the Century" in a nod to the O. J. Simpson case, appeared to offer irrefutable proof of the hypocrisy and injustice of Eastern Europe's so-called democracy. Like millions of his fellow citizens, the Whiskey Robber was outraged.

"Can you believe this Tocsik," he said, herding Gabi into his bordeaux Opel Omega (his Alfa Romeo had been swiped from the parking lot behind Éva's apartment building). "The state is only abusing the people. They just squeeze them up like a slice of orange until they get all the juice out of them. You know, we're robbing the state, but the state is robbing us. The difference is that we're not causing damage to anybody."

"What we're doing is a drop in the bucket compared with the privatization," Gabi said.

They drove south across the metal-framed Szabadság Bridge into Pest and down past the 4 Tigers market, by that point known as a major drug stop on the heroin road from Istanbul to the West.

"You know, in the sixties and seventies, the Sicilian and Marseilles gangs robbed all across Europe," Attila said. "The Red Brigades, the IRA, Che Guevara. They all supported their political causes with bank robberies."

"After all, it's the state who's supposed to be supporting us, right?" Gabi said.

They continued into the industrial southern part of the city and pulled up across the street from a row of two-story buildings. Under a second-floor church was a green and white sign marking a branch of the OTP Bank, the only financial institution in which the Hungarian government still had an ownership stake.

"This money belongs to the people," Attila said, eyeing the concrete-encrusted OTP, which during communism had been the only bank chain in Hungary. "Plus, the more we get, the more we're going to put back into the system over time anyway."

"It's like we're not even robbing. We're just borrowing the money for a while," Gabi added.

"That's why we never take money from customers or employees," Attila said.

"It's out of the question," Gabi said.

When they entered the OTP's large, square, couch-adorned waiting area at 3:30 P.M. two days later, the bank's guard was on the phone in the corner of the room, possibly speaking to a comedian. He shut up mid-cackle when he found his cheek flat against the cold brown linoleum, his Parabellum pistol stripped from its holster, and his back repurposed as a floor cushion for the Whiskey Robber's knee. In the meantime, the bandit's accomplice had unloaded a can of black spray paint into the lens of the video camera above the door.

No one behind the counter even noticed the disturbance until Attila stood up and yelled at the tellers, "Robbery! Hands up and two steps back." There were five employees, all women, and a couple of unintimidating customers. While Attila went behind the counter to work on opening the cash drawers, Gabi yelled something like "No one should hit an alarm because we have other accomplices waiting outside." He was nervous; it was his first bank job.

Attila drained each teller's cash drawer and easily found the small safe that was poorly hidden inside the only wooden wardrobe-like piece of furniture behind the counters. The door to the metal money box itself wasn't even shut, much less locked. After he collected the loot in plastic bags, Attila called the manager over and got the key to the front door so he could lock the crew inside. When they got back out, Gabi broke the rules and sprinted, like Karcsi had three years earlier, back to the car, in this case a taxi, which they had asked to wait for them while they ran "an errand." After thanking the driver for his patience and berating his partner for his paranoia, Attila transferred the money into the Camel duffel bag. They got out at a nearby subway station and, walking through the bustling concourse, stripped off their outer layers of clothes and threw them into garbage cans, then boarded the train. At Moscow Square, they transferred to the no. 61 tram, careful to board separate train cars, and rode to Villányi Street. Once home, Attila removed the cardboard money clips for Gabi to burn in the bathroom and began counting. And counting. It was 7.5 million forints ($49,000) — his second-highest score ever, after the Kemenes Street post office. Attila reorganized the money into two piles — Gabi's share was half minus 10 percent for prep costs — and took back Gabi's gun for safekeeping.

In a red velvet upholstered basement, Keszthelyi and Mound laid out the Whiskey Robber newspaper articles and case files flat on the floor as if dealing a hand of solitaire. Even their publicity-happy host had agreed that whatever transpired that afternoon in the incense-filled chamber would not be disclosed later. The three of them sat in silence for several minutes. Then Józsi Barát spoke. "I see a very large house with a lake," the famous Hungarian psychic intoned, holding out his long hands, one of which carried a gold chain with a round pendant. "Your robber is a rich man from a large and very wealthy family."

In mid-October, Attila and Gabi returned from shark hunting in the Dominican Republic just in time to go swimming with the minnows of the Hungarian hockey league. Several players from the previous season's winless squad had found it a mental imperative to retire from athletics permanently, and Coach Pék had predictably encountered some difficulty retooling his insolvent traveling circus with functioning adults. The three new players he'd managed to sign up were a seventeen-year-old goalie from the junior league with whom Attila would share playing time and two former UTE standouts now in their forties.

A few seconds into the first full practice scrimmage, it became evident to the players that their plight was even worse than it had appeared on paper: the two old-timers no longer possessed the ability to skate backward. A walkout was averted only by Coach Pék's assurances that none of the other players he'd tried to acquire were UTE material anyway. Some had actually complained to Pék during their tryouts that the ceiling in the UTE shower room was collapsing, which, while true, was utterly irrelevant to anyone interested in playing in an open-air stadium, where rain, snow, and batteries regularly fell from the sky.

For his own sanity, Attila pledged he would do anything in his power to make this a better season than the last. He hired a contractor and personally shouldered the cost of having the ceiling in the shower room refinished. He also bought a new refrigerator for the club, which he put in the locker room so that cold beer would be readily and abundantly available.

Gabi had his own method of coping. A few days before the season opener, he quit. Having suddenly become the second-richest player in the league, he realized he had, at twenty-two, accomplished everything he'd ever hoped to do in the sport. He turned his attention instead to his new pastime of snorting cocaine and playing foosball with Gangsta Zoli in the rapper's mom's living room.

Gabi also moved out of his parents' place and into a renovated two-room apartment in Budakeszi, the swanky northwest Budapest suburb, where he enjoyed a panoramic view of the leafy Buda hills, beyond which lay the city.

Budakeszi and its closer-to-town equivalent known as Rose Hill were the Hollywood Hills of Budapest. The underdeveloped, forested clumps that rose from just beyond the western bank of the Danube were home to many of Budapest's highest-profile people, including the current prime minister, Gyula Horn. Gabi had found a several-acre plot listed in the paper and bought it for just 1.5 million forints ($9,800) in cash. Within a few weeks he had hired an architect and was custom-designing a dream house worthy of a Hungarian Wayne Gretzky, complete with Jacuzzi, wraparound balcony, and manicured gardens. To save on construction costs, Gabi picked out a team of workmen from the daily 4:00 A.M. illegal-immigrant assembly in Moscow Square. But his 3.38-million forint ($22,000) share of the last robbery was disappearing quickly.

While exploring his new neighborhood's small commercial strip one afternoon, Gabi couldn't help but notice the quaint local OTP Bank branch. He specced out all the measurements his partner required: distance to the police station (two minutes), number of tellers (five), number of women tellers (five), guards (one), video camera (yes, located above the entrance). One day in November he called Attila with his new cell phone and told him the details.

Attila was skeptical, but after their triumphant evenings skirt-chasing in the Dominican Republic, he'd developed a sincere fondness for his partner and wanted him to feel like an indispensable part of their team. Plus, Attila liked the idea of mining a new part of town. A few days later Gabi was walking around his property when Attila called. "Nice work, Gringo," Attila told him. "I made a floor plan. It's going to work."

In deference to the Tocsik story, Attila began to refer to their robberies as *balhék*, or "little scandals." Mindful of the *Kriminális* broadcast schedule, they set the date for their third joint *balhé* for Thursday,

November 21, conveniently in the middle of the only gameless ten-day stretch of the hockey season. When the 8:00 A.M. practice ended, Attila sped home to his Villányi Street apartment, where only Gabi was waiting for him. (Attila's uncle had finally gone back to Transylvania for good; Éva had caught him washing cars on his own for a cut rate at night and fired him.) It was just after 10:00 A.M., but time was tight: Attila needed to be back in uniform at UTE by five for the afternoon practice, or else he'd lose his alibi and risk finding out that the garbage can that would have to stand in for him was a no less effective goal stopper.

For a couple of hours, Attila and Gabi role-played the *balhé* with Gabi as the guard and Attila's armoire as the safe. But Attila kept breaking and entering the bathroom instead. His stomach was killing him. He did his best to drown his nerves with whiskey, prompting Gabi to make a request. "Promise me you're not going to stop in at a bar again," Gabi said, referring to their first robbery together in August, when Attila jumped in to the Jáger Pub for his customary pre-robbery double. "Okay," Attila said. "I'll fill up here." By the time they left the apartment, he was smashed.

They arrived on separate street corners in clashing wigs and matching trench coats by tram, subway, and a pair of taxis and began their march to the bank entrance at 1:00 P.M. But as they were closing in on their target, Gabi watched Attila peel off course and scramble into the grocery store next door to the bank. "Cramps," Attila said, holding his stomach, when he wobbled out of the market fifteen minutes later. They were about to reach the bank door on the second try when Attila veered off into the grocery yet again. This time he came out carrying a loaf of bread in a plastic bag. He had realized at the last moment that he'd forgotten to bring a sack in which to collect the loot.

Despite all the holdups, the holdup went so well that the flimsy plastic bread bag almost broke from the weight of the haul. It was a new record, 14 million forints ($90,000). By 5:00 P.M. Attila was back in uniform at the UTE stadium, though so stinking drunk that some of his teammates took offense that their unofficial disciplinarian thought he could go on a pre-practice bender now that their record was an abysmal 0–7. When an easy goal trickled between Attila's legs, one of his teammates clobbered him on the head with his stick so hard that a nail from Attila's helmet lodged inside his skull, requiring yet another visit to Dr. Tóth. Attila hardly noticed.

~

In its millicentennial year, Hungary was looking more and more like a rebellious teen desperate for attention than an eleven-hundred-year-old old man who coulda, shoulda, woulda.

Hungary's black market accounted for 30 percent of the country's gross domestic product, compared with 5 percent or less in Western Europe. Arrests for fraud and embezzlement plagued the banking system. The head of Hungary's Olympic swimming federation copped to having invented a swim meet and race times to qualify eleven of the country's twenty-two swimmers for the 1996 Summer Games in Atlanta. ("This is not the Scandal of the Century," he said, defending his refusal to resign his federation post.) Even László Juszt, the *Kriminális* host, made the news when police traced a stolen Mitsubishi to his garage. (He claimed ignorance and surrendered the vehicle.)

It was difficult to know whether to thank or cordon off the FBI's International Law Enforcement Academy. In 1996, 230 Hungarian cops were convicted on charges ranging from bribery to falsifying official documents to using excessive force during interrogations. And their boss, National Police Chief Sándor Pintér — the FBI's primary liaison in Hungary — was in deeper than any of them. Concerns about the crooked associations of the FBI's man in Budapest never made CNN, but they had been building in Hungarian police circles over the summer. They began with his hiring a co-owner of Cats Club (Zubovics's partner) to head up the construction project for a new Budapest police headquarters building, from whose budget hundreds of millions of forints soon allegedly disappeared. Then in November, questions about Pintér's connection to Budapest's underworld intensified, this time because his fingerprints were reportedly found at the scene of a mob-related shooting of a famous horse jockey. When it turned out that evidence implicating the suspects had vanished from the search site, Pintér first denied he'd been at the scene, then clarified his denial to mean that he had been there but only to aid the investigation because it was on his way home from a dinner.

As with the Tocsik case, no one outside Hungary blinked. In Washington, FBI director Louis Freeh donned a tuxedo and was chauffeured to the Kennedy Center in Washington for a gala celebrating Hungary's eleven hundredth anniversary and its smooth transition to a model democracy. Given the festive decor and congratulatory speeches, it appeared that attendees had not been briefed on the fact that the country they were toasting was in tatters. (The party's host, socialite Betty Knight Scripps, announced she'd only recently become cognizant that goulash was a Hungarian soup but did claim to know plenty of Hungarians, such as actor Tony Curtis, who attended the party, and that "you can't help but fall in love with them!")

Two weeks later Hungary's interior minister summarily fired Pintér as well as Pintér's second in command, László "The 12 Percent" Valenta, and several other top Hungarian national and city police brass. With or without the FBI's blessing, Hungary's police department was going to start over from scratch.

In the midst of the turmoil, one lower-level police chief found his image buoyed by contrast: Lajos Varjú, leader of the comparably squeaky-clean robbery division, who watched a remarkable none of his detectives get arrested that year. In the fall, with few choices, a Hungarian law enforcement organization extended Lajos an invitation to speak at its international conference on auto theft. Despite having a month earlier felt so hopeless about the Whiskey Robber case that he approved Detective Keszthelyi's request to visit a psychic, Lajos was re-energized. He not only accepted the invitation to speak at the conference but decided that the subject of his car theft address would be the infamous Whiskey Robber, whom he was going to catch.

To prepare for his presentation, Lajos asked Dance Instructor to come up with a comprehensive, FBI-quality analysis of what was now more than a thousand pages of case files, which had been purged of the report on the session with Józsi Barát, the psychic. On November 21 Dance Instructor sauntered into Lajos's office, wearing a black tuxedo and a top hat, and presented his boss with his latest effort and a map of the city.

"What's this?" Lajos asked Dance Instructor, pointing to the map.

"I also charted the locations of the robberies," he said. "You can draw two concentric circles around the crimes, with the exception of the Sixteenth District. One circle fits within the other. If you connect the dots, a straight line goes through both circles."

Lajos took a closer look at the drawing but was still befuddled by the hieroglyphics.

"What are you trying to tell me?" Lajos asked.

"If you take into account the last crimes, there is also a third circle," Dance Instructor said.

"And?"

"Perhaps the perpetrator wants to spread his activities?"

Lajos thanked the Instructor and began reading the report, which included such witness descriptions of the Whiskey Robber as "he generates trust and gives a very manly impression" and "he is a ridiculous foreign homosexual." Dance Instructor also did what he could to piece together the most telling details of the robber's physical appearance, noting that "his nails are clean. His fingers are long and thin . . . but very little data on the ears."

Lajos was still engrossed in the report two hours later when his phone rang. Two men in wigs and trench coats had just cleared 14 million forints ($90,000) out of the OTP Bank in the hills of Budakeszi. Lajos nearly threw his phone out the window. He rifled through the pages on his desk and pulled out Dance Instructor's map. What was that about the third concentric circle? The call center also mentioned one other thing: though there was no note left at the scene this time, a large round loaf of fresh white bread was found inside the safe.

Eighteen

Just after 8:00 P.M. on a snowy Tuesday evening six weeks later, Gabi's phone interrupted his weekly television ritual.

"Hello," he said, picking up the receiver and hitting the mute button on his TV remote.

"Are you watching this?" Attila asked.

As they were both well aware, *Kriminális* had switched from Thursday nights to Tuesdays at the end of 1996. It wasn't something they could easily forget. On the show's final Thursday broadcast, Juszt had announced that if the Whiskey Robber was out there listening, he should "please move your robberies to Monday or Tuesday if you want us to be able to cover them on that week's program."

Attila and Gabi had intended to oblige. It had been an expensive holiday season for them both. With the earnings from their last gig, Gabi had paid for his and a friend's two-week Christmas safari in Kenya. Attila had gone home and met a stunning woman in Transylvania who had had an effect on him not unlike a casino: once again, his pockets were empty.

The partners had agreed that with little planning they could pilfer the same Budakeszi OTP Bank in Gabi's neighborhood from which they'd gotten 14 million forints ($90,000) in November, and considerate of the *Kriminális* host's request, they would do so on Tuesday, January 14. But it was so cold that Tuesday that neither of them wanted to take public transportation to the gig; instead, they carpooled to the robbery in Gabi's Mercedes, where it was accordingly comfortable and warm and where they had completely lost their focus. Four o'clock came and went while Attila was giving Gabi a report on the two books he'd just finished, one on Hungarian folk hero Sándor Rózsa, the other on the Mexican revolutionary hero of the early twentieth century Emilio Zapata. Meanwhile, the bank had closed. They had no choice but to rob it the following day and wait almost a whole week to see what *Kriminális* would say.

As usual, Juszt's program presented a bit of information about the 8-million-forint ($43,000) robbery that Attila and Gabi had not seen in any of the newspaper coverage. And it wasn't good. According to *Kriminális*, as soon as the robbers had entered the bank, one of the employees had recognized them and phoned the police. She never had time to say anything on the phone, though, because the perpetrators had started the robbery too quickly. But she hadn't hung up. She'd placed the receiver on her desk, where it acted as a microphone for the police call center to record the entire robbery. Hoping to curry some favor with the influential *Kriminális* host, Lajos Varjú had offered Juszt the exclusive, knowing Juszt's show was his only chance to provoke a response from the public. "Bank robbery," Attila had just listened to himself yell on national television. "Everyone on the floor!" (For bigger institutions, he'd gone back to the "floor" method for safety reasons.)

Juszt asked viewers to call the police if they recognized the voice.

"Gabi," Attila wanted to know from his partner. "Can you tell it's me on the tape?"

~

It wasn't so much the cops Attila was worried about as it was the woman preparing to move in with him.

While he was home in Csíkszereda over the holidays, Attila had gone out to the Flash Dance Nite Klub on Christmas Eve, hardly expecting to gamble. But on the dance floor was a gorgeous, shapely long-brown-haired girl that no one could take their eyes off. Attila accepted, and won, a bet from one of his friends that he could pick her up in ten minutes.

Betty Gergely, who was twenty-one and wore a silver stud in one nostril, was from the nearby Székely town of Gyergyószentmiklós (or Gheorgheni, in Romanian). She told Attila she had recently moved back home after being deported from Greece, where she had been working on one of the islands as a dancer. Attila took this to mean she was stripping, got mixed up with the wrong people, and ran. That was okay with him. It meant she was just the type of girlfriend he'd been looking for: someone accustomed to secrecy.

Attila vacated his aunt and uncle's place and spirited Betty off to the Ózon Hotel in the Hargita Mountains outside town. Betty was amazing. She spoke English, was strip club smokin', *and* knew the Székely pig-killing ceremony by heart. After three days Attila had forgotten or waived his rules of female engagement and had invited Betty to come live with him in Budapest. They were going to have the life. He'd help arrange her papers; she wouldn't have to worry about money. "I've got it and that's all," he said. Betty wasn't going to wait for a better offer. "There's just one thing I have to take care of first," Attila told her. He went back ahead of Betty and phoned the day after the robbery during which his voice was unwittingly recorded, telling her, "Come anytime."

There were a few weeks left in the hockey season when Betty arrived by train with a single duffel bag. Attila picked her up at the Keleti train station, where nine years earlier he had experienced his own first taste of Budapest. The delicate arched glass ceiling and the way the trains pulled straight into the middle of the atrium still gave the place a turn-of-the-century aura. The only thing that had changed, Attila knew all too well, was the exchange rates offered by the robed men in the corners.

Quite a lot had turned for Attila, however, in the few short weeks since he'd last seen Betty. In Transylvania he'd been able to imagine himself as a romantic and carefree professional sportsman. But back in Hungary he was inescapably the hockey goalie for a team that hadn't won a game in two years and the fugitive criminal featured weekly in video and audio clips on the nation's top-rated television program. In case that wasn't horrific enough, he was now duty-bound to create a curriculum that would screen all of that from the street-smart Székely with whom he was going to be sharing a pullout couch.

Tuesday evening — *Kriminális* night — was Attila and Betty's special night out. Attila set the VCR to record, then whisked Betty around town to the bathhouses and the *csárdás* for no-frills traditional Hungarian soups and stews. Sometimes they double-dated with Gabi and his new girlfriend, Marian, a blond twentysomething advertising manager whom he'd met the previous summer at Lake Balaton but only had the balls to ask out since he'd become a millionaire. Attila gave Betty an allowance of 100,000–150,000 forints ($550–$820) a month for shopping, the gym, and classes to improve her conversational English — anything to keep her busy so he could just get through the last eight games of the catastrophic hockey season. He would then be able to re-evaluate his situation.

UTE's season had turned so unspeakably bad that Coach Pék had taken it upon himself to redefine the way his team measured success. The coach of the once-mighty hockey club told his players that if they held their opponents to fewer than ten goals in a game, they could consider it a victory. Betty, understandably, could not be allowed anywhere near the stadium. ("I'm superstitious," Attila told her.) The only time she saw Attila play that year was in the season finale, against Alba Volán, which was carried live on national television. Mercifully, Attila played well and UTE salvaged a 3–3 tie. By Pék's standard, that delivered UTE to a modest final 1996–97 season record of 11–13–2. The league office, however, put the tally at a somewhat less impressive 0–24–2.

In late February, a few days after the hockey season ended, Attila took Betty on a ten-day vacation to the Maldives in the Indian Ocean. They got along great, and the trip was the first of many eventful journeys they would soon take, some of them romantic excursions to exotic locales, others mad, unannounced half-hour road trips to the apartment in Érd where Éva, Attila's ex, lived.

As much as Éva had sworn she'd never speak to Attila again after the pub debacle, she knew she couldn't stay angry at him. She and Attila had resumed a close enough friendship that Attila felt comfortable barging into her apartment at midnight with his new girlfriend, demanding cooking lessons. One issue Attila had with Betty was that while she may have been familiar with heating water for a bathtub barrel, she didn't know her way around a kitchen. This was, at first, a relief, given that Attila's had a nonworking oven. But if Attila was going to live with someone, he did expect something in return. And he soon found himself having to explain that his stove — which had separate pilot lights from the oven below — was quite operational and that he preferred his bean soup with a couple of hooves, extra spicy, extra purple onion. Betty's bean soup debut, however, was, in Attila's judgment, a disaster. And before the burners had time to cool, Betty was on her way to meet Attila's former lover. Upon their arrival, Attila introduced the girls, then implored Éva, "Teach her how to cook a bean soup." Éva laughed, hoping it would put Betty at ease. It didn't. Betty was standing in her boyfriend's ex-girlfriend's apartment, being forced to learn to make a gas-inducing soup for a hockey goalie she realized she barely knew.

A week later it got weirder. Betty found herself living with Éva. "I'm sorry," Attila said, dropping Betty off at Éva's place one morning in early March, "but it's for your own protection. I have to take care of something and it could be dangerous. It'll be only a couple of days." Éva didn't want to know what Attila was up to, but he was always generous. She couldn't even keep track of how many times he'd loaned her money or bought her dinner. So she made up the couch for Betty.

On his way back to his apartment alone, Attila stopped downtown, visiting the fashion boutiques on Váci (now called "Vice" Street) for some new Armani suits, then the wig store, where he purchased two new hairpieces. Back home, he pulled his guns and notebook out of the oven and laid the suits and wigs out on the couch; in no time, his little flat was once again a world-class robbery training facility and staging ground.

～

The next day Attila and Gabi emerged separately onto the sidewalk on Kemenes Street near the Danube River in south Buda, Gabi nearly a block ahead of his partner. It was a cold Tuesday in March, and were it not for a dead lawyer, the two of them would have been in another part of town entirely, heading for an OTP Bank on Mester Street across the river in Little Chicago. But the preceding week, as Attila was beginning to memorize the Mester Street bank's layout, it was robbed by an attorney and his driver, whom Attila guessed hadn't accounted for the silent alarm. The driver got away, but the lawyer was shot by police before he could get out of the building. It seemed impertinent to try for that bank now, so Attila went back to his notebook. He figured it would be better to choose a target with which he was familiar, and picked the post office on Kemenes Street near the Gellért Hotel, where he'd delivered the roses and extracted 10 million forints ($62,000) a year earlier.

Attila knew there was a risk in such a selection. If they did the Kemenes Street post office, it would be the third site he was revisiting. (He'd done the bank at Raday Street twice when he was still working alone, and he and Gabi had knocked off the Budakeszi OTP twice.) If the police were paying any attention, they could be monitoring the building. So, to be safe, Attila implemented a staggered entry: Attila would trail behind Gabi to survey the scene. If Attila started coughing, that was the sign to abort.

As Attila approached the post office in his Italian suit and wig, a couple of minutes behind Gabi, he noticed a youngish couple holding hands outside the entrance. As he approached, both of them flashed him a glance. He kept walking past them and down the block all the way to the corner near the silver Erector set–style Szabadság Bridge, where he crossed the street. When he turned around again, the couple was almost a block up the street from the post office, heading in the opposite direction. Attila started back, with one eye on them. When he was almost to the post office's entrance, he saw the couple cross the street and turn back down the hill again. One of them was on a cell phone.

Attila looked through the post office's glass door. Gabi was inside, going through the preliminary motions of distracting the most formidable looking teller with a series of questions and waiting for the word *rablás!* As the young couple closed in, Attila began coughing as loudly as he could, but Gabi was engrossed in an argument about the accuracy of the foreign mail delivery timetable. Attila was almost out of time. He flung open the post office door and hacked so hard that he nearly fell over, then, without looking behind him, turned and began walking briskly back down the hill.

A minute later footsteps closed in.

"What's the problem?"

It was Gabi.

"I told you to fucking pay attention," Attila said over his shoulder as they continued marching in single file down the street like toy soldiers on a conveyor belt.

"I didn't hear you," Gabi said to Attila's back.

"I almost coughed out a lung," Attila said, veering down a side street. Midway through the block, he stopped dead in his tracks and put his hands on his head. His wig was gone. He spun around just in time to see Gabi plucking it off a low-hanging parking sign near the corner.

Later that night Attila unexpectedly retrieved Betty from Éva's place. "What happened?" she asked. "It was fucking canceled," he said. The following week Mr. Romance deposited her at Éva's again. This time Attila drove straight to the Goldberg Pub in Óbuda, or Old Buda, where he met Gabi at a small table in the corner. A man at the next table strained to listen in as Attila described the new target: it was the OTP Bank branch at the end of the busy shopping strip known as Heltai Square, in the northern housing-block-riddled section of town. It was a heavily trafficked pedestrian area, yes, but there were several possible escape routes and the police response would be markedly slowed by the large congested parking lot in front of the shopping area.

Gabi was tiring of all the planning, scheduling, and rescheduling. He proposed that they just go for one massive job — something like the downtown, full-city-block-size treasury building, where they could make enough cash to secure their place in history and then relax for a while. "Imagine what Juszt would say," Gabi said.

"That's why I don't let you keep your gun, Gabi," Attila replied, ready to get the check and go it alone. Gabi's naïveté was almost as annoying to Attila as the robbery chief's had been. Attila wondered, was he the only one who recognized this robbery thing wasn't a game? True, the current political conditions couldn't have been better for the costumed plunder of government symbols, but every other condition Attila could think of that was crucial to robbery success was much, much worse than it had been when he started.

It was plain, at least to Attila, that he had gotten into the robbery racket during a geopolitical hiccup, a brief window of time when there was little need and even less money for sophisticated and expensive security systems. Now, thanks in no small part to his workmanship, even the smaller banks and post offices were installing cameras and hiring armed guards, another hidden downside of great publicity. The majority of financial institutions' silent alarms now rang at both the police station and the office of a private security company, meaning the risk of an armed confrontation had increased dramatically. Then there was the matter of the money. An increasing number of the OTPs were reacting to the robbery boom by installing timelock safes. These primarily state-owned institutions were still Attila's target of choice because their safes remained inferior to the stainless-steel security vaults employed by the wealthier foreign-owned banks, at least according to what Attila read and observed. And the fact that the OTPs still represented the ever-unpopular government was clearly stoking Attila's image as a man of the people. But without his own network of informants and fellow criminals, Attila was struggling to keep abreast of even the most basic technical developments in his field. At the OTPs, for example, the money was no longer stashed in skeleton-key lockboxes. It was now held in steel-filing-cabinet-like units consisting of four drawers, each of which needed a unique key and code to open. From what he learned at the Budakeszi OTP, the lower the drawer, the more money it had inside but also the longer the time limit on the lock. Attila was still trying to figure out the range of time frames. At Budakeszi, the first two drawers opened within three minutes; he hadn't been able to wait for the others. And Gabi wanted to knock off the national mint? "You don't understand the system," Attila said. "The bigger the bank, the more the security; the more security, the greater the risk. That's not a job for two people."

"Fine," Gabi said. "Then why don't we go for two in one day?"

It wasn't a bad idea. The first robbery would attract a substantial police response to one part of town, leaving Lajos and crew undermanned to respond to a second hit somewhere else. But Attila wasn't sure he was up for taking the risk. Maybe the dead lawyer had gotten to him.

"Come on," Gabi said. "We could do five in one day if we wanted."

"Okay," Attila said. "But if we get more than fifteen million [$82,000] at Heltai, we don't do the second one."

On Monday morning, March 10, 1997, two policemen in blue commando team jackets and berets blasted through the door of the Heltai Square OTP Bank, weapons drawn, shouting, "Don't move!"

All eight customers and ten employees in the bank froze as the lead cop trained his gun on the security guard near the door. "We have information that this man is passing counterfeit money through this bank!" he yelled. The guard put his hands up, and the cop began to read him his rights and strip him of his Browning pistol.

"Where's the manager?" the officer called out. "We need to search the safe."

The branch manager dutifully appeared from behind the counter with the key in her hand. The officer who had been dealing with the security guard turned and approached her. "Bank robbery," Attila said, pointing his gun at the woman's chest with a smile. Gabi, standing at the door, motioned with his gun for the customers and the stunned guard to join him in the middle of the room. "On the floor," he said. Attila, handcuffs hanging from his policeman's duty belt, headed to the back.

It had taken almost a week to get the uniforms in order. Gabi had driven fifty miles north to a police supply store in Slovakia to buy the overalls, jackets, hats, and handcuffs. Then Attila spent two full days with tape and art pens, laying down the white block police lettering and perfectly arched insignia on the breast pocket and across the back of the jackets.

But as much prep work as they had done in advance, it was impossible to control everything. While Attila had the manager reciting safety codes for him to input along with the key lock, one of the employees on the other side of the bank hit an alarm. Two minutes into the action, a deafening siren pierced the air, accompanied by flashing blood-orange lights posted inside and outside the bank, as Gabi could see from his post at the door. "Time!" he yelled. "Time!"

Attila had made it down through just two of the four time-lock drawers. He waited about another thirty seconds while his accomplice screamed, then gave up. As planned, they utilized the back exit and within a few seconds were running down an empty alley through a jumble of tall brown apartment buildings to their waiting taxi.

Lajos (as seen on *Kriminális* the following evening) was on the scene soon afterward, wearing jeans and a brown leather jacket, dejectedly fishing through a blue Dumpster in the alley. Unbeknownst to him, the Whiskey Robber and his partner had already devoured a plate of kielbasa and sheep's cheese at their bearskinned headquarters, changed into business suits, toasted — *Egészségedre!* — and were riding over the Szabadság Bridge in another cab toward the opposite side of town. The morning booty was 9.6 million forints ($52,500), not bad but well short of the 15-million-forint minimum ($82,000) Attila had set.

It was nearly four o'clock when they arrived at the designated street corner outside the Kelenföld railway station to put the finishing touches on their crime de résistance. The post office down the street already had its metal grating pulled halfway down when they approached. Attila and Gabi, wearing business suits and baseball hats pulled low over long wigs, ducked under the grate to find two female employees pulling on their coats.

Attila got one of them to open the safe; Gabi watched the other. "It's going to be fine," said Gabi, who looked like a psychopath. Two minutes and 4 million forints ($22,000) later, it was over. Attila and Gabi ducked back under the grating, and Attila pulled the chain door down to the ground from the outside. "You shouldn't leave for ten minutes," he called to the women inside.

As they began walking back toward the taxi waiting for them around the corner, they were startled by loud screams emanating from the post office: "Robbers! Robbers! Get them!" Two men passing on the street heard the cries and lunged at the bizarre duo who'd just left the post office, one of whom was carrying an overstuffed plastic bag.

Gabi took off in one direction, flying past their idling cabdriver, who looked up from his newspaper in bewilderment. Attila ran another direction, drawing, from the sound of it, at least one fleet-footed pursuer. He fled through the neighborhood streets in the darkening day, unable to gain much distance from the man because his dress shoes kept slipping on the pavement. First Attila's baseball hat, then his shoulder-length straight brown wig, and then his sunglasses flew off his head as he ran, but the footsteps and heavy breathing remained close behind. Then just as he sensed his pursuer beginning to lag, another voice maybe twenty-five feet behind him to the right, yelled, "Freeze, police!" Attila lowered his upper body and braced for a gunshot. Instead, he heard the sound of one man tackling another. "I'm not the robber, you idiot," a voice groaned. "He's getting away!"

Attila turned a corner and kept running through backyards, jumping fences and hurdling shrubs but never letting a forint drop. Twenty-five minutes and four miles later, he arrived back at Villányi Street 112. Gabi was there in the stairwell, still sucking wind, his own wig and hat already ditched in a Dumpster he had passed along the way. They were too exhausted to smile. Hands trembling, Attila unlocked the door and leaned back against the frame. Gabi started inside, but Attila pulled him back by the collar. "Shoes," he said.

Nineteen

The day of the double robbery, March 10, was Lajos's wife's, Ildikó, birthday. Lajos had been working around the clock the past several months in hopes of ingratiating himself with the new police administration and had promised Ildikó a special dinner in their two-room Újpest apartment near the UTE hockey stadium (which he'd been renting at a cut rate from the Interior Ministry).

Lajos spent the afternoon sifting through rotten fruit in the garbage bins at Heltai Square. Then as dinnertime neared, he was called to a stinking mess on the other side of town, at the site of the Kelenföld post office robbery. There he found the dimwit police officer who had shouted, "Police!" then tackled the man who'd had the best chance in years of catching the Whiskey Robber. The officer was so drunk that he had no recollection of what had transpired. Nor, it turned out, had he ever been a policeman.

Lajos was despondent. As soon as his bosses picked up a paper in the morning, he was sure his already falling stock was going to plummet. At least the man who had given chase until being sideswiped by the "cop" had been able to lead Lajos to three pieces of evidence the robber had lost during his flight. The first was a white baseball cap with blue-outlined lettering that read LEVIS above the smaller embroidery, AMERICA'S ORIGINAL JEANS. Nearby was a choppily styled long brown wig stiff with gel. And, on a side street, a pair of sunglasses.

After collecting the items, Lajos headed straight to HQ to hover over the forensics department and begin writing up his report. By the time he paused long enough to remember dinner, it was well after midnight. He fell asleep on the cigarette-singed couch outside his office, hoping Ildikó would forgive him.

In the morning he phoned home for his castigation and then immediately went to work tracing the evidence his team had gathered at the scene. Keszthelyi sourced the wig through its manufacturer in Korea to the only store in Budapest that carried it: a boutique on Váci Street. But the only male customer the owner remembered was a man who came in saying he needed three wigs for a Beatles cover band minus a George, and there was no receipt for the sale.

The Levis hat turned out to be an officially trademarked edition. According to the company, it was one of only 308 such caps that had been shipped to Hungary, which meant it had almost certainly been sold from one of the company's four Budapest outlets. Yet while this discovery sounded good for about ten minutes, it turned out to be the most common type of robbery department lead. It meant nothing because there was no way to follow up.

So Lajos turned once again to his most promising investigative tool. He phoned the *Kriminális* offices and offered up the Whiskey Robber's disguise to László Juszt as long as the television host would show a phone number for viewers to call with tips. The following week Juszt displayed the accessories on his program, and once again the robbery department was bathing in leads.

On March 20 Keszthelyi had the pleasure of spending two hours with thirty-six-year-old Ágnes Hornyák, a *Kriminális* viewer who showed up at the robbery offices with what she said was "important information." Hornyák said she had closely observed three perpetrators before the robbery at Heltai Square. "They are the heads of three gangs who will soon hit all the post offices in Budapest at the same time and rob them all," she told Keszthelyi. "I can help because I always have a camera and I can take photos."

"Although I'm not a psychiatrist," Keszthelyi wrote in his summary of Hornyák's visit, "this lady shows definite signs of being on the edge of a nervous breakdown. I am 100 percent sure she had no idea what she was talking about."

One man phoned to say that a few days before the robbery, he was at the Goldberg Pub, where he overheard two men discussing how to make fake police jackets to rob a bank at Heltai Square. Lajos was able to get the new police chief to approve a shortwave radio for the pub, and the wait staff was instructed how to use it to contact the police in case either of the men appeared on the premises again.

Several people, all with prior criminal records, were taken into custody, including the first of many sets of brothers erroneously linked to the case, József and Lajos Budai. But they were released after going unrecognized in the police lineups staged at the Gyorskocsi Street jail, the city's famous clink where Imre Nagy, the hero of the 1956 revolution, had been hanged.

Finally, on April 21 the robbery department appeared to get the break it had been waiting for. A call came from a guard at the Tököl juvenile prison on Csepel Island, the strip of land in the middle of the Danube River as it enters Budapest from the south. A credible inmate claimed to know the identities of both the Whiskey Robber and his accomplice. Keszthelyi and Mound borrowed a police car and made the half-hour drive to Tököl, where they met the juvenile institute's oldest prisoner, thirty-five-year-old László Klányi.

Klányi had been sentenced to four years in prison in June of 1996 for fraud. He was serving his time at the juvenile facility because he had a serious leg injury that needed further treatment and Tököl had just hired a new orthopedic specialist, the well-regarded former UTE hockey team doctor, Attila Tóth.

When Keszthelyi and Mound arrived, Klányi was waiting in the visitation room behind a glass panel. He told the detectives that before he was convicted the previous year, one of his friends had confessed to him that he was the Whiskey Robber and had even admitted that he was going to rob a bank and leave a red rose and a letter. Klányi proceeded to describe both the Whiskey Robber and his accomplice in detail. He said he had even seen the police uniforms used at the Heltai Square OTP Bank robbery and the wigs. "They asked me to join, but I refused because of my family," Klányi said. "I was going to be the driver."

Keszthelyi and Mound took Klányi into another room and showed him the discount-bin security-camera video they'd brought of the bank robbery on Lajos Street in June 1995. "That's him," Klányi said. "He is the brain behind everything. You have to be careful when you go to get him because he won't hesitate to use his gun. And he's very fast. Like a grasshopper."

That night Keszthelyi led commando units into the apartments of both men Klányi had identified. They were booked and brought to police headquarters. The suspects certainly fit the descriptions of the Whiskey Robber and his accomplice, and in the first apartment, as Klányi had described, Keszthelyi found a police uniform, two wigs, and a likely excuse. "I used to be a police officer," said thirty-four-year-old János Kis. "And if you want me to try on my mother-in-law's wigs, I will."

"If you're not the Whiskey Robber," Keszthelyi asked, "why would [Klányi] accuse you?"

"I don't know," Kis said. "I should report him for this."

The apartment of the other suspect, in Szentendre near the Cats Club, was the home of forty-two-year-old breadmaker Józsi Benedek. It was suspiciously clean of evidence.

The pair was held while Keszthelyi frantically sought other corroborating data and witnesses. For the next two days, he, Lajos, and Mound pored through police records and conducted nearly a dozen interviews.

Kis, it turned out, really had been not only a cop but also a Parliament guard, which meant that he had some specialized knowledge of police and security methods that could have helped him stay ahead of the law and perhaps to have a police uniform or two lying around. With his bushy mustache, curly hair, wide symmetrical face, and easygoing manner, he indubitably fit the images and descriptions the police had of the Whiskey Robber. Famous among his peers for wearing nothing but sweatsuits and slippers, Kis was described by one associate as "a nice person but he drinks his portion."

The baker was more of an enigma. Known throughout the pubs of Szentendre as Dadogós Józsi, or Stuttering Józsi, he clearly spent a good deal of time with Kis. But none of the robbery witnesses had ever mentioned a stutterer.

Keszthelyi didn't go home for two days. On the second night, while digging through the police employment archive, he found the missing link he needed: motive. Kis, it turned out, had been fired from the police department for stealing mountain bikes on his off days. He might well have an axe to grind with the force.

Lajos was intrigued, but he wanted Keszthelyi to drive down to the juvenile prison to reinterview Klányi. If they were going to close the book on the Whiskey Robber case, they had to be sure they had the right guys. Unfortunately, Keszthelyi's second visit with Klányi raised more questions than it answered. Klányi, too, seemed to have an axe to grind — with his old friend Kis. Klányi kept mentioning to Keszthelyi that Kis was also profiting from the fraud for which Klányi was convicted. "I didn't mention that at my court hearing," Klányi said.

Later that afternoon, back in Budapest, Keszthelyi interviewed Klányi's ex-wife. She told Keszthelyi how Klányi's leg had been mangled. Klányi's friend Kis was at least partly to blame. Klányi had been riding on the back of Kis's motorcycle when Kis had gotten into an accident. Now Keszthelyi had a better context for Klányi's apparent hostility toward the man he claimed was the Whiskey Robber. But it didn't mean Klányi was lying.

"Do you think I should trust your ex-husband?" Keszthelyi asked Klányi's former wife.

"He's a complete liar," she responded. "You can't even believe what he asks."

Keszthelyi's head was spinning until late that afternoon, when he got an unexpected tip that helped clear things up about Kis, Klányi, and Stuttering Józsi: while that trio was still locked up, the Whiskey Robber and his partner had hit again. And this time the details of the robbery were somewhat heartening. Upon learning how little money was in the safe, the "gentleman bandit" had begun racing up and down the bank's small foyer, screaming, "Fuck! Fuck! The life, the LIFE! It's unbelievable! I'm too old for this shit!"

At least, Keszthelyi thought, he wasn't the only one losing his mind.

⌒

Attila was twenty-nine years old. He was a hockey goalie and a building superintendent. He had a beautiful Székely girlfriend. He lived in Budapest. He was, as far as he could tell, the most prolific and well known thief in Eastern Europe. Except for cleaning the stairwell of his apartment building and taking out the trash once a week, he had the life he'd thought he wanted. He was the well-loved star of the most popular TV show in Hungary. He was rich. And yet he was going mad.

He hadn't been able to sleep since the day two months earlier when he'd almost been caught running from the scene of the second of he and Gabi's two robberies. He'd spent many of those nights imagining Betty asking where he'd put that Levis hat she'd bought him — or worse, her seeing it on television in the hands of László Juszt. Attila was so consumed by keeping up on where the police stood with the investigation that he often arrived at 5:00 A.M. at his pal Frici's newsstand to get the papers. And with his friend Dr. Tóth now working up at Tököl prison, Attila was so paranoid that he had started checking medical journals out of the library in hopes of self-diagnosing his deteriorating stomach condition rather than see a strange doctor.

The last thing he needed was to be told that the bank he was in the process of robbing had just emptied the bulk of its coffers into an armored vehicle for deposit. But that's what had happened during his last robbery. He left the OTP with just 1.5 million forints ($8,200), his worst showing since the debacle at the Ó Street travel agency three years ago. Subtracting Gabi's share, it was his lowest take since December 1993. When he and Gabi had gotten back to his apartment, Attila was still fuming. "I'm not getting caught with a couple of hundred thousand forints," he said, taking back Gabi's gun and giving him the few cardboard clips from the bill bundles to burn. "I'm not going to look like some loser, some novice. I'd rather shoot myself in the head."

Attila's twenty-three-year-old partner was also losing his edge, though he'd been at the game for only eight months. Gabi didn't tell Attila, but while Attila was having his meltdown inside the bank, Gabi realized he'd forgotten to spray the video camera. Fortunately, when he remembered, he saw that the camera's cord was hanging loose along the wall. It wasn't even plugged in. "Shitty OTP," he'd muttered, kicking a dent in the bank's cheap wall.

The partners had agreed that although they couldn't end their careers on such a sour note, they had to shut down the business. They both had substance-abuse problems, digestive trouble, and anger-management issues. They couldn't take it anymore, and neither, it should be mentioned, could their girlfriends, who were sick of the boys' foul moods, unexpected absences, and monopoly on the bathrooms. Attila and Gabi decided they would do one more job — Attila's twenty-second, including the single failed attempt at the train station travel agency in 1993 — and call it a career.

Attila steeled himself for one last round of preparations. It would be his and Gabi's eighth robbery in nine months. He found a department store outside town where he could buy wigs. He re-examined his robbery book as if it were the last skin mag in the Milky Way. He even snooped around the Interior Ministry garages to see which precincts had more squad cars in for repairs. And then he made his decision. They would go after the same OTP Bank on Grassalkovich Street, in the southern industrial Pest outskirts, that they'd robbed after buying their trip to the Dominican Republic. It was a sleepy area, it was farthest from a police precinct, and two of the cop cars from the district were out of service.

On May 27 Attila dropped Betty off at Éva's, went home, and started drinking. At eight o'clock the next morning, Gabi showed up to find the door to the apartment unlocked and Attila asleep with the lights on and a wig draped over the lampshade. After waking his partner, Gabi played the role of the guard for their dress rehearsals. Then they pulled their business suits over their clothing, painted their mustaches, fastened their wigs to their heads, and headed out for the grand finale.

Twelve customers were inside when they entered the bank. Attila started anyway, pouncing on the guard and taking his gun. Gabi remembered to spray the camera. Attila finished before Gabi could call time. If an alarm had been activated, it was silent. Attila locked the door to the bank from the outside with the key the manager had given him, and he and Gabi walked swiftly back to their waiting cab. "To the HÉV, please," Attila told the driver, referring to the southern station of the city's aboveground train network. In the concourse bathroom, they slipped out of their sports jackets and dress shirts, transferred the plastic bags of money into the Camel duffel, and hopped onto the train heading back toward the city. Attila could tell by the weight of the bag that it had been a big score. As the train slid north past Grassalkovich Street, he looked wistfully out the window at the police cars surrounding the bank. Someone tapped his arm. "Can you imagine having that kind of courage?" a woman next to him said, nodding at the cordoned-off crime scene. "I bet that's the Whiskey Robber." Attila was going to miss robbing.

The next day, before he picked up Betty but after he and Gabi had counted up a record 25-million-forint haul ($138,000), Attila pulled a batch of guns out of his oven, most of which were pieces that had been fleeced from bank guards. He dismantled them on the floor, dropped them into a sack, and waited for Gabi to show up. They got into Attila's red Toyota Land Cruiser and drove south past the Danube's Csepel Island, past the abandoned factory buildings, then the sandy dunes sprouting grape vines, until neither the city nor the pollution cloud around it was visible. At a remote section of the road, Attila pulled over to the shoulder. He and Gabi tramped through the muddy reeds and mosquitoes to the bank of the river, where one by one, they tossed the tools of their former trade into the brackish, still water.

Twenty

So they're dealing with this Whiskey Robber again," the man with the newspaper in the backseat said to the taxi driver.

"Yeah, I saw that," the driver said, weaving through traffic along Stefánia Street near Heroes' Square.

They drove in silence for a few minutes.

"What would you do if he got into your cab?" the passenger asked.

"I would probably recognize him," said the mustachioed driver, who himself bore a resemblance to the thief. "But I've never seen anyone similar."

"Where do you think he goes, the casinos?" asked the mustachioed passenger.

"Probably," said the driver, looking in the rearview mirror at his fare. The man in the backseat had long dark hair under a baseball hat and bushy eyebrows sticking out of his Ray-Ban sunglasses. "I don't mind playing the tables a bit myself," the driver offered.

"Really?" his passenger asked. "What's your game?"

"I like them all," the driver said. "Blackjack, roulette."

The cab pulled up to downtown's Deák Square. "The corner here is fine," the passenger said, digging into his pocket with effort. "Can you hold this for a minute so I can get my wallet?" he asked the driver, passing him a half-empty can of Coca-Cola. A moment later the man in the backseat pulled out a thousand-forint bill ($5.50) and handed it over the seat. The driver gave him back the Coke. "Thanks," the passenger said. "Good day."

Then Lajos Varjú climbed out of the back of the cab, hurried down the pedestrian underpass and back out the other side in front of police headquarters, where, once inside, he pulled off his wig, hat, and sunglasses, and rushed the Coke can to forensics to be tested for fingerprints. Unfortunately, the mask of desperation he wore was his own.

That summer Lajos and his robbery team became the last Budapest police division to vacate the hundred-year-old downtown headquarters next to Planet of the Zorg and relocate to a tinted-glass space needle in northern Budapest. The new nine-story HQ, topped with radar towers and satellite dishes, was an impressive sight, particularly as it was set on the edge of the city's largest communist-era housing block, a colorless diorama that resembled a meeting of disorderly cereal boxes. Locals quickly dubbed the sleek new police palace the Death Star. Indeed, image was everything. In order to get out of the state-of-the-art structure's parking garage, Keszthelyi once had to dismantle the malfunctioning parking arm that drooped down after the passage of each car. And because several hundred million forints had allegedly been embezzled from the construction fund, the building's design plans had to be altered in progress. Instead of a seamless cylindrical design, the new HQ was completed in the shape of one wide half cylinder abutted by another much narrower half cylinder. It was a true testament to just how little anything had changed.

For Lajos, however, the new surroundings were invigorating, at least briefly. After working the city's busiest beat from an oversize closet overlooking a band of outlaw ragamuffins, he would command his 103-member division from a spacious, carpeted office with a view of the one-bedroom apartment Hungarian rapper Gangsta Zoli shared with his mother. In contrast to what Lajos had become accustomed to at the old HQ, thinking like a cop no longer required an active imagination or a lukewarm tonic. His new digs featured an arrestee tank, entire hallways lined with one-way-mirrored interrogation rooms, and a press center stocked with pretzels and refrigerated beer in which he would soon long to swim.

With Sándor Pintér and his cronies off the police force and the next year's national elections in sight, Prime Minister Horn had underscored his commitment to winning Hungary's war on crime. Aside from promising an end to the crime wave, Horn created an expanded public relations department and a new special operations force, the KBI (Központi Bűnüldözési Igazgatóság, or Central Criminal Office). The KBI, also known as the Hungarian FBI, quickly arrested the owners of Attila's preferred auto dealership, Conti-Car, on organized crime charges, a bust that resulted in an internal staffwide police request that the ubiquitous "I Love Conti-Car" stickers be removed from all police cars and offices. But it was the KBI's follow-up bulletin that began to ruin Lajos's mood. The blueprints for the new police headquarters building had been stolen from the KBI director's car, and the KBI was warning that a group of mafiosos linked to the arrested Conti-Car kingpins had phoned *and* faxed the Death Star to report that they were about to destroy the building with shoulder-fired missiles. With his marriage suffering from a lack of attentiveness, Lajos had hoped the new green velvet couch in his office might offer him comfort in times of need, not a cushioned landing in case of a projectile attack.

And to think he'd actually been almost giddy after the Whiskey Robber's last strike. The Grassalkovich Street OTP that the robber and his partner had pilfered for the second time was one of the banks that Lajos had successfully persuaded to store marked bills in its safe — and sure enough, the bait was among the 25 million swiped forints. All Lajos had to do, he'd somehow assumed, was be patient and eventually he would reel in his robber. He was, of course, mistaken. When he arrived at the bank and asked the manager what system would be employed to detect the bills when they re-entered circulation, the manager told him simply, "Neither the OTP nor the post offices have the technical capacity or human resources to do such a thing."

He'd then interviewed the robbery's twelve uninjured victims, among whom was Ms. Plóder, a seventy-five-year-old woman who had entered the bank while the crime was in progress. Ms. Plóder described being rudely ordered by one of the perpetrators to get on the floor, which she naturally refused. "I will not," she had told one of the robbers. "And don't ever talk to me like that again." The young perpetrator, apparently the Whiskey Robber's accomplice, had then apologized and helped her into an armchair. "It almost seemed like a robbery," Ms. Plóder told Lajos. Then she opened her purse and offered Lajos a small gratuity for his kindness.

It wasn't the first time Lajos had been treated like wait staff. Everyone in Hungary knew how badly the police were paid. But he hated the presumption of helplessness. Unfortunately, the kind of tips Lajos wanted were harder to come by and often worth even less. For example, it was a call from one of the casino managers that had led Lajos to don a wig and makeup in search of the roulette-playing taxi driver. But the cabbie's fingerprints did not match the few prints the police had managed to collect from the Whiskey Robber.

Despite the trail of evidence and phone book's worth of tips Lajos had collected on the case in the past two years alone — the videotape, the audiotape, János Kis and Stuttering Józsi, the wig, the rare-edition Levis hat — he was no closer to knowing the identity of the thief than he was when the series began in 1993, twenty-two robberies and more than four years ago. Everything, including the shiny new building in which he worked, was beginning to make Lajos feel like a joke.

Given his team's investigative track record, he decided his best chance to catch the robber would be in the act, which at the current rate was almost once a month. He signed up for a course offered by the FBI, a series of weekly trainings role-playing bank-heist scenarios at the Citicorp bank in downtown's touristy Vörösmarty Square across from the famous Hapsburg-era Café Gerbeaud. The rest of the week, Lajos and his team patrolled the top projected Whiskey Robber targets both in and out of Dance Instructor's concentric circles, stopping in to make sure the employees were properly prepared for their impending melodrama. And they waited for the call to come. But the summer of 1997 passed into the fall and fall became the holiday season, and there was no sign of the Whiskey Robber.

Twenty-one

For just 5 million forints ($27,300) in cash, Attila had bought a one-bedroom town house with a small backyard on suburban Rezeda Street in the XX District, straight across the river to the east from his old place on busy Villányi Street. Rezeda was a quiet, unassuming middle-class block in south Pest, all the way on the opposite side of town from his partner's opulent new digs in the Buda hills. But to Attila, who had never lived anywhere with more than one room since he occupied the couch in his aunt and uncle's apartment in Csíkszereda, his new home was luxurious enough.

It was also the first time he was officially living with a woman. And with his winless hockey season — and, dare we say, his robbery career — over, Attila was prepared to make a real transition. It wouldn't be like last time with Éva. He went shopping with Betty for new furniture — an L-shaped couch, modern Formica dressers, big-screen television, an expensive stereo system — and even let Betty do the decorating. Eschewing the peasant motif of Attila's Villányi Street pad, Betty selected pastel paints for the walls and a pink carpet. For the small courtyard in back, she went with sculpted fir trees and a gas barbecue grill. It was no place for a bandit. When Betty was done, Attila went out and bought a shark head and mounted it on the peach-colored living-room wall. He was trying. These were big changes.

As summer arrived, there were still no UTE workout sessions to attend, because the team was in the process of being taken over by new management and coaches. Even General Bereczky had finally left the team. Attila had never had so much time on his hands. He and Betty took another luxury beach trip in June to the Seychelles, where they talked about having kids but agreed instead to raise an animal. When they returned from the trip, they bought Don, a Bernese mountain dog whom they named for the Russian river that flows through the mountains south of Moscow into the Black Sea.

Attila stayed away from the newspapers and tried to stay out of trouble. He couldn't go to the Cats Club anyway, because his contact there, co-owner Gyula Zubovics, hadn't survived his car bombing that May. Attila and Betty puttered around the food court and multiplex of the first American-style shopping center in Eastern Europe, Budapest's $60 million Duna Plaza, built on a former Soviet military base. At night they hosted Gabi and Marian and Bubu and some of Attila's other teammates for barbecues. Sometimes they went downtown to the gay bars, where the good jazz and rock bands played.

But despite the loss of Cats, Budapest was still a city with more casinos — nine — than anywhere in the world except Las Vegas, Atlantic City, and London. And on some days Attila couldn't resist their call. He would tell Betty he was going out for an errand and end up at the roulette wheel all night, returning the next morning drunk and despondent, pleading with Betty to forgive him for his "illness."

The real problem was that Attila was hedging his bets. What if Betty left him? What if he were arrested several years down the line when they had kids to worry about? Or what if those fears were just a distraction meant to keep him from getting too deep into a relationship he didn't know how to have and a life that was quickly becoming very average?

As the summer wore on, Attila began picking fights with Betty, once losing his temper upon sighting a spiderweb in the bathroom she was supposed to have cleaned. Betty knew something was wrong, but Attila swore it didn't have to do with her. One night she awoke from bed to find Attila on the kitchen floor with Don, crying with the dog in his arms. Attila didn't understand exactly what was going on with him, but he surely did know one thing: he hadn't thrown *all* of his guns into the Danube River that day with Gabi. And even though he no longer lived at Villányi Street 112, he'd kept the apartment, where two of his pistols and his robbery encyclopedia remained in the bottom of the oven.

The hockey season couldn't come soon enough. It was impossible to say what kind of team would emerge from the ashes, but at least it would keep Attila occupied. At the end of August, when *Népsport* published the league's rosters for the season, Attila made a special trip to Frici's newsstand to check out how his club was shaping up. It took several minutes of scanning the paper before he understood what he saw. After toiling for seven years as an unpaid goalie who'd almost never missed even a practice, no one had bothered to let Attila know he was no longer a member of the team. His name did not appear on the UTE roster.

~

December 1997

Attila's metallic gray Mitsubishi Pajero wound around a final turn on the thin dirt road and down a small hill to an opening in the trees. There in the clearing was Gabi's nearly finished Budakeszi dream house, an A-frame, dark wood Swiss chalet with a wraparound balcony on the second floor that looked out onto a December-brown valley. Attila pulled his car into a paved square driveway and parked it next to Gabi's truck.

"Don't you love the air out here," Gabi said, coming around the corner from the back with Marian. Marian said hello to Attila, who was wearing his black leather jacket over a pair of OshKosh B'Gosh overalls, then kissed Gabi good-bye and climbed into her apple red Opel to run some errands while the former teammates caught up.

Winter was on its way and a cold wind was blowing through the trees. "Let's go inside," Gabi said.

Gabi hadn't seen Attila since Attila's thirtieth-birthday dinner in early October at the Chinese restaurant that had been blown up in a mafia hit the following week. Attila seemed okay then, but Gabi couldn't say for sure because there were nine of them dining there — Attila, Betty, Gabi, Marian, Éva, Bubu, the grocery clerk Zsuzsa and her daughter, Sylvia, with whom Attila was still friends, and Sylvia's policeman boyfriend. (Betty had made Attila a cake shaped like a stack of U.S.

$100 bills.) The only thing Gabi had gleaned from the evening about his former accomplice was the news that Bubu had scored Attila a goalie position with UTE's rival, FTC.

The former partners went through the sliding glass door into the basement, where Gabi and Marian had been living while the construction on the main level was being completed. Piles of dirty laundry were clumped in mounds on expensive, colorful Persian rugs.

"I don't know how you live like this," Attila said, looking around the bar area for a whiskey. There were boxes of old pizza sitting on the counter. The refrigerator smelled like rotten fruit and sour milk.

"It's just temporary," Gabi said. "It should be done in a couple of months."

Gabi had forgotten to buy whiskey. He apologized, poured two vodkas on the rocks, and brought the bottle over to the kitchen table, where they sat down.

Aside from living in squalor, Gabi seemed to be doing well. He had traded his BMW for a Dodge Stealth before he got the truck that was sitting in the driveway. The Stealth was like a spaceship, he said. Once, he was pulled over by the police, who only wanted to see how fast he could go. But he had to get rid of it; it was costing him a fortune in gas. And he needed a truck anyway, to ferry construction supplies to the house. This was his life in a nutshell.

Attila filled Gabi in about life with FTC. "I'm sure it's worse than when you and your dad were there," he said. Gabi could imagine. The three things everyone knew about the Chicky Panther were that he was filthy rich, he'd had two of the worst seasons in Hungarian hockey history, and he was a career UTE guy. That wouldn't go over well at FTC, where the abhorrence of all things UTE was still so strong that in May, during an FTC-UTE soccer match, FTC fans set the UTE stadium on fire. Even Bubu couldn't protect Attila from that kind of odium. For the first time in years, Attila had to deal with being called a *bozgor* — a "worthless homeless guy" — by both his opponents and his gracious new teammates. And the FTC gang invented a new insult just for Attila that he'd never heard before: they called him a *bocskoros*, a slang word for a Transylvanian-style sandal.

Attila acted as if he found the whole situation funny. Laughing, Attila told Gabi that he'd gotten so mad on a recent road trip when a teammate claimed Attila was in his bus seat that Attila got out on the M7 highway and hitchhiked home, skipping the game. But he didn't care, Attila said. He had other plans. "I'm thinking of opening up a 24-hour liquor store," he told Gabi. "Can you believe they don't have one in south Buda?"

"No," Gabi said. "Really?"

Both sufficiently drunk by now, Gabi figured it was as good a time to ask as any. Betty had called him a couple of weeks earlier to tell him that Attila was on a gambling binge. It was a sensitive topic, Gabi well knew, but Betty had asked for his help. Plus he had his own reasons for wanting to know if it was true. "So, have you been seeing the casinos?" Gabi asked.

"Just a little," Attila acknowledged, filling his glass with vodka again. "Easy come, easy go."

"Don't you think it's suspicious with you spending so much money there?" Gabi asked, trying not to flinch.

Attila put his glass back down on the table, empty. "Gabi, don't keep your money in your pillowcase," he said. "Have as many experiences as you can. That they can never take away."

Gabi could see where his partner was going with the conversation, and as much as it scared him to acknowledge, part of him missed the life. Growing up in the Orbán family, any respect and praise was always directed toward his dad and his elder brother, the goddam "Goal King." Gabi's partnership with Attila was the most successful team he had ever been part of. On the other hand, Gabi now had a big house, nice cars. His brother didn't have that. Gabi was even thinking about asking Marian to marry him. He wanted a family, too; the whole package. He and Attila had had too many close calls. He didn't want to risk everything all over again. "Betty seems like the type of woman who would be great with kids," Gabi said, trying to change the subject.

"Marian's not what's going to make you happy," Attila said, getting up and going over to the sliding glass door. After a minute he came out with it. "I think we should do another job."

"I'm going to sell the house," Gabi countered. "I think I can get at least twenty million forints [$109,000] for it. When I do, I'm going to give you some of the money. You helped me, and I'm going to help you."

"You'll never sell it until it's completely finished," Attila said, returning to the table. "You're going to need a lot more money to finish this place. I already have the plan."

"I don't know," said Gabi. "You see what's going on."

The papers were full of crime news, portraying a city falling into the grasp of a violent and unforgiving underworld. As evidence mounted that the Russian mob was controlling Hungary's billion-dollar-a-year oil-importation industry, it seemed as though every new purported witness to the corruption was being silenced; three Hungarian cops investigating the case became victims of suspicious suicides. Another story that led to a strident outcry from several foreign embassies in Budapest involved two Danish businessmen who had picked up two Hungarian women and taken them to eat at a Budapest nightclub. When the dinner bill came, it was for 1 million forints ($4,300), which the Danes stopped protesting when a battalion of muscle-bound men arrived at their table to collect. Crime was becoming an epidemic. Even the hot dog buffet at the Keleti train station was damaged by a hand grenade.

With national elections just six months away, the government was making pronouncements about strict new national law-and-order programs, which themselves had provoked new violence. The offices of all five of Hungary's political parties (and Budapest's mayor's office) were threatened and in several cases attacked by crude explosive devices that failed to kill anyone but succeeded in helping vault safety past the economy as the public's number one concern. It also made the Whiskey Robber look like the Tooth Fairy.

"We can do Grassalkovich again," Attila said, referring to the OTP in the southern industrial part of the city that they'd already robbed twice.

"You're crazy," Gabi said. "They must have a cop on duty there full-time by now. They're going to be waiting for us."

"Fine," Attila said, smashing his fist down on the table and standing up. "I can get someone else. But in four or five years, I'm not going to take the blame for the gigs you did!" Gabi watched him leave, raging. Betty would not be pleased.

The next day Attila phoned his partner. He wanted to apologize, he told Gabi. "I'd like to take you for an ice cream," he said. Attila's bluster the previous afternoon had been just that. He'd read about the police's new Dolphin motorcycle unit that could respond twice as fast to calls; he needed Gabi. But by the time they met for dessert, Gabi didn't need any convincing. He'd thought about it and decided that Attila was right. The garden in back of his house had been swept away in a heavy rain, and it would take more money than he had to refurbish. He was in.

Twenty-two

February 1998

Lajos sat in his office, holding two new case files in his hands and no new people in his custody. Was it possible? he asked himself. The crimes in question bore every stamp of the Whiskey Robber — two men, good looks, bad wigs, hats — everything but the gunfire.

The old Lajos would have found it inconceivable that the first robbery had even occurred at all. He'd been conducting constant business-hours drive-by surveillance of the Grassalkovich Street OTP. Not only had it just been robbed again by two men in Whiskey Robber-esque costumes, but this time one of the perpetrators had squeezed off three shots from a Parabellum pistol. None of them hit anyone; they were all fired at the video camera, prompting, according to witnesses, an argument between the two robbers about following directions. Could the Whiskey Robber's accomplice have forgotten his spray paint?

Then, six weeks later, on February 5, 1998, two men with similar physiques, without masks, and said to be wearing hairpieces robbed another city OTP. Again gunfire, though only a single targeted shot this time that destroyed the NOW SERVING board. What really set the robbery apart, however, was the shot that didn't go off: after taking out the service board, the perpetrators had pulled out a wired explosive device and placed it on the counter, announcing that it was a remote-controlled bomb. Actually, it was two premium Cuban cigars wrapped with transistor radio wire to a battery, a bullet cartridge, and the face of a digital watch. But as a bluff, it had worked to perfection. If these gigs were the work of the Whiskey Robber, he'd certainly shown a willingness to up the ante.

Both robberies were covered by a burgeoning media that now included two more Hungarian television channels. The government had finally privatized the airwaves, and the two new commercial networks launched with *Kriminális* copycats as their showpieces. But aside from the lone account of the second robbery in *Népszava* (THE ROBBER IN A JOKING MOOD), the media did not attribute the bullet-marked heists to the Whiskey Robber. To Lajos's relief, he wasn't even pressed for comment.

At eight years of age, the independent Hungarian media was hardly a model of journalistic rigor and responsibility, unless perhaps if judged against its nonexistent past. For the majority of local journalists, covering crime was a privilege, and the pervasive aura of criminality in the nation's capital lent an air of exhilaration and significance to even the shoddiest tabloid operations. In that regard, the postcommunist 1990s in Hungary was not unlike the fabled golden age of American sports in the 1920s and 1930s, when journalists rode the rails with the ballplayers they unapologetically mythologized. The tall and handsome chief of the Budapest homicide department, Péter Doszpot, happily became a larger-than-life celebrity. A regular on *Kriminális* and the other crime shows, the thirty-five-year-old Doszpot was invariably shown wearing black leather jacket and sunglasses, riding in to fight the city's dark side in his red Alfa Romeo convertible (a gift from the Italian carmaker). The only thing he lacked was a theme song.

Lajos, who wore the same style jacket, didn't have the right look — or an evil nemesis — and wasn't offered a free car. But on the days when he didn't have use of one of the department's Volkswagens, Lajos could usually hitch a ride with the affable reporters to the crime scene.

Kriminális host László Juszt, who had been given an entire wing of offices at Hungarian Television, spun off his television show into a theater production, the *Kriminális Cabaret*, which caricatured the country's crime problems and government corruption scandals. The show, which ran for three months in Budapest's Little Broadway theater district, featured the harmless Whiskey Robber as Hungary's court jester, a lovable lout in an out-of-control lot. (The actor who portrayed the Whiskey Robber — wearing a business suit and wig, and carrying flowers and a whiskey bottle — was József Zana, father of Gabi's and Attila's friend rapper Gangsta Zoli.)

But though the media had no shortage of crime material, it was getting harder to make light of it. That spring a Bulgarian diplomat was found stabbed to death in his home with his mouth taped shut. A member of Parliament was killed when he was hit by an oncoming car while trying to fend off an attacker attempting to steal his parked vehicle. And since January, a serial killer had been stalking the city's shop clerks.

Needless to say, Prime Minister Horn could have picked a better time to have to make the case that Hungary was the safest and most progressive country in the former Eastern bloc. But with only a few months left before two momentous votes — his own for re-election, and that of the U.S. Senate on Hungary's acceptance into NATO, a key endorsement for foreign investors as much as a military safeguard — that was the task ahead for Horn.

Like both of Hungary's democratically elected prime ministers before him, Horn would fail to make his case for re-election. A month before the first round of voting, a Hungarian media mogul, János Fenyő, was gunned down in broad daylight on Budapest's streets by men in balaclavas, sparking a national outcry. Even the prime minister angrily declared, "Whatever this is in Hungary, it is not public safety!"

The blame game quickly began. Horn announced that he would fight for stricter immigration laws, claiming that 80 percent of the country's robberies and murders were committed by foreigners. The interior minister, who oversaw the police department, accused Parliament of neglecting to adequately fund the police. (Adjusted for inflation, the police department budget was 14 percent lower than it had been in 1995.) And inside the Death Star, Budapest police chief Attila Berta began sniping about a certain robbery chief. The city's robbery division, Berta had said, was suffering because Lajos Varjú was upset about not receiving kickbacks.

Berta's charge drifted down to Lajos's office in early March. Upon hearing it from one of his colleagues, Lajos dropped what he was doing and headed to the emergency stairwell. He'd had it. He'd been running one of the busiest departments at the police with less than half the cars, equipment, and people he needed. The KBI had refused his requests for help tracing the marked bills. Dance Instructor was threatening to quit to devote himself to his new and possibly more lucrative hobby of training carrier pigeons. With no more cars to crash, Mound had lost interest in everything but fishing. Of course, Lajos hadn't hidden his dismay at the fact that his request for pay raises for his staff had been denied for the nth year in a row. But unlike many of his colleagues, he had never asked for or accepted bribes. Lajos bounded down two flights of stairs to the fifth floor, walked straight past Berta's protesting secretary, and flung open the door to Berta's office, where the city police chief was in a meeting with several other top cops.

"You're stupid and you're a liar," Lajos bellowed at Berta. Then he turned around and stormed out, slamming Berta's door shut. After sixteen years as a cop, Lajos had just turned over an hourglass on his career. His only chance to save his job now would be to catch the Whiskey Robber. Quickly.

Twenty-three

Budapest
March 11, 1998

Three minutes!" Gabi yelled. The sirens were sounding just as they had when he and Attila had been here in police uniform almost exactly a year ago. But Gabi needed to remain calm. He'd remembered to bring the paint this time and to use it. He was watching the door and the customers and the time. And he was trying to keep one eye on his partner — but he had no idea where his partner was.

"Three and a half minutes!" Gabi yelled, looking out the glass double doors behind him at a piece of the Heltai Square shopping center. In the reflection of the glass store windows across from him, he could see the bank's orange outdoor alarm lights spinning.

Gabi couldn't believe he'd let Attila persuade him to do this bank again. After the December OTP robbery at Grassalkovich Street, he had actually started to believe Attila was too good to ever allow them to be caught. When they had arrived there that day, a police car was parked outside the bank. It had pulled away a few minutes later, and Gabi jumped out from the bush in which they were hiding and began moving toward the bank. Attila yanked him back. "They're going to circle around," Attila had said. "They always circle around." Sure enough, a minute later the car had appeared behind them, drove slowly past the front of the bank, then moved on. Gabi was awed. His partner had a sixth sense, he had concluded. Now, panicking, Gabi wondered what he had been thinking. Attila wasn't a psychic. He was a drunk.

"Four minutes!" Gabi yelled over the alarm. "Do you hear me, Mr. X?"

Attila was in the back, hovering over the chief teller while she fumbled around with the keys to the cash drawers. But his pickled head was somewhere else. Betty was gone. Attila's relationship with her had been going downhill since the summer, but it ended for him a few weeks ago in Aruba when he'd started to tell her his secret one rainy day in their hotel room. "I don't want to know," she'd said, stopping him. After that he'd lapsed into a stoic silence, anesthetized by the realization that the woman he'd contemplated marrying didn't want to know who he really was. He was still in a sort of shock when, last week, he was walking around the neighborhood with Don and saw Betty sitting in the McDonald's with another man. Something snapped. He ran inside and slapped Betty across the face right in front of her lunch companion. Gave her three days to move her things out. She left, and he was glad — he certainly didn't need a woman like that. But he hadn't been able to take down the note she'd left on the refrigerator that morning. "Hi, can you take my black dress to the cleaners?" It seemed so normal, he thought, so *nice* — so much like something he would never have. Attila hadn't cried so much since the time with Éva at his grandmother's grave. He felt as though he didn't know anything anymore, only that he was alone, again.

"Five minutes!" Gabi was screaming, but Attila didn't much care. He'd started the timers going on the file cabinet safe first before going back to collect the contents of the teller drawers, and now he was back at the safe. The first two drawers were open, but he was going to wait at least until he got to the third. "Open it now!" he yelled at the teller with the key ring. "I know you can open it." He'd read somewhere or other that there was a special code that could override the time lock in an emergency.

Vegetable vendors, whose carts were parked just outside the bank, were gathering around the front door.

"Five and a half minutes!" Gabi shouted. "Mr. X, *there are people outside!*"

No response.

"Six minutes!" Gabi yelled. "*Six minutes!*"

Attila finally appeared from behind the counter, waving his arms. He was wearing a long wool coat and a dark beret over a long dirty-blond wig. With his small round glasses, he resembled a shorter, stouter John Lennon in the Yoko years. "Let's go," he said to Gabi. Gabi ran from the front door toward the counter, where Attila pulled him through a doorway. Like last time, they headed to the back exit that opened onto the alley. But this time, when they crashed through the steel door, a crowd of ten or twelve people were waiting for them. It was the vegetable vendors.

A weak sun strained through the early-morning sky. Attila and Gabi had wanted to wait for rain or snow so that the police response would be slowed, but today's chance of flurries was the worst weather in the foreseeable forecast. It was cold but clear. The vendors began to make their move.

Girding for a challenging flight, Attila had already dumped the loot into his Camel duffel bag, which hung from his right shoulder. "Stay back!" Attila yelled, firing twice into the air with his Tokarev pistol.

The produce personnel backed up, and Attila and Gabi bolted down the alley along the back of the shops. When they passed the Jéé discount department store, Gabi tore off one way through the apartment complex and Attila went another. Most of the group followed Attila because he was the one with the gun and the bag, presumably carrying the bank's money.

Hearing the clamoring vendors in tow, Attila fired two more shots in the air without looking back, in hopes of forcing another retreat. Two blocks ahead, along a footpath, an off-duty policeman, Ferenc Laczik, was on his way to the shopping center's post office when he heard the shots. To his left, he saw a man in a business suit running directly toward him, followed by a pack of apron-clad vigilantes.

Attila didn't see Laczik until they were only forty feet apart. "Don't come near me, or I'll shoot!" Attila shouted as he approached the policeman in a dead sprint. Laczik didn't have his gun with him. He backed up onto the grass on the side of the path with his hands up as the bespectacled thief ran past him and turned a corner at Building 7 in the apartment complex. "Keep going!" some of the vendors shouted to Laczik, who took off ahead of them in pursuit. "He's getting tired!"

As Attila ran, he fired one more shot, then another. Laczik knew the gun had at most a ten-bullet chamber, and he'd already heard at least four shots. "Fire!" Laczik yelled, trying to egg on the perpetrator. "Go ahead, try to hit me!"

Attila turned down a walkway and kept running, past a kinder-garten building and playground. At the end of the winding path, he emerged onto the main boulevard, Pünkösfürdő. He burst into traffic on the road, heading for the nearest intersection, Király Street.

At that corner another off-duty policeman, István Tamari, was waiting to cross the street on foot. Tamari heard car horns and then saw a man with a gun running ahead of a trail of people, all yelling, "Robber! Robber! Get him!"

Tamari pulled out his gun and pointed it at the man. "Freeze!" he shouted at Attila. "Police!"

Attila ignored the warning. The light had turned red and a line of cars was stacked up at the intersection. He approached a small white Czech-made Škoda 120 and put his Tokarev up to the driver's window. "Get out!" Attila yelled. The man and his wife leapt from the car with their hands in the air.

Attila jumped in and started driving even before he could close the door. Tamari, now just thirty yards behind the car, fired twice. One of the bullets shattered the Škoda's back window. Attila crouched so low in the driver's seat that he could barely see the road as he lurched out into the intersection, ran the red light, and turned left down another major boulevard.

The first police unit on the scene arrived from the opposite direc-tion and, seeing the Škoda run the light and the people pointing after it, gave chase — as did four of the vegetable vendors, who hailed a small Volkswagen. The three cars swerved and sped along through the morn-ing rush-hour congestion, drunken-caravan-style. Before a Shell gas station on the corner of another intersection, Attila turned left onto a smaller road, swerving into oncoming traffic. The police car and the vegetable vendors followed. The vehicles darted and weaved through traffic, traveling in circles until, after about twenty minutes, the other two cars lost sight of the Škoda.

The Whiskey Robber had eluded capture again.

⁓

Gabi cautiously approached his mansion an hour and a half later, after a circuitous route using several modes of transport took him back to the car he'd left at the Déli subway station, the last stop in suburban Buda.

Attila and Gabi had made a rule after Attila was nearly nabbed by the pedestrian pursuer almost a year ago to the day: if either of them was ever captured, he would wait at least three hours before giving up the other's name. It wouldn't be fair, they decided, to expect the captured party not to talk at all. But a three-hour window would allow enough time for the other to make it over the Romanian border to freedom. Gabi hadn't seen Attila since the discouraging glimpse he got over his shoulder of the screaming vegetable vendors charging after his partner. If Attila had been caught, Gabi had only ninety minutes left to get out of the country. He needed his passport.

He entered the house from the sliding door in the back, half expecting to find a commando team hiding under his dirty laundry. But there was nothing out of the ordinary that he could see, except for his answering machine, which was blinking with twenty-five messages on it, all hang-ups. Within a minute, the phone rang again. Gabi picked it up and said nothing.

"Gringo?" Attila's voice said.

"Where the hell are you?" Gabi asked in a whisper.

"I'm at the border at Ártánd," Attila said, referring to one of the checkpoints on the Hungarian-Romanian border.

"How did you get there so fast?" Gabi asked.

"You're not going to believe it," Attila said. "It's safe to come back?"

Two hours later Gabi heard the sound of a car pulling up the gravelly road. "Where the fuck are you?" Gabi heard Attila yell as the car pulled to a stop in the driveway. "You wouldn't believe it, Gringo," he kept on. "They shot the window out of my car. It was really like in America what happened to me."

"What car?" Gabi yelled out his second-floor bedroom window. "Wait, I'm coming down."

Gabi came outside and shut Attila up long enough to proffer the important question: "Do you have the money?"

Attila had left his outer layer of clothes and (accidentally) the dependable Camel duffel bag in the stolen car when he parked it near the HÉV station. But before jumping out to catch a subway to a tram back home for his own car, passport, and Don (who was now panting in his backseat), Attila had transferred the money from the plastic bag to the inside of his jockey shorts. The 5 million forints ($23,600) was sweaty but safe. It was time to celebrate.

⌐⌐

There was also a small celebration taking place across town at the Death Star, though it was not in the robbery offices. That day the violent crime unit, with the help of the KBI and the FBI, had captured the serial killer who had been stalking the city since January, stabbing to death four shop saleswomen. The arrest was trumpeted at a special news conference in the media room, where champagne was served. If the bubbly gathering went the way the public relations department and Lajos hoped, no one in the media would be left with the time or faculty to ascertain that in other news, the Whiskey Robber had just knocked off his twenty-fourth bank, shot up a street, stolen a car, and outraced the police through morning-rush-hour traffic.

Lajos was clinging to his job by a thread. In the month since telling his boss that he was an idiot, he had been summarily rejected on every request he'd made for equipment or assistance. The new KBI was unwilling to provide him any personnel, and had reiterated its lack of interest in helping him trace the marked bills that the Whiskey Robber had stolen last May. So while Lajos appreciated the press office's maneuvering on his behalf that afternoon, he couldn't take it as anything more than a token bearing the inscription: *You'd better come up with something, or your time is up.*

An hour after the Heltai Square shoot-out, Lajos was on the scene with his entire department. One witness told investigators that he had seen one of the perpetrators arrive that morning in a sedan. Mound of Asshead had managed to borrow a video camera from another department and began recording pictures of every car, and license plate, in the shopping center lot, beginning near the bank door. Unfortunately, the police administrative office had refused Lajos's request to restock his department's depleted battery supplies, so halfway through Mound's filming, the camera went dead.

Later, back at HQ, while the serial killer press conference dragged on downstairs, a group of Lajos's men played back what they had on tape, then ran every license plate through the vehicle registration system. If you had a criminal record and a good enough parking space at Heltai Square that day, there was a 100 percent chance you would be arrested.

Brothers Norbert and Tamás Gergely were the first. Tamás'
car parked near the bank, and when police stripped and searched
home later that day, they found a Chinese throwing star, two 9mm gas
guns, and a stolen ID. Norbert was positively identified by a five-year-
old who was in the kindergarten playground when a band of angry men
had stampeded past the school.

The Gergelys were booked but would be home in time for dinner,
as the focus of the investigation quickly shifted to another set of brothers, Gyula and Péter Szűcs. Péter, thirty-one, claimed that his Audi 100
was parked at the shopping center because he was taking his daughter to
the kindergarten, where she was enrolled. Though that was apparently
true, the Szűcs brothers were also out on bond, awaiting sentencing for
the robbery of a department-store van. In addition, a police dog confirmed that the Szűcs brothers' unique scent matched the odor police
collected by pressing an Ágnes-brand baby diaper against the safe inside
the bank. The Szűcses were arrested and taken to the Gyorskocsi Street
jail, pending witness identification.

The next morning the Szűcs brothers were brought to a room with
a long, dark one-way glass along one wall and placed in a lineup with
three other inmates. They were handed lumpy farmer's hats, fake plastic glasses, and dime-store wigs by a jail guard who unironically choreographed the vaudevillian production. On the other side of the dark
glass stood several witnesses of the robbery, including the bank's security guard, some of the vegetable men, and an anxious Lajos Varjú. It
was pure, unscripted democracy. All of the witnesses fingered the taller
Szűcs brother, Péter, as the primary perpetrator, and Gyula as his
accomplice. Lajos was dubious. He knew the Whiskey Robber and his
partner were an athletic duo, and frankly the stick-thin Szűcses didn't
look as if they would pass a physical, much less be able to outrun a team
of steamed produce men. But later one of the undercover policemen
who had chased after the robber, Ferenc Laczik, affirmed that he was
"certain" the police had the right men. Never mind that unlike every
other witness, Ferenc identified the guy he'd run after as the *smaller*
brother, Gyula.

For the Szűcs brothers, the case against them was not easy to contest, largely because it wasn't clear what it was. And like most arrestees
in Budapest, they had no legal representation or financial wherewithal

to suggest a timely court hearing would commence. So they resorted to reason. Lajos Varjú listened to the Szűcses' pleas and agreed to conduct one final test of their guilt at a special facility by the incorruptible three-dog canine unit. But there the brothers crapped out again. The city's top two police sniffer dogs, Galopp and Pátz, positively identified the Szűcses in all five tests. Only Nanzi contradicted her canine colleagues — not enough to spring the brothers.

Lajos was under no illusion that he'd caught the Whiskey Robber and his accomplice, but the Szűcses did appear plausibly guilty of some of the crimes that had perhaps erroneously been on the more famous robbers' account. The Szűcses were charged with not only the most recent Heltai Square robbery but also the similar robbery of the same OTP Bank a year earlier. In addition, they were charged with the post office robbery that had occurred later that same day. Then more than a month after the Szűcses' arrest, a ballistics report proved that the shot fired through the NOW SERVING board at the OTP robbery in February was from the same gun used at the latest Heltai Square robbery. Suddenly the Szűcs brothers were facing charges for four robberies, all of which had previously been thought to be the work of the Whiskey Robber. Unless further evidence surfaced definitively clearing the brothers, Lajos wasn't in any position to risk setting them free.

Twenty-four

Two months after the Szűcs brothers were optimistically pinned to a slate of unsolved robberies, Hungary elected a telegenic new prime minister, Viktor Orbán, who had cast himself as the man to finally unite the country and bring it the long-awaited international stature that had already been accorded Lech Walesa's Poland and Václav Havel's Czech Republic. At thirty-five, Orbán would be the youngest leader in all of Europe, a soccer-playing, Oxford-educated man who exuded a Clintonian optimism and whose Alliance of Young Democrats Party vice chairman wore an earring. It was a far cry from Antall, the medical museum curator, and Horn, the graying former communist minister. A few weeks before the May 1998 election, Hungary was provisionally approved by the U.S. Senate to become a member of NATO. And after Orbán's victory at the polls, he received a letter of congratulations from President Clinton and an invitation to the White House.

But many of those who believed in Orbán had their hopes shattered before he was even inaugurated. After promising to clean up crime and corruption, Orbán appointed as his new interior minister the disgraced former national police chief, Sándor Pintér, who in turn hired as his top deputy another name familiar to those at the police department, László "The 12 Percent" Valenta. Then, a few days before Orbán's July inauguration, the most deadly bombing in Budapest since 1956 ripped through the walls and windows of Váci Street's landmark McDonald's, killing four people and injuring more than a dozen others. Among the dead was the apparently intended target, "Big Tom" Boros, a former mafia chieftain who had been working as a government informant on an investigation into the mafia-controlled oil business — which was by that time believed to be the largest and most lucrative criminal operation in Eastern Europe, siphoning billions of dollars a year from several countries in the region.

If nothing else, the mob hit got America's attention. The U.S. government formed its first-ever joint international police force with the new Hungarian government to probe the Boros murder, and, inexplicably, U.S. vice president Al Gore sponsored Sándor Pintér as a keynote speaker at a Washington law enforcement conference — on ethics in crime fighting.

Meanwhile back in Hungary, Pintér's controversial Interior Ministry appointment generated an outcry that lasted until late summer, when the prime minister's office made an announcement that would reclaim headlines for the foreseeable future and ultimately put *Kriminális* host László Juszt out of a job. According to Prime Minister Orbán's office, the former prime minister's Socialist Party had spied on Orbán's conservative Alliance of Young Democrats during the campaign. It was "Hungarian Watergate," according to the scandal-addled media, and for the time being, the punch it packed was more than enough to send the country back to licking its wounds and mumbling to itself in the corner. As Hungary's biggest newsweekly, *HVG*, remarked of the latest disgrace, "It is small, it is sour, but at least it is ours."

As Orbán had promised, wholesale changes in Hungarian law enforcement soon began. The KBI was disbanded, and KBI director Ernő Kiss, who was captured by a Death Star security camera peeing on the building, was fired.

The police also saw the exit of another embattled police chief: robbery head Lajos Varjú, who turned in his resignation soon after Orbán's election.

POLICE CHIEF RESIGNS, read the headline in *Mai Nap.*

Asked by the paper whether he quit over the Whiskey Robber case, Lajos said no but added, "I wouldn't be surprised to learn he [the Whiskey

Robber] is already in a jail somewhere." The real reason he left, Lajos said, was his dissatisfaction with the direction of the police force. "The police department is under shameful management," Lajos told *Mai Nap* in the kind of assessment for which the tabloids lived. "I always believed police should take their job seriously, but I'm not sure that applies today. The corruption is unbelievable."

As the Whiskey Robber read the *Mai Nap* story, he couldn't believe his eyes. He'd done it. Attila had not only outlasted his archnemesis, but now the guy was confirming his beliefs about the rotten system.

As the worlds around them imploded, both Lajos and Attila tried to salvage what was left of their personal lives. But picking up the pieces wasn't easy. Lajos separated from both his formerly beloved job and his formerly beloved wife, moved into another apartment, and went about trying to start his own private detective agency, the Blue Moon.

Attila, in the aftermath of his Hollywood-style car chase, was struggling to keep his sanity. The bullet that had gone through the back window of the getaway Škoda he'd stolen had nicked the windshield right in front of his head. He couldn't stop thinking that he'd escaped a grisly death by inches. Reading that the Szűcs brothers had been arrested and charged with several of his crimes brought no relief. He felt for them, but he didn't have the stomach to try to communicate to the police that they had the wrong robbers. He had to lie low for a long while if he was going to get through this. He knew the police knew he was still out there.

To distract himself, Attila spent two evenings at the Vidám Theater, where László Juszt's *Kriminális Cabaret* was playing. On his second visit, Attila secured a second-row seat from which he howled at Gangsta Zoli's father's portrayal of the Whiskey Robber. But there wasn't much else Attila could think of to keep himself occupied except carrying a silver flask of Johnnie Walker everywhere he went, sipping from it even at traffic lights. With Betty gone and his longtime relationship with both UTE and Lajos Varjú over, Attila was as adrift as he'd been since he climbed out from under a train ten years earlier. He spent a few weeks forlornly chopping trees on Éva's new property to help finish clearing the forested plot on which she was building a house. At night he went to the clubs alone, buying whole bottles of liquor from the bar and inviting everyone in the joint to drink with him. When the bottles were empty, he smashed them on the floor to cheers, then set about finding a woman to take home for the night.

In May, with the hockey season still months away (if he even decided to go back to FTC at all) and a few million forints (about $15,000) he was going to have to make last, he took a trip home to Transylvania. He had planned to stay with his aunt and uncle, but when he'd phoned to tell them he was bringing Don, they said they didn't want the dog in the apartment. Attila took Don to Transylvania anyway and, in protest of his relatives' shunning his only friend, stayed in a hotel and didn't bother visiting his family. He spent several days hiking with Don, picking wild mushrooms, and cooking his own meals on a camping stove. He stayed for a week, until he started feeling as lonely as he had been in his empty house in Budapest. He didn't know what to do with himself.

Gabi was also alone, having broken up with Marian and having had a falling-out with his parents after an argument with his father about his rudderless, spendthrift lifestyle. He also parted ways with his oldest friend, UTE forward Krisztián Nádor, during a vacation to the Greek island of Corfu. Krisztián accused Gabi of having become an egotist, dictating and altering their plans as if he expected to be addressed as Your Majesty.

As summer began, Attila's old friend Gustáv Bóta returned to UTE as the general manager and offered Attila his goalie position back, which Attila immediately accepted. (As usual, no pay.) Gabi too was offered, and accepted, an invitation to come out of retirement and start playing for UTE again. The boys were back together again, though not happily. They kept careful distance from each other, afraid of the spark that might ignite if they got too close. Robbery, it went without saying, was on neither one's agenda.

The team had chosen as the site of its preseason training camp the Transylvanian mountain town of Gyergyószentmiklós, where Betty was from and which Attila knew like the inside of a Budapest bank. The club was going to be there over October 6, Attila's thirty-first birthday. Attila got Bóta to approve a team outing to a special spot Attila knew, suitable for a celebration. He wanted to be the Chicky Panther again.

Attila called his uncle Dénes in Fitód and arranged for a freshly killed whole pig to be sent to the dormitory where they would be staying. Once the team arrived in Gyergyószentmiklós, Attila went to a restaurant and hired a trio of Gypsy musicians with accordions and the eatery's two cooks. And he rented an old school bus. On the day that Hungarian prime minister Orbán sat in the Oval Office in Washington discussing the fight on international crime with an embattled President Clinton reeling from the Monica Lewinsky scandal, the Whiskey Robber, his partner, and their UTE teammates were devouring pork and swilling *pálinka* on a freezing Transylvanian hillside. Attila regaled his teammates with tales of the fabled Székelys and taught them to sing the Csíkszereda hockey fight song:

MOM, SWEET MOM,
WHAT EVERY SZÉKELY BOY WANTS
IS A HOCKEY STICK.
A HOCKEY STICK
A HOCKEY STICK
THAT IS THE DREAM OF EVERY SZÉKELY BOY.

One by one Attila's teammates lined up to give him a birthday toast. It felt like the best night of his life. He'd nearly forgotten his troubles, believing he could be happy and safe again, have friends, a laugh, a life. Those hopes were gone when the sun rose the next morning.

Back in Budapest, the newspapers provided a constant reminder that crime didn't pay. The highlight of Attila's days was going to McDonald's with Don, where he would order each of them a strawberry ice cream cone. But most of the time he was angry — at his teammates for being so lazy, at his country for being such a wreck, at himself for shutting so many doors. Sometimes when he was stuck in bumper-to-bumper traffic, he got so frustrated that he flashed the pistol he'd begun keeping under his seat to clear other drivers out of his way. Some of his friends' girlfriends who used to say how sweet the Chicky Panther was became afraid to invite him to their apartments for fear he would drink too much and do something they wouldn't be able to repair or forgive.

As for UTE, the club was at least better than the 0–24–2 disaster that Attila had last played for two seasons ago. With Attila as the second-string goalie, the team was pulling out a victory in almost half its games. But the team's new coach wasn't impressed by Gustáv Bóta's Panther. He could smell the liquor on Attila's breath every day. He stopped playing him in games and by December stopped putting him on the ice even in practice. A week before the holiday break, Attila confronted Coach Alexander Vlasov. "I'm the only one that shows up every day," Attila barked at him in the hallway of the UTE facility. "I should at least get to play in practice." Vlasov told him to stop showing up at all.

It had been more than six months since Attila had spoken to his aunt or uncle, and without anywhere else to go for the holidays, he rented a place at his regular hideaway, the Ózon Hotel in the Hargita Mountains outside Csíkszereda. He invited some teammates to go up and ski with him, advertising the area's natural beauty and the free lodging. The only one who stopped by for more than a day was Zsolt Baróti, a young Transylvanian forward who had joined UTE the previous year. On New Year's Eve they stayed in, drinking and talking, and in the first few hours of 1999, the party-hardy Chicky Panther surprised Baróti. He pitched over, head in hands, and began bawling. Baróti knew Panther was something of a streak player in the game of life, but he never imagined he got this low. "I'm so lonely," Attila said, sobbing into his drink. He had been running with every gauge on empty for far too long. Something had to give.

Twenty-five

Budapest
January 15, 1999

The alarm clock jolted Gabi awake at 4:30 A.M. He dragged himself out of bed and stumbled over to the storage room beneath the basement stairs, where he had stowed a curly black wig, mascara, glasses, a disposable Gillette razor, and a can of black spray paint. He collected it in a blue sports bag and traipsed out into the cold garage. It was still dark as he steered his Suzuki Samurai through the hills, Vivaldi's *Four Seasons* in the CD player, trying not to think too much about the hours that lay ahead.

They both needed the money. It had been ten months since the shoot-out at Heltai Square. Gabi had tried to save every forint he could, but there was still more to be done on the house. Most recently, the outdoor wooden staircase leading from the back to the deck had cracked from the weather.

For his part, Attila owed 2 million forints ($8,600) to the Atlantis casino, which he tried to get from Éva, who owed him that amount for a loan he gave her for her house. But Éva didn't have it. He'd have to do this one job and then figure out the rest. He didn't really care. Truth be told, if it weren't for the visceral memories of those adrenaline-charged robberies, he might have believed he didn't even exist anymore.

Ten days earlier, on January 5, after a light snow had left the streets icebound, Attila and Gabi pulled off another OTP robbery. But the guard put up a serious fight with Attila, and a few minutes went by before Attila could pin him to the floor. Gabi had held the rest of the customers and employees at bay during the scuffle, but too much time had elapsed. Attila could only do a quick sweep of the teller cash drawers before they had to split. The 297,000 forints ($1,250) they collected was Attila's lowest take ever.

Normally, Attila and Gabi prepared at Villányi Street, but for the last two robberies they hadn't had the energy to bother. Plus there was no one else living at Attila's place on Rezeda Street now but Don. At 6:00 A.M. Attila answered the door in Bermuda shorts and fuzzy red Fila slippers, stinking of alcohol. "I have to go back to sleep, Gringo," he said, heading back into the bedroom. "Wake me at seven."

Gabi lay down on the couch and watched soccer highlights on cable. As the sun began to rise, he could see that it looked like yet another nice day, which wasn't very nice if robbery was on the docket. At 7:00 Gabi pulled on Attila's big toe and his partner rose from the bed in one motion, saying, "What's with this weather?"

"I don't like it," Gabi said. "Are we still going to do it?"

They'd been trying for bad weather for a week. "We can't keep waiting," Attila said. "Our freedom is everything, but it's not worth anything without money."

They began their preparations in silence.

At 8:30 A.M. Gabi left the house, followed a few minutes later by Attila. They were to meet on a corner near Frankel Leó Street, a cobblestoned pedestrian road just off the Danube River on the Buda side of town. Gabi had argued against doing this OTP because the street was too choked with people. But there weren't any easy targets left, and Attila felt it was too dangerous to do another site they'd robbed before. The upside of this bank, which rated a 4 in Attila's book, was that it was likely to carry big money because the branch was a major OTP hub for foreign currency and transfers.

They had observed the place three times in the past week. It sat in a crowd of stores on either side of the street — a fruit and vegetable grocery, a hairdresser, a copy place, a café, and a supermarket. The police station was at least three minutes away by car every time they clocked it.

When they arrived at about 9:00 A.M., the street was still relatively quiet. It was Friday; Attila hoped people would be tired from the long week. He sure was.

Attila had his raincoat draped over his arm, which Gabi knew meant that his gun was already in his hand. Attila entered first and quickly sized up the scene. The bank had a split-level layout: a wide, open staircase rose up from one side of the room. All told, he counted about fifteen people, employees and customers.

When Gabi entered a few seconds later, Attila was already moving at the guard. Gabi positioned himself in front of the door, while Attila tossed his coat off his arm and attacked the unsuspecting security man, forcing him onto the floor. In seconds, Attila had taken possession of the guy's small black Russian TT gun and turned toward the counters, shouting, "Bank robbery! Hands in the air!"

There were so many customers that Gabi was worried some of them hadn't heard Attila's order. He fired a shot into the ceiling and yelled, "Everyone! On the floor!" Then he froze. He'd forgotten to spray the camera. He was already beyond the entranceway when he spun to find it staring straight down at his face. He pulled out his paint can and doused the lens.

Meanwhile, Attila had his gun to the manager's head. If she didn't open the safe immediately, he said, he would shoot her. "I need another key from upstairs," she told him calmly. He let her go.

Gabi took a canvas bag from his pocket and tossed it over the counter so Attila could start on the drawers. Almost three minutes had passed by the time the manager reappeared with the key ring.

"Time!" Gabi yelled as two women wandered through the front door behind him. "On the floor," Gabi said, turning to face them and shaking the nose of his gun at the ground.

Attila stood with the manager at the safe. She said the time lock was set for five minutes. "Open it now!" he yelled, then went back and finished clearing out the rest of the teller drawers.

"Four minutes," Gabi yelled. He was looking out the door. Was that a siren?

Attila was back at the safe. He noticed a separate drawer on the top part of the cabinet vault with its own latch. He got the woman to open it. There looked to be at least 10 million forints ($43,000) inside. He stuffed it into Gabi's duffel.

"Five minutes," Gabi called. "Five minutes! Five minutes!" Attila waited another minute until the next drawer opened, bagged the cash, then ran around to the front, where Gabi was nervously waiting. Before they could open the front door, the sound of the sirens was loud and clear.

There was only one way out. They charged through the front door as a voice to their left shouted, "Freeze! Police!" They turned right, ran down the street, then bolted through the garden in back of the sixteenth-century domed brick Lukács bathhouse. They rounded the next corner, where Attila had left his cab. "We're in a hurry," Attila said as they climbed in and thrust their heads between their legs to stay out of view. "Take us to the HÉV station." The driver pulled out into the traffic-logged street. After traveling only a few blocks, the sirens got noticeably louder. "We'll get out here," Attila said, throwing a 5,000-forint note ($21) at the driver and pushing Gabi out the left side. Attila's muffled heartbeat pounded in his chest. It was good to be alive.

Ahead of them was the flat cement Margit Bridge, which led straight into Pest just north of Parliament. They stormed down the stairs of the pedestrian concourse that ran beneath the bridge traffic, pulling off their wigs, hats, and outer layer of clothes and doing their best to shave off their mustaches with their Gillettes and saliva. When they came out on the south side of the bridge, sans disguises, the sirens sounded as though they were converging on them from every direction except for the river to their left.

Heading south, Attila and Gabi made their way onto the river's scenic jogging path, across from Parliament and the poor-man's-Paris east Danube bank. Glancing over his right shoulder, Attila saw three cops trying to negotiate their way across the crowded boulevard that separated them. To Attila's left was a fifteen-foot drop toward the cement highway at the edge of the river. "We have to jump," Attila yelled to Gabi; then he threw the bag over the edge, crouched, and jumped after it. He hit the cement hard, and a sting rang all the way up his spine. "Jump!" he yelled again to Gabi, but his partner didn't appear.

Two hours later, as the UTE-FTC game got under way at the UTE stadium, Attila was in his purple Opel Omega, speeding down country road E4 toward the Romanian border with the money, three guns, his robbery encyclopedia, and Don pacing back and forth in the backseat.

As he passed the fragrant fertilizer plant outside the frozen Tisza River town of Szolnok, he heard on Hungarian radio: "UTE ice hockey player Gábor Orbán, son of coach George Orbán, has been arrested for robbery. Police are still searching for his accomplice." According to the news, the robbers' taxi driver, whose name also happened to be Orbán, was being questioned as a possible third accomplice.

Attila jerked the wheel and peeled off the road into a gas station. Into the bathroom he went, carrying the most incriminating piece of evidence he owned: the notebook that had guided him through six years of robberies. Standing over the open toilet, he tore the book apart page by page, ripping each information-packed folio into confetti and flushing it into the sewers of the eastern Hungarian plain. Then he shuffled inside the station mart and bought a bottle of Johnnie Walker. He just needed a quick freshener. He was about sixty miles from the border with less than an hour to go before Gabi was allowed to spill the beans about his identity. Before getting back on the road, he stuffed the cash and all but one of the guns under some clothes in the bottom of a blue Budmil hiking backpack and stuck it in the trunk. The other gun he loaded and rammed into the shoulder holster beneath his shirt.

Back at the UTE stadium, the game's first period came to an end with an eruption in the stands caused not by fire, a hail of batteries, or the fact that UTE was actually leading FTC, 4–2. It spouted from the mouth of a balding radio journalist who was covering the event from the top of the bleachers while listening to a small transistor radio. He'd just heard a bulletin about the arrest on bank robbery charges of UTE forward Gábor Orbán, one of two UTE players that the reporter had noted earlier had failed to show for that afternoon's game. The other was the wealthy goalie. . . . The man sprung from his press seat at the top of the metal bleachers and bounded toward the rink, shrieking out the scoop of his lifetime: "Attila Ambrus is the Whiskey Robber!" he cried. "Attila Ambrus is the Whiskey Robber!"

One hundred fifty miles to the east, the flat, frozen fields of western Romania stretched out before Attila like a welcome mat. He checked the digital dashboard clock: 3:31 P.M. In approximately fifteen minutes it would be three hours since he last saw Gabi on the jogging path by the river. Attila pressed the gas pedal to the floor.

At 3:40 P.M. he reached the multilane Ártánd checkpoint station at the Hungarian-Romanian border and picked an empty slot. He pulled his car to a stop in front of the guard and rolled down his window. "*Jó napot,*" he said, smiling. *Good day.*

The guard bent down and glanced into the car at Attila and Don, and asked for Attila's papers. Attila handed over his passport and car registration and reclined his seat while the guard took his information back to the booth. Inside the adjacent station, the fax machine was kicking up a document titled "Emergency National Search Warrant."

A few minutes later Attila watched the guard head back in his direction. He put a smile back on his face. "Step out of the car, please," the guard said, as six marksmen with rifles crawled toward the car.

third Period

Twenty-six

The thief had been in custody for a little over an hour when Mound of Asshead burst into the precinct house near the Danube River jogging path. So far, the cops who'd been questioning Gabi had succeeded only in getting him to ante up the name of a common rodent. "*Patkány, patkány, patkány,*" Gabi said like a broken record. *Rat, rat, rat.* He repeated the word for so long, you could almost count time by it, which, since there was no clock in sight, was precisely what Gabi was trying to do.

Normally, the undersize Mound wasn't much use as an intimidator of anything but inanimate objects. But the Whiskey Robber case had shaken something deep in his potbelly. To him, it was the reason his best friend, Lajos, had been driven from the force. And thus it was the root cause of an even more painful development: the ascension of the most condescending member of the robbery squad, József Keszthelyi, to robbery chief, even though Mound had been the longtime deputy and had more years on the job.

Mound descended on the cell where Gabi was being held and asked the precinct cops to step out of his way. That was the moment at which two distinct versions of how Gabi came to cough up his own name, and then that of his accomplice, were born. One version, Mound's, involves precision psychological pressure; the other, Gabi's, entails a series of crushing body blows, which, since he was handcuffed, he was helpless to deflect.

Either way, just under three hours after his capture, Gabi provided the details necessary to enable Lajos Varjú's successor, József Keszthelyi, to become the first member of the robbery department to meet the Whiskey Robber. Like Gabi, Attila had given himself up without a fight. But Keszthelyi wasn't taking any chances. When word came in from Ártánd that Attila was in custody, Keszthelyi ordered the border guards not to transport him from the premises. He wanted Attila handcuffed and put in the holding pen in the border station's basement. He was coming to pick up the robber himself.

When Keszthelyi pulled up to the border about 7:00 P.M., a television truck bearing the insignia of Hungary's MTV broadcasting channel was already parked outside. Keszthelyi went inside, brushed past *Kriminális* reporter József Jónás, and bounded down the stairs to the station's basement, where he found exactly what he hoped not to see in the holding pen: nothing. No Whiskey Robber, no guards, not even a note.

Keszthelyi scrambled back outside. One of the border guards pointed him toward a cornfield behind the building, where the outline of two men was barely discernible in the early-evening light.

Keszthelyi drew his Jericho pistol from his belt and began walking toward the figures, watching the steam from their breath waft into the January night. As he got closer, he could see they were both looking away in the direction of Romania. Then, without turning, one of the men called out to Keszthelyi. "Regards, Mayor," the voice said. Keszthelyi stopped in his tracks as Attila looked back over his shoulder at the new robbery chief. It was then that Keszthelyi got his first look at the man the Budapest police had been chasing for just a week shy of six years. He was attached by a thick leash to a border guard, taking a leak in the field.

When Attila finished urinating, Keszthelyi wordlessly herded him into the back of his car, along with the evidence the border guards had collected from Attila's purple Opel: a Browning, a Parabellum, and a Tokarev pistol, 18 million forints ($77,000), a bottle of whiskey, and a Bernese mountain dog. After giving a short statement to the *Kriminális* reporter, he cuffed Attila's hands to a metal bar in the backseat and took off for the Death Star.

Back in Budapest, news of the Whiskey Robber's capture had spread like syphilis, and reporters who had never covered hockey before were homing in on the UTE locker room like flies around an outhouse. After the radio reporter's shrieks reached the bench at the end of the first period of the UTE-FTC showdown, the shaken UTE players gathered to discuss forfeiting the game. But they were ahead, 4–2, and without confirmation of the rumors about their teammates, they decided to continue. In the remaining two periods, UTE surrendered five unanswered goals and lost, 7–4. (They would also lose all twelve remaining games that season.) When the final horn sounded, the players tramped back to their smelly quarters in a stupor. Even Bubu, still a member of FTC, hypnotically followed his former UTE teammates instead of going to the visitors' changing room, where his clothes were hanging.

The players sat mutely at their lockers. The information about their teammates — which judging by the number of reporters stationed conspicuously around the room appeared to be true — was difficult to digest. Hungary hadn't had such a universally well regarded figure as the Whiskey Robber since anyone could remember. The hats, the wigs, the headlines, the demoralized officials, all that stunning criminal work — had it been the Chicky Panther all that time? And what about Gabi? On the one hand, the squirt had become even flashier than Attila with his cars and fancy house, and it was no secret that he experimented with expensive drugs. But donning police uniforms and robbing banks? He'd grown up in housing *built* by the OTP.

Bubu was afraid, correctly, that Attila's arrest meant he was already under suspicion of having been involved in the Whiskey Robber's six-year spree. Zsolt Baróti, who'd just spent New Year's with Attila, was sure the police had the wrong guys. No one with as much fame and money as the Whiskey Robber could possibly be as unhappy as Attila. Some of the other guys were stoked, though they weren't about to admit it. The few who agreed to talk to the media expressed surprise.

"He didn't look like a gangster," Kercső Árpád, an ex-captain of UTE who was at the stadium, told *Mai Nap* of Attila. "I'm shocked by the news, although I remember when he arrived to practice in an exquisite car, several people joked, 'Look, the mafioso arrived.' But I never thought he would rob banks."

"He stood out as a hardworking man," the diminutive UTE manager Gustáv Bóta told *Magyar Hírlap* of his Panther. "If Attila Ambrus needs anything in prison, he can count on me."

On the opposite side of town, three robbery department detectives crashed through the door of the superintendent's flat at Villányi Street 112. Only one item, found under the sink in the kitchen, was seized as evidence: a plastic bag stuffed with dozens of neatly clipped newspaper articles chronicling post office, travel agency, and bank robberies dating back to January 1993.

Lajos Varjú was behind his desk at the Blue Moon, trying to go home for the night if only his phone would stop ringing. First it was Mound, relaying the news that the Whiskey Robber and his accomplice had been caught. Then it was a reporter from *Mai Nap* looking for a reaction. "Aren't you bitter that you weren't present at the arrest?" the reporter asked the former robbery chief, with tabloid tact.

"To me, the police is in the past," Lajos said, lying. "I'm happy for the success of my colleagues and I congratulate them."

Click.

~

The elevator doors on the seventh floor of the Death Star opened just before midnight, spilling the contents everyone had been waiting hours to see and someone's Bernese mountain dog.

Keszthelyi and Attila confidently walked each other down the hall, stone-faced, the way men do when pretending not to want an audience. Attila, hands cuffed in front of his waist, walked ahead of the robbery chief. What did Keszthelyi care what his arrestee did? As soon as they reached the end of the hall, the Whiskey Robber's show was over.

Keszthelyi had already planned it out. On the ride back from the border, he hadn't said one word to Attila, letting him boil in his own soup all the way to Budapest. Keszthelyi knew Mound had gotten only vague details related to seven or eight robberies out of George Orbán's brother, but Keszthelyi wasn't going to stop at that. Nor would he perform his interrogation in one of the closet-size one-way-mirrored rooms, where Gabi had been sweating until only an hour ago. Keszthelyi wanted everyone to watch him pick apart the Whiskey Robber. When he and Attila reached the open secretary's station between his corner office and the conference room, the robbery chief directed Attila to sit down at the large triangular table as the detectives fanned into positions from which to observe.

Everything was set for Keszthelyi to begin when Attila committed yet another robbery. Before Keszthelyi could start, the Whiskey Robber turned his hazel eyes up to his captors and announced, "Gentleman, I have failed." Then he asked for a map. If the moment had belonged to the robbery chief, it didn't any longer. For the next sixteen hours, as Don bounded up and down the hallway, sniffing shoes, the police listened as Attila detailed all twenty-six of his robberies over the past six years as if he were delivering a keynote. Attila recounted in chronological order disguises, bank tellers, video cameras, escape routes, and the exact count of his bounties. Every couple of hours, Keszthelyi sent another member of the robbery department charging to the archive room to search for files that had been gathering dust for years. Not even the typist could keep up with Attila's story. At 4:00 A.M. her hands cramped into bear claws and she had to be replaced.

Attila was still going the following morning when the Hungarian media gathered on the main floor of the Death Star in the large auditorium normally reserved for conferences. Keszthelyi, who had gone downstairs to listen, looked on as the new Budapest police chief, Antal Kökényesi, announced that the dangerous serial robber known as the Whiskey Robber had been captured. Yes, he was the UTE hockey goalie known as the Chicky Panther. Yes, he had been part of the Interior Ministry's team since 1988. Yes, his accomplice was George Orbán's kid. No, not the Goal King, the other one. The thief had indeed confessed to several of the robberies, Kökényesi reported, though he could not give a number yet since it seemed to be increasing by the hour. Asked how many heists the police had physical evidence to prove were committed by the Whiskey Robber, Kökényesi glanced over at Keszthelyi, then back at the reporters in front of him. "Eight," he muttered.

In another part of the city that Saturday morning, Éva Fodor was at the Keleti train station, seeing her mother off after a visit from her home in the countryside. As they were walking through the concourse, the back page of *Mai Nap* jumped off the newsstand at her:

WHISKEY ROBBER CAUGHT?
IS THE UTE GOALIE THE ONE SOUGHT FOR YEARS?

Suddenly Éva felt as though she couldn't breathe. She hurried her mother onto the train, then sat down on a bench inside the station, dizzy. Hundreds of pieces of a puzzle were swirling into place in her head.

⁓

Later that day Attila was transported by van across the Danube to his sixth home since arriving in Hungary eleven years earlier: the city's oldest and largest jail, on Gyorskocsi Street, final resting place of 1956 hero Imre Nagy. Built in 1907, the red and brown brick building took up a whole city block in the center of downtown Buda, just three blocks off the Danube River, directly across from Parliament and not far from the spot where Attila leapt off the ledge the previous afternoon, temporarily shaking the police. From the outside, the jail could easily have been mistaken for a century-old four-story office building, save for the barely visible black bars set into the square windows on the upper three floors.

Attila was assigned to one of the two hundred identical, small, square cement-floored cells. The room was appointed with two steel beds, a sink, and a lidless toilet. His cellmate introduced himself as Killer. Three times a day a tray containing a purported meal was pushed through the slot in the wooden door.

Attila couldn't remember when he'd felt so welcome. Aside from his almost daily interrogations in the adjacent administration building, he was allowed out of his cell two times a day, once for a shower and again for the morning walk outside in a cement-walled box in the building's inner courtyard. Like the others, until convicted, Attila could wear his own clothing, a bag of which was ferried to him by the police after an unenlightening search of his Rezeda Street apartment. There was no television, but his cellmate had a radio; and Attila found the guards more than willing to bring him the newspapers, all of which were filled with his story. *Magyar Hírlap* wrote that he and Gabi were "the century's most persistent, cautious and most wanted armed robbers. . . . If it is proven true that Attila Ambrus is the noted Whiskey Robber, then one-fifth of the robberies in the capital are on his account." The article went on to describe Attila as a "strikingly intelligent man, who pays attention to every detail, who is definitely daring, who was courteous in the beginning but became harsher in his methods toward the end." The nation's largest and most respected newspaper, *Népszabadság*, referred to Attila as "the master." Attila's fellow inmates at Gyorskocsi dubbed him simply "the King."

He didn't request bail, a lawyer, or even a phone call.

⌒

Now that Attila and Gabi had been arrested and charged, a new team of police investigators was responsible for preparing the case for trial. The five-member unit, headed by thirty-seven-year-old Colonel Zsolt Bérdi, met each morning on the fourth floor at the southeast end of the jail.

Bérdi, a medium-size man who wore suits three sizes too big and spoke only in a whisper, did not always have an easy time impressing his concerns upon his staff. And he had some very big concerns about this case. For starters, it wasn't just the prison population that was treating Attila like a film star. When reporters got wind that Attila had been captured at the border with his dog, several tabloids wrote that it was the Whiskey Robber's devotion to his pet that led to his arrest. In response, more than a thousand people phoned the Death Star offering to adopt Don, among them the cabaret and television star Zsuzsa Csala, who quickly became a vocal Whiskey Robber advocate. "Here's a guy who dares to rob directly," Csala said to the media of Attila. "He's not hiding and he's not denying. He's confessed to everything. Actually, he's even helping the fact-finding. This is rare in our society. Where I live [in the Buda hills], I'm surrounded by crooks. One of them has built a bobsled track. Another has a moat. You have to approach the house by boat. There's no way you can get this money in a respectable way. They're all robbers."

Bérdi looked at Attila's case through a different lens. What kind of person, he wanted to know, admitted to committing twenty-six robberies? Attila had even confessed to an attempted robbery back in 1993 at the Nyugati train station travel agency. Bérdi had never seen such a thing. He didn't trust Attila and he wasn't going to let himself or his investigative department be played the way the robber had played the robbery department for the past six years.

At his daily 8:00 A.M. meetings, seated at a long wooden table upon which two black miniature FBI flags flew from a pencil holder, Bérdi told his team that while it was indeed good news that Attila was still maintaining his complete guilt, they could not lose their focus. If the thief backed out of his confession, they had almost nothing to go on except an extended vacation, because they would surely be fired. "Where's the hundred and forty-five million forints?" Bérdi whispered, referring to the approximately $600,000 total Attila and his accomplices had snatched over the past six years. "Do you really believe he's squandered all of it at the casinos?"

Valter Fülöp, the handsome young lead investigator who had been questioning Attila, was a believer. "It's possible," he told Bérdi. "He's an adrenaline addict. He told me he loved nothing more than hearing the police car sirens when he was robbing a bank."

"Don't fall under his spell," Bérdi emitted. "Remember, this guy shot at police officers. We need to look at proving attempted murder. But don't tell Attila. We can't afford to lose his trust or cooperation."

⌐

Attila and Gabi didn't see each other for six days after their arrests. Bérdi wanted them kept on separate floors to ensure that they couldn't coordinate their stories. That was fine with Gabi, who had no idea if Attila held him responsible for his capture and wasn't looking forward to finding out.

On Thursday, January 21, Gabi was led down to a small empty holding cell. A few minutes later the door was unlocked and Attila was pushed into the room. As the door closed behind him, Attila looked at his flinching partner and smiled. "Here I am," Attila said. "It's what it is."

The reason the two UTE players had been brought together that morning wasn't clear until they were ushered into another larger room, where three other men were standing in handcuffs, guarded by two jail officials. As soon as Attila and Gabi entered, one of the cuffed men made a run at Attila, flailing at him with his scrawny arms, which were latched together at the wrists. "Why didn't you send a message," the pipsqueak shouted. It was Péter Szűcs. Brother Gyula also made a feeble attempt to swipe at Attila, but he'd recently contracted tuberculosis from his cellmate and was so weak, he could barely wipe his own ass.

The Szűcs brothers had been Whiskey Robber fans before their arrest and had been convinced that once the bandit heard that they had been charged with some of his crimes, he would get word to the police of their innocence. Instead, not only did no word come, but no new vindicating robberies came and the Szűcses had spent the past ten months in jail. (Hungary had no limit on how long the accused could be kept in custody; one man spent more than a year awaiting trial on charges of stealing 138 rolls of toilet paper.)

After a guard jumped in to pull Péter off him, Attila apologized. *"Bocsánat,"* Attila said to Péter. *Sorry.* And he really was, but he also didn't know what the Szűcses were still doing there. It had been almost a week since he had confessed to the crimes with which they were charged.

As soon as the room was back under control, the guards began to pass out white placards numbered one to five and asked the men to stand facing the glass. It was a lineup. On the other side of the one-way glass was a group of witnesses from the Heltai Square OTP robbery, recalled for another look at possible culprits. For an hour Attila, Gabi, Péter, Gyula, and an undercover cop were handed a variety of cheap wigs, plastic glasses, tall felt hats, and fake adhesiveless black mustaches that required them to pucker their lips in order to keep on their face. While a police photographer snapped shots with a Polaroid, the five men traded disguises, shuffled places, and repeated phrases, including "Bank robbery," and "Don't you dare hit the alarm like last year," which were overheard during the second of the two robberies at Heltai Square, nearly a year earlier.

Now that Attila and Gabi were in the tank along with the Szűcs brothers, several key witnesses from the robbery, including Ferenc Laczik, the plainclothes cop who had chased after the robber that day at Heltai Square, were adamant about the perpetrators' identities: according to Laczik, the main perpetrator, identified by his placard number, was the diminutive, unathletic Gyula Szűcs. When the order of the lineup was switched and the hats but not the wigs, mustaches, or glasses were removed, Ferenc's conviction did not waver. As he said before, it was the one standing second from the left: Péter Szűcs.

That afternoon Bérdi made an assessment he hadn't expected to make. He determined the Whiskey Robber's word to be more credible than the memory of one of the case's best witnesses — a cop, to boot — and thus ordered the Szűcs brothers' release.

Twenty-seven

Despite the level of public interest in the case, it was three weeks before the Hungarian public was able to see Attila speak for himself, because that was how long it took for Bérdi and *Kriminális* host László Juszt to agree to the terms of Attila's first television interview. Juszt had been holding out to do the show live from Attila's jail cell while he and Attila sipped whiskey, but eventually he consented to taping the interview in Bérdi's office (where Attila would appear without handcuffs) and merely presenting the robber with a bottle of whiskey that would remain unopened.

The special edition of *Kriminális* aired in prime time on Wednesday, February 10, at the end of a news cycle that, even by Hungarian standards, was remarkable. The previous Tuesday one of the country's most dangerous criminals, György Döcher, was assassinated while having coffee at a downtown café. The next day preliminary disciplinary proceedings were launched against the prison official who had permitted Döcher to step away from his jail cell for an afternoon refreshment.

Then on Monday Márta Tocsik, the lawyer who had presided over the Scandal of the Century, was found not guilty on all charges. And earlier in the day of Juszt's Whiskey Robber interview, the police launched a massive investigation into the financial improprieties of Gábor Princz, one of the best-known and wealthiest Hungarians, who had famously run Hungary's largest bank chain, Postabank, into the ground and stuck the Hungarian government with a 152-billion-forint ($652 million) bailout bill while he fled to Vienna.

But that night one-third of the country tuned in for Juszt's Barbara Walters–style sit-down with the Whiskey Robber. After the *Kriminális* theme, Juszt appeared at his podium in the newsroom and introduced the night's show by calling Attila's story a "serial fairy tale." Then he rolled the tape of his interview from earlier that day at the jail.

The cameras followed the beefy Juszt, dressed in an olive double-breasted suit and yellow designer tie, into Bérdi's dowdy, dark office, where the Whiskey Robber was leaning against an empty bookshelf as if waiting on a librarian to return with his periodical. Wearing a peach-colored button-down and three-day-old stubble, Attila looked relaxed and rested; his short dark hair was combed and slightly wet from a recent shower. Juszt, grinning like a politician, handed him a bottle of Macallan whiskey, "just to be stylish. Unfortunately, we cannot drink it together."

Reaching out for the bottle, Attila laughed, showing his deep cheek dimples. *Köszönöm szépen,* he said. *Thank you very much.* He was more handsome and telegenic than even Juszt could have hoped.

The two men sat down in Bérdi's office. "I'm glad to finally meet you," Juszt said, beginning the interview. "We've worked together for so many years."

Attila spoke briefly of a hopeless childhood in Romania, characterizing his escape into Hungary as a second chance, a shot at a better life that never materialized despite his best legal efforts. "I did everything," Attila said of his job history. "I don't have a skill for anything, but I did everything." He was humble and reflective, and though his background said one thing, he neither looked nor sounded anything like a former animal-pelt smuggler who'd never finished high school and had just landed in the slammer.

Twice during the half-hour interview, Juszt suggested that Attila's style was like Robin Hood, but Attila wouldn't accept the comparison. "I'm a criminal," Attila said. "But the goal was not to get money at all costs. There were many cases where I was in a situation where I could have shot somebody or been shot, but the most important thing was that there would be no violence, no blood. If the situation got too hot, I just took off. . . . But I really want to emphasize that I'm very sorry. I didn't want to, but I did point my gun at some people. I may not have caused physical injury, but there was surely a psychological reaction, and I am apologizing to them now."

Attila hit every note perfectly without even sounding as if he was trying. He sidestepped the folk-hero comparison as ably as he painted his case in political terms. Asked by Juszt what type of prison sentence he expected, Attila said, "I know about [Márta] Tocsik, for example. The two cases have nothing to do with each other. But she took money from the state. I took money from the state. It's not my place to judge, but she was released. I know I will not be released. I'm expecting ten or eleven years."

By the end of the interview, Attila's sincerity and poise had surrounded him with a sheen of moral clarity. By comparison, his interviewer appeared fawning and awkward. Noting that the newspapers had previously reported that Attila had been to see his play, the *Kriminális Cabaret,* Juszt asked what Attila thought of the production. "I don't want to be too personal about it," Attila said, "but I think if someone is a reporter, he should be a reporter. For instance, I am a bank robber, so I don't try to be a gravedigger, though, actually, I used to be a gravedigger. But I don't try to be Tolstoy. It was good, but I thought it was too slow."

To end the program, Juszt turned to the camera, saying simply, "He was the Whiskey Robber."

Not surprisingly, the *Kriminális* interview was a public relations hat trick for Attila. He came off as handsome, intelligent, articulate, courageous, self-effacing, and even penitent — not exactly qualities Hungarians associated with someone sitting in jail or, for that matter, elected office. Yet despite all of his star qualities, Attila also appeared unmistakably like so many of his countrymen — another guy who had struggled to make a life for himself in an unfair system. As unlikely as it was, the man behind the legend of the Whiskey Robber actually seemed to live up to the myth.

Budapest's bars and coffeehouses buzzed with tributes to Hungary's "modern-day Sándor Rózsa," the eighteenth-century Hungarian Robin Hood. Gangsta Zoli, moved by the audacity of his occasional drinking companion, began writing a new single that would soon climb the charts, "The Whiskey Robber Is the King." Even some of the victims of Attila's robberies came to his defense. "It's a shame we were hit at the beginning," one of the tellers from an early post office robbery told *Mai Nap*, "because we didn't get the flowers."

For the next month Attila lived out a fantasy. After what felt like a lifetime forcing himself not to talk — first under Ceauşescu in Romania and then as a hunted criminal in Hungary — he was free to say anything he wanted. And for the first time in his life, everyone wanted to hear what he had to say. Almost every day he received, and accepted, a media request. He sat down for interviews in room 309 of the jail's adjacent administration building with all three of Hungary's major television networks and every newspaper. Back in his cell, he yapped so incessantly that his cellmate, Killer, who signed his letters to his wife in blood, finally threatened to stab Attila if he didn't shut up (which worked).

Because Attila was feeling so chatty and still had no lawyer, Bérdi seized the opportunity to ask if he would agree to speak with a forensic psychologist as part of the investigation. Attila not only obliged, he filled up the doctor's notebook. At the end of one several-page-long answer in which Attila described to the shrink his hockey career, his childhood, and his odd job history, the psychologist wrote in the margin of her notes: "Only asked about physical injuries!"

Gabi, on the other hand, who had had no contact with Attila since the Szűcs lineup, was a far more reticent resident of the jail. There were still two robberies of the thirteen he had committed that he was maintaining he didn't remember, even when investigators prompted him with such details as a loaf of bread in the safe and a cigar bomb on the counter. And after the publication of Gabi's interview with the daily newspaper *Népszabadság*, his lawyer, Péter Bárándy, the president of the prestigious Budapest Chamber of Lawyers and the country's future justice minister, advised his client against talking to the media ever again. Perhaps it was Gabi's description of life on the run that prompted his lawyer's concern: "It was so exciting, seeing the huge-lettered headlines on the front pages about the Whiskey Robber," Gabi told *Népszabadság*. "And I'm sitting there with the front-page guy. We're friends! We're partners! And I know things that any cop would give his arm for!"

In March, when the media's golden glare began to recede, Attila got a good look at his new, lonely reality. He was surrounded by metal bars, guards, investigators, and boxes of chocolate and love letters sent by anonymous admirers. But none of his friends or hockey teammates had come to visit. He assumed that his former compatriots were tired of being interrogated about him, especially since he hadn't been such a good friend the past couple of years. The last time he'd seen Éva, a few weeks before his arrest, he'd stomped out of her house after screaming about the money she owed him. And as for Bubu, it was unlikely Attila could have reached him even if he had tried: his old billiards companion was now an investor in a group of brothels, a career move that had made him so paranoid that he had changed his phone number and traveled around town only alongside his six feet six Székely business partner, both of them packing loaded pistols under their leather jackets.

The only two people from Attila's past life who remained in his present one were Zsuzsa, the maternal grocery clerk who thought of Attila as the son she never had; and a blond, leggy eighteen-year-old national figure-skating competitor named Virág who'd had a crush on Attila ever since he played hockey with her brother for a season at FTC. Each of them arrived once a week, bearing a bag full of the items Attila requested: a half kilo of crispy, all-meat Kaiser bacon (presliced); two packages of smoked broiled chicken legs; one poppy seed roll and one walnut roll (both from a decent confectionery and not a supermarket so they wouldn't dry out); two or three pieces of vacuum-packed smoked salmon; two pieces of halva; and, most important, whiskey — as much of it as they could sneak in, which turned out to be easiest to do in emptied-out soda bottles.

There was no official visitation room, so the jail's visitors met their loved ones in the same office in which they were interrogated, room 309, the little rectangular chamber next to Bérdi's office. Just as for press sessions, Attila was freed of his handcuffs so he could sit comfortably in the old green armchair near the door. Often the guards left him alone and stood outside during his visit, which they usually allowed to slide past the thirty-minute limit. Only once did Attila emerge from a visit (with Zsuzsa) so smashed that they had to help carry his leftover food and "soda" back to his cell.

Attila was aware that he was getting special privileges. He was allowed more than one shower a day and could leave his light on as late as he wanted. Colonel Bérdi had even agreed to give him an old type-writer for his cell so that he could begin writing his life story. But as the days wore on and Attila continued to be questioned about the Heltai Square shoot-out while not being told anything about when or how his sentence would be handed down, he grew wary of his captors' goodwill.

One day when the lead investigator Valter Fülöp called Attila upstairs to ask him some more questions, Attila decided to ask one himself: he wanted to know if he could talk with Colonel Bérdi about his seemingly inert case. After all, he'd confessed to everything, yet still hadn't even been formally charged, much less sentenced. Attila wanted to know what the holdup was. But Valter dismissed Attila's concerns, saying, "There's no problem. Everything will be cleared up in court."

Attila was stunned. There was only one reason he could think of that his case would end up in court, and that was if the government planned to charge him with a crime other than those to which he'd confessed.

Standing in the hallway outside the interrogation room, Attila nearly lost it. He'd done everything the police had asked and more. Didn't even have a lawyer to run interference. Valter let Attila rant until he was finished. Then the guards took him back downstairs.

A few days later Attila got a message to Valter through the guards that he wanted to see his ex-girlfriend Éva. Valter had the number; he'd already questioned Éva several times. Valter made the call, and a week later Éva nervously arrived at the jail and was led up to room 309.

She got to the room first and tried to be patient while she waited for the guards to get Attila. She was ready to forget the fight she and Attila had had the last time they were together, but the one thing she couldn't help feeling angry about was just how much Attila had kept hidden from her even on that day in Csíkszereda at his grandmother's grave. She wasn't sure how she would feel when she saw him, nor what he would want from her now that he was a big celebrity in a load of trouble.

When Attila arrived, Éva was shaken by his downcast, alcohol-reddened face. He looked a lot worse than he had during his *Kriminális* interview. She could tell he was hurting, and when the guard unlocked his cuffs, she reflexively grabbed his strong, familiar hands. Their conversation was stilted at first, both because of their recent fight (for which they each apologized) and because of the guard in the room. After a few minutes, though, he left them alone, and as soon as the door closed, Attila told Éva the one thing she wished he'd been able to say to her years ago: "I need help." He told her he knew the Szűcs brothers had been facing attempted murder charges for the shooting following the robbery of the OTP Bank at Heltai Square on March 11, 1998. But, Attila told Éva, even though he had repeatedly sworn to investigators that the shots he fired that day were only warning shots — in hopes of warding off his pursuers — Attila was afraid the police didn't believe him.

"I need you to believe me," Attila said.

"I do," Éva told him.

She said he needed to get a lawyer, immediately. She would take care of everything.

A few weeks later Attila was summoned from his cell and taken upstairs to Colonel Bérdi's office. He walked into the room to find not an attorney but the former robbery chief, Lajos Varjú, sitting on the couch.

Lajos had received a call the previous week from Judit P. Gál, the lanky enterprising reporter for *Mai Nap* who had done the bulk of the paper's coverage on the Whiskey Robber case. She wanted to know if Lajos would be interested in going to see Attila with her so that she could write a story about their meeting for the paper. Initially, Lajos was reluctant. He still wasn't over his bitterness about his treatment by police brass, and no other case symbolized his frustration like this one. Directly or indirectly, the Whiskey Robber had brought about the loss of his job, his reputation, and, most recently, his marriage. But ultimately he was too curious to say no.

Lajos could see right away that Attila wasn't faring well in captivity. His hair was greasy and matted down on his head, he had a scruffy Fu Manchu mustache, and his chest and arms were bulging unnaturally out of his shirt like a steroid-filled bodybuilder. But he still had that disarming grin. When Attila recognized who was waiting for him, his face brightened and he reached out his hand to his longtime foe. Lajos shook it and his own head. Life was a pisser.

"You were the only true professional at the police," Attila told Lajos, then added before Lajos could answer, "but I was always one step ahead of you."

Lajos laughed, hoping he wasn't going to regret having come. As he listened to Attila talk, Lajos noticed two things about his old nemesis. First, he was stinking drunk, and second — which he figured flowed from the first — he sounded dangerously wistful about the past.

"Remember the time I sent you a note?" Attila asked as the *Mai Nap* reporter scribbled notes and a photographer snapped pictures.

"Yes," Lajos said, forcing a smile. "I nearly blew up inside."

After about twenty minutes, there was little left to say. Lajos took some satisfaction in seeing that Attila wasn't much different from what he'd expected. Even though they had just met, he felt that he had a pretty good bead on Attila. He was a simple guy with a decent heart and a screwed-up life who made some terrible choices. He had also spent his hockey career at the rink less than a mile from the Újpest apartment where Lajos had lived until last year. Lajos could be *extremely* annoyed by Attila, but he couldn't hate him. He did, however, want to ask him something. As Lajos got up to leave, he saw that no one else was paying attention and he leaned in toward Attila.

"Have you already figured out how to get out of here?" Lajos asked.

"*Persze,*" Attila said. *Of course.*

Twenty-eight

Bérdi's team was trying to wrap up its investigation. Though Gabi hadn't been as forthcoming as Attila early on, he'd finally confessed to all thirteen robberies in which he had participated and even allowed investigators to confiscate his house as stolen property. It was pretty clear to Bérdi that he was merely the sidekick.

So far, Attila's stories about gambling the money away and spending it on cars and trips for his girlfriends had checked out. Technically, he owned no property: the Villányi Street apartment was a rental, and the town house on Rezeda Street was in the name of his grocery clerk friend Zsuzsa's daughter, Sylvia. But Bérdi still hadn't found Attila's first two accomplices: Károly "Karcsi" Antal, his former UTE teammate, and Attila's cousin László Veres, whose names Attila had belatedly surrendered in what Bérdi interpreted as a desperate attempt by the robber to appear cooperative and trustworthy. Bérdi believed those accomplices — both Székelys from Attila's hometown — could provide key information about any leftover loot. The only question was how long it would take to find them, because apparently they had fled Hungary. The Romanian authorities said they were "working on it," which, given the absence of an extradition treaty between the two countries and Romania's warm feelings toward Hungary, might have meant "fuck off."

Worst of all, Bérdi was finding that solidifying the attempted murder charges based on evidence from the Heltai Square shoot-out was a nightmare of Dallas book repository proportions. All that was certain after two inconclusive sets of ballistics tests was that there were bullets fired from several directions, from different guns, some of which had ricocheted off cars and apartment buildings. As far as who was aiming where and why, the best thing he had to go on was a sworn statement from Ferenc Laczik, the sight-challenged policeman who had chased after Attila. Laczik attested that at least one shot fired by the perpetrator was targeted directly at him, because he remembered looking straight down the barrel of the man's gun.

It wasn't until sometime in April that Attila had legal representation. The lawyer Éva had found had refused to take the case after reviewing Attila's file full of signed and detailed confessions. It was Zsuzsa who finally netted a counselor through one of her relatives: failed mayoral candidate George Magyar.

It was only a matter of time before someone like Magyar would enter the picture. The fifty-one-year-old attorney had brown eyes that darted around in their sockets when he spoke, as if he were calculating the potential earnings of each syllable. Though he had never handled a criminal case before, he was certain Attila's would be a success. "Your confession is absolutely illegal," Magyar told Attila during his first visit to the jail, unveiling his defense strategy. "There was no lawyer present."

Attila didn't know what the slope-shouldered attorney was talking about. He reminded Magyar that on the night of his capture he had signed away his right to a lawyer twenty-six separate times. But Magyar, who was pondering a second mayoral run after commanding 1 percent of the electorate in 1994, was not easily deterred. He kept Attila talking and soon seized upon another trifle: According to Attila, the police had (appropriately, Attila thought) given him some whiskey during his confession that long night at police headquarters. ("Never," Keszthelyi later said of the charge; "Only at the end," said Mound.) Magyar nearly jumped out of his chair. He'd hit pay dirt. His client had been hauled off to the Death Star, deprived of a lawyer, and then induced into a drunken stupor before being forced to confess. Johnnie

Cochran, eat your heart out. If there was ever a case made for the International Court of Human Rights in Strasbourg, Magyar told Attila, this was it. As for his fee, Magyar understood that Attila was broke, but he had some ideas. He planned to market Attila's story; they would split the profits. Attila mentioned that he'd been typing up his life story. A wonderful idea, Magyar said. He would start working on a book-publishing deal, perhaps with the *Mai Nap* reporter Judit P. Gál as cowriter. And another thing: no more media interviews without his approval and receipt of a negotiable payment.

Attila wasn't sure what to make of Magyar. But he could appreciate his pluck, and at this late stage and with no other options, Attila had to hire him. After crossing out the lines in Magyar's contract stating that Attila was responsible for reimbursing Magyar's gas and parking costs, Attila signed Magyar's agreement for representation. But there was still one thing that Attila wasn't sure his new lawyer understood: he had no intention of retracting his confession. He'd robbed banks until he was caught, at which point he gave himself up and ended the game. He'd played by the rules, as far as he understood them, and had no intention of starting to lie now just as a legal strategy. Fair was fair.

If the police or the prosecutors were going to change the rules, however, that was another thing. Attila went to both Valter and Béla "Blinky" Bartha, the two main investigators on the case, and told them straightaway that if they charged him with attempted murder, he wasn't going to stand for it. He would escape.

Valter had heard such a threat a hundred times before and no one had ever escaped from the Gyorskocsi Street jail. He told Attila to sit tight; he would be able to read his case file soon enough. Attila spent his mornings typing and jogging in circles around the outdoor exercise walk box, waiting for the other sandal to drop. He traded candy with the guards for getting the cook to make him scrambled eggs, and he drank whenever he had a supply on hand. In the afternoons he did push-ups and leg-sits and played Pente with his new cellmate, an Ecstasy dealer called Zoli. Loser had to do sit-ups. At night Attila didn't do much sleeping.

Finally, on July 2, nearly six months after his confession, the investigative phase of the government's case against Attila Ambrus was complete. Bérdi put the final evidentiary file listing the charges against him into the cabinet in room 309. Attila was informed that he was free to read the file, and he asked to see it immediately. He was led upstairs, where he took his regular seat in the green armchair and began to look at the documents. It didn't take long for his eye to settle on the word he was looking for: *gyilkosság. Murder.*

As far as Attila was concerned, his case was settled. Just as he did that autumn eleven years earlier in Romania, he granted himself permission to leave the prison in which he was wrongfully being held. He would do whatever was necessary to get out.

Overtime

Twenty-nine

Buda Castle
Budapest
July 3, 1999

You are beginning your careers at an auspicious moment," said Prime Minister Orbán, looking out at the graduates of Hungary's Police Officer College seated before him. "The past year has brought a breakthrough in the fight against crime. We have made it clear that Hungary will be a peaceful, honest, and respectable country. . . . The police force today is managed by efficient and strong-handed leaders. And the government is fully behind the police."

~

Gyorskocsi Street jail
Budapest
Seven days later
9:01 A.M.

Károly Benkő stood in walk box number four for several seconds before he could believe what his heavy-lidded eyes and overtired brain were registering. He was sure that six minutes earlier he'd locked Attila Ambrus into this sunny twenty-six-by-sixteen-foot space and gone to the chair at the end of the courtyard to smoke a cigarette, as he always did. Then, thirty seconds ago, when a conspiratorial squawking began to emanate from the open-air boxes, he had walked back to peer through the doors' round porthole-like windows.

Numbers one, two, and three were okay. But there was indeed an irregularity in number four. The inmate was gone. The Whiskey Robber was gone.

Károly's reaction surprised even himself. Instead of hitting the alarm, he took off past his chair, into the jail, and down the hall toward the kitchen, yelling, "Lock up the knives!"

Attila had to be somewhere on the premises.

Károly grabbed two other guards, and the three of them burst into the parking lot in the jail's inner courtyard. Attila couldn't have exited through the walk-box door; it was still locked. The only other way he could have disappeared was by somehow scaling the thirteen-foot cement wall of the box. That would have put him on a thin path leading to a guard tower, which was empty today because of a shortage in staff. The only way down from there was through the building's inner courtyard, which mostly served as the employees' parking lot.

Károly and his men looked under the dozen or so cars. One of them dove into the garbage Dumpster. Nothing. They bounded up a small set of metal stairs that led to the door to the administration building. It was unlocked, as it never should have been.

They spread out through the hallways on every floor, but everything looked agonizingly unremarkable. As on any other Saturday morning, the long corridors were empty and still. The only sounds came from a few clanks of an odd typewriter and the giggle of a secretary making a personal call.

A few minutes later Károly and one of the other guards spilled out the main entrance, gasping in the morning air like a pair of desperate fugitives. Two joggers heading toward the Danube sneered at them. Then, from behind a city bus, the third guard came careening around the corner with a message suited for an urgent telegraph or Károly Benkő's gravestone: There was a rope! Dangling from the window! Of Blinky Béla's office!

Wooden clubs drawn, Károly and his men raced back inside and up three flights of stairs to room 309. The door to Béla's office was jammed shut. Károly kicked it in.

The office was empty. The computer and fax machine were on the floor. The seat cushion from the armchair was sticking up from the chair's base. The green grating on the window had been pulled out of the wall, and a thin rope of pink, red, and blue bedsheets — the same ones Attila used in his cell — was affixed to the steel radiator and led out the open window. He was gone.

Károly had no choice but to call HQ. He picked up the phone on the desk, but there was no dial tone or, now that he looked, any cord attached to the unit. Like the wires from the fax machine and the computer, the phone cord had been reappropriated as the last several yards of the escape rope, the end of which dangled a mystifying seventeen feet above the sidewalk outside.

At 9:14 Károly made the unhappy call from an office down the hall.

The Death Star dispatcher's first call was to Bérdi, who was preparing to leave for a weekend in the countryside with a group of friends to celebrate his having passed the Hungarian law bar exam. The next call went to the robbery chief Keszthelyi, who was also at home, eating breakfast and preparing for a summer break at Lake Balaton. Neither of the men believed the news at first or, when convinced of its validity, had any idea what to do. No one had ever escaped from the Gyorskocsi Street jail before. There was no procedure to follow.

Budapest police chief Antal Kökényesi was already on holiday, so technically his deputy Jakab Géza was in charge of the city. When Géza heard the news, he went straight to the Death Star and phoned national police chief Péter Orbán (no relation to the prime minister or the Whiskey Robber's accomplice or the taxi driver who was briefly arrested after unwittingly carting Attila and Gabi to and from their last robbery). Neither Géza nor Orbán wanted to send the matter any further up the ladder. They knew that their boss, Interior Minister Sándor Pintér, was with the prime minister that weekend, preparing for the arrival on Monday of an FBI delegation from the United States. There was an international crime conference beginning in Budapest on Tuesday.

The Whiskey Robber problem needed to be disposed of quickly. Géza saw only one way to ensure that. It was going to be one hell of an inconvenience, but at 10:50 A.M., he issued an emergency decree sealing the capital, a measure no one could remember having been taken since 1956.

About that time, Bérdi was arriving at the Gyorskocsi Street jail to find the halls echoing with inmates' cheers and chants. Fearing an uprising, he called Géza at the Death Star and asked for three commando units to be sent over on the double. At 11:54 A.M., as the muffled chop of low-flying police helicopters rumbled through the jail's corridors, thirty-six special troopers in riot gear fanned out through the building, beginning a systematic search of each cell.

The city's entire police force — more than two thousand cops — was called into action. They were divided into four groups and sent out to comb every block of the city. Roadblocks, manned by cops in bulletproof vests, were set up at every bridge and all seven highways leading out of the city. Searches of the bus, subway, and train stations were made top priority. After witnesses reported seeing a motorboat take off from a nearby dock about the time of the escape, the Danube Water Police was also enlisted. Budapest's Ferihegy International Airport was put on a high-security alert.

Bérdi believed that Attila was still inside the jail. The rope was too short to provide a safe landing on the street. It had to be a decoy. When the first search by the commando teams was finished, he ordered another, including checks of the closets, heating ducts, and the roof. "Again," Bérdi whispered when they finished, sending them back for a third sweep.

In cell 312, where the Whiskey Robber had resided until a few hours ago, the troopers picked up two items of note just as the television crews arrived: a sixty-five-page typed autobiographical manuscript and a heavily thumbed copy of Aleksandr Solzhenitsyn's *Gulag Archipelago,* volumes one and two. Of even greater interest was what was missing from the cell: under Attila's bed, behind a stinking clump of old bread crusts, was a hole in the wall two feet deep.

Attila's cellmate István Szopkó, the check fraud specialist who had opted not to go out for the walk that morning, pleaded ignorance of Attila's escape plans. He'd been transferred into the cell only a day earlier — when he arrived, he had mistaken Attila for the infamous Duna Bank embezzler — and he was too tired to go for the walk, he told the commando team. Of the morning, he said, "We got up around eight-thirty. They told us, 'It's a walk.' He [Attila] was already dressed, had black jeans, a cream-colored short-sleeved T-shirt, and white athletic shoes. Before the walk, he shaved off his beard but left the mustache."

All four of Attila's former cellmates, who had been rotated in and out so as to limit Attila's opportunity to form alliances, were also interviewed. None of them claimed to know anything of his plans or even about the bread-encrusted tunnel in their former cell. Tibor Benyó, who had been Attila's cellmate until only two days earlier, remembered that Attila had recently told him, "In this world, it's not worth it to be fair or sincere." Gabi, who was being held on another floor, was about as helpful as usual: not at all.

About 2:00 P.M. the skies darkened and a heavy rain that would not stop for days descended. The police issued a national alert to the media and all law enforcement officers in Hungary that the fugitive Attila Ambrus should be considered armed and dangerous. Despite Attila's cellmate's description of what he was wearing, the communiqué stated that Attila was last seen wearing purple pants, a cream-colored shirt, and a full beard and mustache.

George Magyar also contacted various media outlets to let them know that his client would never be caught. "The only way he can be caught is if he dies," Magyar told one reporter when pressed. "Defeat for him is not an option." Indeed, for Magyar, victory was at hand; forint signs danced in his head.

Acting police chief Jakab Géza had never heard such proclamations come out of the mouth of a lawyer. Géza put Keszthelyi in charge of coordinating the search effort while he frantically attempted to acquaint himself with every aspect of the case. He had Bérdi fax Attila's entire file, and his partially written autobiography, to the Death Star. When Géza learned how Attila had entered Hungary, he refined his previous search order, specifying that the transportation searches include the bottoms of every vehicle and train car. Hysterical from the time pressure, Géza called Bérdi so many times with questions that Bérdi eventually cracked, smashing his telephone into his desk until it splintered into pieces.

As darkness fell with no letup in the rain, the Danube River began overflowing onto the side streets, submerging cars and halting traffic. The troops who had been searching the city all day still had nothing, and inside the Death Star, hopes for a quick resolution to the crisis were fading. At 11:00 P.M. another national alert was transmitted to all checkpoints and news bureaus, reading, "Instead of bordeaux-colored pants, his pants were black. Instead of a cream-colored T-shirt with no pockets, he had a cream-colored shirt with two pockets; and instead of a beard, he was freshly shaven but wore a mustache." There were still no photographs available; eight hundred copies of Attila's mug shot were being slowly reproduced in the bowels of HQ.

Just before midnight Géza reluctantly ordered the city reopened. Bérdi, Keszthelyi, and most of the two thousand cops who had worked all day went home hoping to catch a few hours of sleep before the newspapers hit the stands. But the night would not end without at least one arrest. Károly Benkő, finishing up what was now a forty-two-hour shift, retired to a cot in one of the jail cells he normally guarded. He had been taken into custody and charged with suspicion of aiding and abetting Attila's escape.

⌒

When the FBI conference began in Budapest on Tuesday, the country was just beginning to dry out from the worst flooding in decades. The three-day intelligence meetings were to center on the progress of the historic joint Hungarian-American law enforcement team that had been formed the previous summer to fight organized crime and corruption in the region. Despite the hoopla surrounding the formation of the task force, however, the unit had not arrested anyone, and the man whom many in international law enforcement believed to be the most dangerous criminal in the world, Semion Mogilevich, was still living comfortably in Budapest, reportedly dealing, among other things, nuclear materials. Maybe no one back in America was concerned about the historic force's ineptitude, but in Hungary it had fueled the already rampant skepticism about the credibility of both countries' governments. After all, how else to explain why the White House would welcome Sándor Pintér, the least-trusted government official in Hungary, to speak at an anti-corruption conference?

Yet while American representatives to the Budapest congress were prepared to address concerns about the joint force's efficacy, they were not prepared for the news that greeted them upon arriving in the soggy city. Local journalists barely had time or space to play up the theft that morning of Prime Minister Orbán's car, the second vehicle stolen from his office in only a few months. The papers and airwaves were instead overflowing with coverage of the Transylvanian hockey goalie

who had departed from the city jail on a bedsheet, the same character some FBI agents recognized as the Lone Wolf. According to public opinion polls, between 80 and 90 percent of Hungary was rooting for the Whiskey Robber to outrun the authorities. On the city's streets, vendors were doing a brisk business selling T-shirts and coffee mugs proclaiming, I ♥ THE WHISKEY ROBBER! and GO WHISKEY ROBBER! "Would you have climbed down from the window on a shoelace?" inquired an unscientific poll of Hungarians in *Mai Nap*. "I wouldn't have done that, because I would have been so scared," answered one man, "but this guy is so skilled, I can imagine him doing anything." Officially, Hungarian authorities had no comment on the matter; they had yet to figure out what in hell they would want to add to the dialogue.

On Wednesday *Blikk* ran a double-page story in which Dr. Hegedűs Magdolna, a plastic surgeon, offered suggestions as to how Attila could better his chances of remaining at large. (She recommended a chin reconstruction — "It's too wide, I'd make it a bit more narrow" — for 400,000 forints [$1,700] but offered a full array of procedures and prices.) *HVG*, Hungary's largest newsweekly, wrote breathlessly of Attila's escape, dubbing him the "Hungarian Butch Cassidy."

The only member of the media not participating in the furor was one of the men who helped create it, *Kriminális* host László Juszt. After Juszt had reported one month earlier that Prime Minister Orbán's infamous "Hungarian Watergate" spy charges had been declared baseless by a parliamentary committee investigation, Juszt was arrested and charged with "revealing state secrets." The prime minister explained that the parliamentary committee's findings (of nothing) had been classified material and, thus, Juszt had jeopardized the country's safety with his story. Juszt was also fired from the supposedly independent Hungarian Television.

On Wednesday afternoon the Hungarian police finally made a statement regarding the Whiskey Robber case. An hour after George Magyar held a televised news conference announcing that he'd copyrighted, in Hungarian and English, the name Whiskey Robber (which was true) and struck a "Hollywood movie deal" with an unnamed producer for film rights to his client's story (which wasn't), police spokesman Dézsi Mihály emerged from his Death Star office to brief reporters. "This is human stupidity," Mihály said. "It was twenty-seven counts of armed robbery. Full stop."

⌒

Once again, robbery chief József Keszthelyi found himself in charge of finding the man he'd just been promoted to colonel for catching. Things were, of course, markedly different this time, and not just because Keszthelyi knew who he was looking for. In the six months since he'd caught Attila, Keszthelyi had become, literally, the poster boy for Hungary's new and improved police force. To counter flagging public confidence in his government, Prime Minister Orbán had launched what was known as the "public image" campaign. As part of the program, the police introduced a new slogan — "Let's Serve Together" — which was emblazoned on publicity materials distributed across the country. Above the block-lettered banner, the posters and pamphlets featured a large color photograph of none other than the smiling blue-eyed robbery chief astride a police motorcycle, flanked by two other bike-riding cops. Given the public reaction to the Whiskey Robber's escape, it was plain that a lengthy manhunt threatened to undo any progress the campaign might have made. For Keszthelyi, it also had the potential to destroy his promising young career. Not finding Attila Ambrus wasn't an option.

Keszthelyi replaced his cell phone with a new one that allowed him to program in different rings for different numbers, enabling him to ignore calls from the media. He rarely went home, most of the time curling up for a few hours of sleep on the green velvet couch in his office that had once billeted Lajos. The top brass at the police gave Keszthelyi the authority to choose his own special seven-member squad to work exclusively on the case. Among those Keszthelyi chose for his team were two of Bérdi's investigators, including Valter Fülöp, who relocated their offices from the Gyorskocsi Street jail to the Death Star. Keszthelyi also picked up the police department's top undercover investigations expert, László Kozák. Noticeably missing from the search team was Mound, who had quit the police force a week before Attila's escape to join Lajos at Blue Moon, and Dance Instructor, who had been transferred into an administrative post.

Each morning Keszthelyi went to the bathroom and mussed some water around in his crew cut, then headed into the seventh-floor conference room at 7:00 A.M. to meet with his group around a large

U-shaped conference table. Copies of Attila's partially written auto-biography lay marked up on the table. Maps of the city were tacked to the wall. The file cabinets in the corner were stuffed full with more than ten thousand pages from the case.

There was no consensus in law enforcement circles as to whether Keszthelyi would succeed. Many, including Lajos Varjú (whose speculation frequently appeared in the papers), believed the Whiskey Robber was already long gone into the Transylvanian mountains.

But Keszthelyi disagreed. He was sure Attila was laying low in the city somewhere, trying to figure out how to score enough money to get somewhere far away where he could live under a different identity. He didn't buy the rumors that Attila had left a hidden stash somewhere that he'd by now grabbed and taken off with. Nonetheless, he wasn't leaving any possibility unexamined. Keszthelyi sent a special request to Romanian authorities, asking for their help in apprehending Attila. ("Ambrus Attila is an especially dangerous criminal," the letter stated. "He may be armed. We are requesting you make this your top priority.") He also called in INTERPOL, specifically to track several of Attila's hockey teammates, including Jenő "Bubu" Salamon and Zsolt Baróti, whom Keszthelyi's men were not able to locate in Budapest. The names of Károly "Karcsi" Antal and Lázsló Veres, Attila's first two accomplices who had never been apprehended, were also forwarded to INTERPOL.

On street corners and subways around Budapest, Keszthelyi's investigative team put up menu-size WANTED signs, using a menacing picture of Attila from his initial arrest, wearing a black leather jacket and looking straight at the camera. And in case Attila had heeded *Blikk*'s advice and gone in for plastic surgery, doctored photos of him were also made and sent to all of the country's police precincts and the media.

As for undercover surveillance, Keszthelyi's team targeted several locations, including hotels, high-class brothels, casinos, and "places visited by Romanians" — bars, low-class brothels, train station corners, and Transylvanian restaurants. The robbery chief didn't expect Attila to be stupid enough to reach out to any of his previous contacts, but just in case, he had Éva's house in Érd surrounded, as well as the home of Zsuzsa Csala, the actress who had famously offered to adopt Don after Attila's arrest. Keszthelyi also had a unit watch Lajos Varjú, as well as

Don the dog, who was living in the suburbs with a relative of Attila's grocery clerk friend, Zsuzsa. Two hundred fourteen people's phones were tapped, fourteen of whom (including Éva and the actress Csala) were followed around the clock by four officers, two at a time in twelve-hour shifts.

But as the police soon began to realize, all the official manpower in the world might not make a difference. As Keszthelyi's men circulated around town, they found that virtually no one they questioned was willing to help them catch the Whiskey Robber. Many Hungarians even appeared to relish the opportunity to assist in the authorities' demoralization. From law-abiding citizens to career stool pigeons, people told Keszthelyi's men that even if they saw Attila, they would never admit it. The case had become a referendum on the government.

On July 22 Interior Minister Sándor Pintér made a rare appearance before the media, appealing to their sense of moral responsibility. The media printed his warning verbatim. "All I would ask of you is that you ask the people who were the victims of these robberies about this," Pintér said. "Ask the people he threatened with his gun, the people who were present when he fired bullets into the walls, shooting right past their ears, the people whose money he took. He stole over 130 million forints [$560,000]. Ask them how much of a hero they reckon him to be."

Needless to say, Pintér's voice did not carry much weight as a defender of the people.

THE HERO OF OUR TIME, THE BANK ROBBER, read the headline on the editorial page of *Magyar Hírlap* on July 29.

> In a time bereft of morality, can anyone regard the deeds of the Whiskey Robber as a crime? And if so, what about the everyday "business" of the so-called elite. . . . [People] understand that they are locked out of the privileged class, which can do anything without punishment. Attila Ambrus had the courage to make an attack against this unjust system. He didn't rob a bank. He just performed a peculiar redistribution of wealth, which differs from that of the elites only in its method.

That afternoon Keszthelyi recalled all of his men from the field for a special meeting.

"We need to rethink our approach to the investigation," he told them. They needed to stop relying on the public's help to catch the Whiskey Robber, he said, and start becoming proactive. The robber's success had always come because of his ability to think like the police. Now they had to think like him. After nearly seven years on the case, Keszthelyi was confident he could help them do that.

"There are only two places Attila knows well," Keszthelyi told his team. "Transylvania and Budapest. And there aren't any banks in the mountains of Transylvania. Eventually, he's going to turn up where the money is." (Just as good old Eddie Sutton said.)

Keszthelyi wanted his group to come up with a list of potential financial targets where they could set up shop and wait for the robber to come to them. If Attila was in Hungary, he obviously knew every cop in the country was after him. And he was a careful criminal. Keszthelyi didn't believe Attila would risk venturing out to scope out a location before robbing it. Since he knew Attila didn't like surprises, Keszthelyi was betting that he would show up someplace he'd already robbed. Valter, who'd spent more time interviewing Attila than anyone, agreed.

Over the next hour the group sifted through the case files and narrowed Attila's past hit list down to four likely targets, easily eliminating the post office and travel agencies where he couldn't score enough loot to make it worth the risk.

One of the four remaining targets was the Frankel Leó Street OTP, the last place Attila and Gabi had robbed before their arrest in January. But Valter felt that Attila was too superstitious to go back to the spot where his streak had ended.

"What about Heltai?" one of the investigators suggested. But it was deemed unlikely for similar reasons. It was where the shoot-out had taken place. Unlucky.

That left the post office next to the Gellért Hotel, where Attila had famously brought the bouquet of roses for the tellers and absconded with nearly 10 million forints ($65,000), and the Grassalkovich Street OTP, in the industrial southern outskirts of town, which he'd already robbed three times.

One of the investigators had recently been to the Gellért and thought he saw scaffolding in front of the nearby post office. They phoned the post office switchboard and were told that, indeed, the branch was closed for renovations. That left only Grassalkovich.

Just then Keszthelyi's mobile phone began ringing — sounding the jingle that indicated it was the emergency dispatcher, who was on strict orders to phone him immediately if any information came in.

"*Igen?*" Keszthelyi said. *Yes?*

"Robbery in progress," he was told. "Grassalkovich Street OTP."

Thirty

Attila entered the bank in a blue and white canvas baseball hat, sunglasses, and a windbreaker, shouting, "You know who I am, I have nothing to lose!" The guard had recognized him even before he got inside, and tried to lock the door, but Attila was too fast and too strong. Most of the tellers had been on duty during at least two of Attila's previous three robberies at that branch and knew the drill. They got down in their regular positions against the wall while Attila went to work.

Somewhere around the three-minute mark, the sound of sirens became audible along with another, more alarming noise — the low, rhythmic patter of helicopter blades. Attila stood up from his crouch in front of the time-lock safe and, with only the teller-drawer money in his bag, broke for the door in a dead run, feet flying, arms flailing. Across the street a postal worker saw a man racing from the building and, hearing the sirens and knowing the bank's reputation as a Whiskey Robber feeding trough, jumped on his motorcycle to give chase.

As two helicopters wafted over the city's southern horizon behind him, Attila turned left down one of the small streets leading toward the Danube and disappeared into a cluster of grass and trees behind a row of dilapidated wooden farmhouses. He hurdled some sagging wire fences and arrived several minutes later at a dirt road, beyond which stood a tall row of reeds at the marshy bank of the river.

The sound of the helicopter blades was starting to drown out the sirens. Attila looked up. The choppers were circling only a few blocks away.

He squatted in the grass, tied the plastic money bag as tightly as he could, and began wading into the mucky river. The current wasn't bad, but his clothes were so heavy with water that once his feet could no longer touch bottom, he became afraid he might drown. There was splashing in the reeds along the bank, but from where he was, Attila couldn't see the postal worker wading into the water after him. Holding the bag on the surface of the water, Attila took a deep breath and dipped his head under, kicking and stroking with his free hand.

When he hit the pavement outside the jail nineteen days earlier, it wasn't as if Attila hadn't considered swearing off crime entirely. If there was any upside to throwing yourself out a fourth-floor window on a short rope, it was that it likely followed a pledge of self-improvement. Attila had managed to land on his feet, but he severely twisted both his ankles, and the escape rope had torn up both his palms.

Needless to say, the death rope hadn't been his top getaway choice. Attila had been working on ideas on how to get out for nearly two months before he read the attempted murder counts against him. Once, he offered to Bérdi that he could help the police do a re-enactment of the Heltai Square shooting, during which he hoped to make a run for it. When the request was denied, he considered claiming that he could lead Bérdi to a pot of hidden money somewhere in the woods. But it seemed too obvious, and if it didn't work, he'd be stuck with a (false) admission that he had a cash stash.

Then Attila had his friend Zsuzsa bring him a screwdriver during one of her visits, which he used to begin tunneling through the plaster wall of his cell. But after chipping away for a few weeks and getting only an arm's length in, he saw that plan wasn't going to lead anywhere further than solitary confinement.

The only other possibility he could think of was the administration building window escape. He began stocking up on bedsheets and even asked Éva and Zsuzsa to bring him extra running shoes so he could use the laces. He'd carefully kept track of the placement of the few Khrushchev-era cameras in the corridors and walk boxes, and during his trips to the administration building, he had practically memorized its blueprint. He'd also noted that on summer weekends, there were far fewer guards around. If he could just make it over the walk-box wall without being seen, he figured he would make it — that is, as long as he could go out a window on the *second* floor.

Unfortunately, when he got into the administration building that morning, he'd heard voices on both the second *and* third floors, and with no time to waste, he headed instead for Blinky Béla's office on the fourth floor, where, in preparation for just this scenario, he'd stashed an extra line of bedsheets under the armchair's seat cushion one day while pretending to look at his file.

The sheet and rope combo wouldn't reach the ground, so he ripped off the cords from the phone, fax, and computer and added them to his line. It still wasn't long enough, but by the time he stepped out onto the window ledge, he was going down regardless of his uncertainty about the condition he would be in upon landing. Not even the horrified look on the face of the old woman on the sidewalk outside the Chang An Chinese restaurant directly across the street was going to stop him. At least the rope didn't break. Once he reached the end, it was too painful to hold on and he let go, dropping to the concrete with a thud and a groan. It took a few seconds to swallow the shooting pain in his legs. Then the adrenaline took over. He began to run as best he could on two twisted ankles toward the Danube, where his first sight across the river was Parliament, spread out on the bank like a big, proud turd. Once at the jogging path, he turned north and continued past the same spot where Gabi's fear of jumping six months earlier had led to their arrests.

When he reached the Margit Bridge, about half a mile from the jail, the mustard yellow 4/6 tram was screeching to its last stop in Buda. He hopped on and rode over the bridge to the Pest side, where he got out at the first stop, a small square with a fresh flower stand, and ducked into a nearby pub. The liquid-breakfast Saturday crowd was small. "Two beers," Attila said to the bartender, but she recognized him anyway. "Aren't you the Whiskey Robber?" she asked. He laughed. "I always get that," he said. He slugged back the drinks and paid with some of the 25,000 forints ($110) he'd borrowed from Zsuzsa during her visit the previous afternoon. Then he went into the pub's bathroom, where he stuffed his cream-colored long-sleeve shirt and black jeans in the bottom of the trash and pulled out the razor he'd brought from his cell. A few minutes later he walked out of the bar, clean-shaven and wearing shorts and a dark T-shirt, on his way to make a phone call to János Kovács, a man he'd never met before.

János was a contact Attila had been given by one of his cellmates at the jail. He was a real "musician," Attila had been told, someone who worked on his own and knew the right notes to play for any occasion. Attila didn't tell János who he was on the phone, only that he needed to see him right away.

They met at the market hall in the XV District, a sprawling several-story food and furniture bazaar. Attila told János he'd be in a red baseball hat, which Attila bought at one of the booths and pulled low over his head. When Attila's searching pupils met with the bulging eyes of the thin balding man approaching him, Attila was pretty sure he'd found his maestro. "János," the man said, reaching out his hand. *A Viszkis,* Attila said unnecessarily. *I'm the Whiskey guy.*

Attila told János he needed a place for a little while and offered to pay as soon as he had money. But János said he didn't want Attila's money. He put the Whiskey Robber up in his third-floor apartment downtown and went to stay with his brother-in-law. He said he'd check in on Attila in a few days.

Once safely ensconced in János's flat, the first thing Attila did was to shave his head, which gave him the nerve to step outside a few times for food and supplies. But soon the increased police presence on the street began to scare him. He debated going to a brothel but, on his fifth day in János's pad, he ordered a call girl to the apartment. Despite his shaved head, she not only recognized him instantly but started screaming about her brother, a cop. She clearly wasn't one of Attila's fans. Attila freaked. He grabbed the woman and told her that if she said anything to her brother, he would have his associates kill her. Then he pushed her out the door, went down to a pay phone, and called János. He had to get out of there quickly, he told him. But he had no idea where to go.

János knew exactly what to do. He called his friend Domonkos, a Székely from Székelyudvarhely, or Odorheiu Secuiesc in Romanian, a Transylvanian town just twenty-five miles west of Csíkszereda. As János correctly assumed, Attila's support among Transylvanians was nearly unanimous. In Csíkszereda, Whiskey Robber T-shirts were all over the city. BIG CITY COWBOY was the headline in *Hargita Népe,* the main local newspaper. The biggest Hungarian language daily in the country, *Magyar Szó*, based in Bucharest, wrote, "Attila wanted to taste the kind of life which for us is unattainable," and compared him with Australian folk hero Ned Kelley. There was no way Domonkos would refuse to help the most famous living Székely.

Domonkos, a thirty-five-year-old unemployed plumber working part-time at a fruit market, had recently split up with his wife. And for reasons he was in therapy to explore, he preferred sleeping in his metallic green Honda at gas stations than in his studio apartment in northeast Budapest. Attila could have the place.

Domonkos wouldn't accept any compensation from Attila, either, and he definitely did not want to know any of Attila's plans. It was a deal. Attila had one small request: gauze and Neosporin for his palms, which were still so deeply scarred from the escape rope that he couldn't make a fist. That was no trouble. Domonkos also agreed to come by the flat twice a week to restock Attila with food, whiskey, and all of the newspapers. So that Attila would know it was Domonkos at the door, they decided that before entering, Domonkos would knock twice quickly, then pause and knock again. Attila was not to leave the apartment.

Attila spent the following days crawling around the parquet floor, afraid to raise his head above the level of the windowpane. The apartment was on a busy intersection, above a 24-hour food mart. Often he jolted awake at the sound of a car horn.

Attila knew that if he wanted to make it out of Hungary and survive in an unfamiliar place without being discovered, he needed enough money for fake papers and the start-up costs of a new life. He estimated it would take between 20 and 25 million forints ($85,000–$110,000) to get somewhere safe like Brazil, where his hero Ronnie Biggs of England's Great Train Robbery was living peaceably without fear of extradition.

And thus the visit to Grassalkovich Street, where — to his surprise and dismay — the staff had moved the safe since his last visit. When he heard the helicopters, he'd only just found the main repository for the bank's cash. After running to the river, he swam through the Danube to Molnár Island, the piece of residential land in the middle of that section of the river. He pulled himself out on the Molnár Island bank, stripped off his clothes, and was standing naked with them in his hand when an old man chased him away, hollering about trespassing. The plastic bag

Attila was carrying held only 1.5 million forints ($6,500). Nowhere near enough.

Later that day, when Domonkos came into his apartment with a bag of groceries in his large arms, he saw wet clothing strewn around the room and Attila sitting on the floor in a towel. On television was live coverage of the search for the Whiskey Robber, who had just made a dramatic return to robbery by pulling off his fourth job at the OTP Bank on Grassalkovich Street. There were conflicting reports as to how many policemen the robber had outswum through the Danube during his getaway. According to George Magyar, it was three hundred; according to the police, none.

Domonkos had known Attila for only twelve days, but the two of them had already developed their own shorthand. "Where have you been?" Domonkos inquired of his roommate.

"Yes," said Attila.

~

The robbery at Grassalkovich Street was a disaster for Keszthelyi in virtually every way but one — at least he now knew that Attila was still in Budapest. And since the Transylvanian had gotten so little money from the job, Keszthelyi was sure Attila would be a city resident for at least a little while longer.

Keszthelyi was sure he would get another chance to catch Attila but for the time being he was the one who felt caught, presiding over a public relations disaster of capitalist proportions. THE INTELLIGENCE OF THE HUNGARIAN CRIME SQUADS COULD NOT BE LOWER, read a headline in *Népszabadság*. And it wasn't just the Hungarian media covering the story anymore. The latest installment of the Whiskey Robber saga had awakened the international media, who appeared delighted to find that Hungary had finally produced something they could understand and admire: a folk hero. HUNGARY'S ROBIN HOOD was the headline in the *Christian Science Monitor*. WHISKEY ROBBER WANTED BY POLICE AND PR PEOPLE BECOMES A HUNGARIAN FOLK HERO, touted London's *Independent*. "Despite the fact that authorities are emphasizing the danger he poses, [Attila's] popularity among the people continues to rise," wrote France's *Le Figaro*. Even the world's largest sports magazine, U.S.-based *Sports Illustrated*, celebrated Attila as "one of the best goalies in his country's top pro league." Attila was already becoming part myth. It was a long way from the horse paddock.

Keszthelyi was approved to put full-time surveillance at ten banks around the city. But the real shift in police tactics was behind the scenes. With the help of the police public relations department, Keszthelyi and Géza launched an effort to destroy Attila's public support. At one press conference Géza refuted Attila's reputation as a man of modest upbringing, exclaiming, "Ambrus had *more* possibilities than the average citizen. He could have chosen legal ways." Some articles, based on carefully leaked information from the police, also portrayed the hidden side of Attila to be that of a coarse, violent alcoholic who tried to kill two police officers. The police also successfully spread the not wholly untrue story that Attila had Don with him on the day of his arrest not because of his love for the dog but because he'd needed to go home for his passport and, while there, also grabbed the canine.

The most creative smear, however, came directly from Keszthelyi, who in interviews normally expressed himself in Terminator-style statements such as "I am the cop; he's the thief. I will catch him." But tucked behind a keyboard, Keszthelyi loosened up, penning an entirely fabricated article for the police newsmagazine, *Zsaru,* which ran under the headline IS THE WHISKEY ROBBER ATTRACTED TO BOYS? The two-page article, which claimed to be written "by our colleagues," cited several anonymous people saying that Attila was gay. As soon as it hit the newsstands in early August, László Garamvölgyi, the national police spokesman, made the Hungarian radio and television talk-show rounds to break some hearts about the sexy bandit.

One morning in August, Attila and Domonkos were sitting on the floor of Domonkos's apartment watching *Napkelte (Sunrise),* the Hungarian version of the *Today* show, when Garamvölgyi came on the set and began to talk about Attila's homosexuality. Upon hearing the charge for the first time, Attila jumped up from the floor and bolted for the front door with the intention of going straight to the Death Star to do some damage. Fortunately, before he could get the door open, Domonkos tackled him from behind. Domonkos knew how hotheaded Székelys could be, and he wasn't going to let their new Sándor Rózsa go down over something like this.

~

When Attila calmed down, he was no longer as intent upon getting out of the country so quickly. Just as Keszthelyi thrived on putting criminals away, Attila thrived on avoiding getting put away. And the latest emasculating smear amounted to real fightin' words. The police had just upped the ante and Attila was going to see their bet and raise it. Over the past month, as the Hungarian media regularly compared Attila with Sándor Rózsa, who had stood for the rights of the common man in his series of maverick robberies and attacks against the ruling Hapsburgs, it had been getting harder for Attila not to think of his fight as something bigger than just a bid for his own freedom. That the police had now resorted to spreading lies about him to win back public opinion gave Attila renewed purpose. Lest he forget, this was about the truth. He wasn't a murderer and he wasn't a man of privilege and he wasn't gay and he wasn't going to stop until he exposed the government and its minions for the fraudulent malefactors they were.

As he did when he first dedicated himself to becoming a robber — after nearly getting caught attempting to rob the travel agency at the train station in 1993 — Attila put himself on a strict regimen designed specifically for only one purpose: to triumph over his pursuers by intuiting their movements and exploiting their weaknesses. Every day, he spent two to three hours doing push-ups, sit-ups, and leg-sits, a minimum of a thousand each. He'd already acquired one gun, using Domonkos as an intermediary, and now he got another. He placed them on opposite corners of the wooden frame under the futon he slept on, one near his right hand, the other near his left foot so that he was never more than a split second away from protection.

During the days, he crawled around on the floor like a crab, careful to keep his head below window level. At night he sat on the small cement balcony in the darkness, listening to the sounds of the street below. He never used more than a small reading lamp on the floor. He did crossword puzzles to stay relaxed. But as the weeks passed, the pressure of being on the run with nowhere to run was getting to him. He'd left one cell and was now a virtual prisoner in another. He felt worse than he did that summer in 1995 when he was caught on camera at the Lajos Street bank. Attila allowed himself to drink every other night, and when he did, he usually finished two whole bottles of whiskey by the time the sun came up, hallucinating about the halcyon days as UTE's Zamboni driver. But he had a responsibility to the people now.

Attila tried to recount the pages in his robbery book that he'd flushed down the gas station toilet in January. He could picture almost every entry, but the problem was, there wasn't much left worth remembering. By the end with Gabi, there weren't any easy targets left that they hadn't already done. And Attila knew his next hit couldn't be a site he'd done before: the police would have all of those bases covered by now. He decided to bide his time until things cooled down a little and he might be able to sneak out for some location scouting.

That left Attila with nothing to do but keep up his workouts and follow his saga in the media. He read the papers every third day, when Domonkos arrived to restock his food and reading materials. And on television, he followed the latest on the manhunt, a pastime that required nothing more than lying inanimately on the floor and consenting to being dragged through unpredictable emotional terrain. Sometimes the news of his story made him laugh out loud, such as when he watched a prominent television journalist call the Whiskey Robber case "the Monica Lewinsky story of Hungary" because of how embarrassing it had become for the government. Sometimes it made him sad, such as when the guest on *Sunrise* was his dog, Don. Sometimes he was amazed, such as when his lawyer went on television to announce his completion of a deal with an Austrian company to produce Whiskey Robber energy drinks. And often it made him angry, such as when he saw special reports that belittled his past, claiming that he had had "numerous brushes with the law" earlier in life and that, once he got rich, he had "failed to provide for his impoverished parents in Transylvania."

Only rarely did the news inform him of the progress of the police, but when it did — such as on September 1 — it was always heartening. On that day Attila watched as every channel carried live coverage of the police shutting down and sealing the Flórián shopping mall at the foot of the city's northernmost river crossing, the Árpád Bridge, because he was supposedly inside. They were still chasing shadows.

In the third week of September, Attila finally steeled himself to go out. He shaved his scruffy beard into a Fu Manchu, put on a baseball hat, and took public transportation to a motorcycle dealership on the southern outskirts of town, where he paid cash for a moped. He drove in the direction of Budapest's tiny international airport, Ferihegy, fifteen miles southeast of the city. A few miles beyond the airport, he turned down a dirt road into the town of Vecsés, home of the celebrated *Vecsési káposzta,* or pickled cabbage, and one humble OTP Bank. Attila wasn't sure how much money it would carry, but he was sure it wasn't in the jurisdiction of the Budapest police. He didn't want any part of Keszthelyi. He knew the robbery chief well enough to know that this case was personal for him; Keszthelyi wasn't very easily going to be made the fool again.

After locating the OTP in a shopping plaza off the main road, Attila ferreted out the local police precinct house. At one minute and forty-five seconds doing 60 mph, the bank was a bit closer to the police station than he'd hoped. But he didn't think it was likely to be equipped with a direct alarm to the station, like those in the city. Plus, it was real small. He would be in and out.

He parked the scooter at a McDonald's on the other end of the little shopping center and went to check the layout. Mentally, he wasn't ready to do the job right away, but he didn't want to go home, either, now that he was finally out of Domonkos's apartment. After his assessment, he got back on the bike and drove into a nearby wooded area, where he spent the night under the stars. In the morning he awoke with the sun and drove west, across the Danube River to Érd, where Éva lived. He had to be careful. She was an obvious target for surveillance. But he needed to see a familiar face and she was the only one he felt sure he could trust.

Éva's neighborhood was a hilly and heavily wooded area. When Attila got near her street, he walked the bike up the road and sneaked onto her property through the trees. He didn't see any suspicious cars around, so he darted toward the house, where, through a window, he could see Éva inside on the couch watching television. For a moment he had to wonder what his life would have been like had he not let those 2 million forints ride on black 17 the night before he and Éva were supposed to close on the pub. Then he knocked on the glass.

Éva was shocked. She'd figured Attila was in Transylvania by now. She yanked him inside and shooed him upstairs. Though she hadn't seen it for the past few days, an unmarked car with two men in it had been parked just down the street for weeks. And thank God he was smart enough not to have called. The phone, with all those strange clicks, was surely tapped. But it was a most excellent reunion — in almost every way. Éva was dating another man, with whom she was getting serious. She wasn't going to sleep with Attila, but she would let him stay for a week if he promised not to leave the house or use the phone. For Attila the sex thing was a serious buzzkill, but he would have to adjust if he wanted to enjoy the pleasures of freedom even briefly. He spent most of the days in Éva's loftlike upper floor, playing pool on the competition-size table he'd helped her acquire a couple of years earlier.

Attila's hair had grown in since he'd shaved it at János's place, and, as he was talking about needing to transform his appearance, Éva had a suggestion. Her son, an eighteen-year-old aspiring hairstylist whom Attila knew, was a huge Whiskey Robber fan, and she was sure he would give Attila a makeover free of charge. Attila agreed, and Éva's son came over and dyed his hero's hair and eyebrows peroxide blond, transforming him into a stockier Billy Idol. Attila looked like a new person, and he had a new idea. On one of his last days at Éva's place, he took a white T-shirt from one of her drawers and drew on it with a black Magic Marker:*

Then Attila wrote a note to his lawyer with a request he assumed Magyar wouldn't mind granting. When he heard about a robbery on the outskirts of Budapest, Attila wrote in his note to Magyar, he should phone the police, tell them it was the work of the Whiskey Robber, and then deliver the T-shirt and a special message to them, which Attila enclosed. Then he gave the shirt and the note to Éva and told her to get them to Magyar right away.

*BM stands for Belugium Ministerium, or Interior Ministry, which oversees the police.

On the morning of Tuesday, September 28, Attila kissed Éva good-bye and drove out to the OTP Bank in Vecsés to look it over one last time. He'd taken a bottle of whiskey with him from Éva's cupboard and gone to the train tracks nearby to drink and wait until it was almost closing time. He finished off the entire bottle and fell asleep. When he woke up, it was nearly four o'clock. He got on the bike and motored back up the hill to the bank.

It wasn't until Attila got inside that he realized how drunk he was. He must have been slurring his words, because when he asked the tellers for the money, they started laughing. Attila waved his pistol and yelled, but it didn't help. He watched dumbly from the wrong side of the counter as two employees punched a lock on the safe. Finally he summoned enough force to launch himself up and over the divider, where he grabbed as much cash as he could from the teller drawers and lumbered back out the front door.

Thirty-one

The report of the Vecsés OTP robbery didn't get to Keszthelyi until the next day. The perpetrator of the crime had gotten away with just 224,000 forints ($960), less than the price of the scooter he'd forgotten in the parking lot, which was found with the key in the ignition and the helmet on the seat. If the job was the work of the Whiskey Robber, he'd set a new all-time low for himself.

The next day the bank camera's videotape was delivered to the Death Star, and as soon as Valter and Keszthelyi watched the film of the robber jumping over the counter, they knew it was Attila. They also knew that the last thing they needed was to make any public acknowledgment of the out-of-town hit, so the robbery went unreported by the media and George Magyar held on, for the time being, to the T-shirt that Éva had delivered to his office the previous day.

It was probably just as well for Magyar, whose weekly press conferences about the Whiskey Robber case were beginning to grate on the public. Not that he wasn't a compelling showman. At his last event, he had sat next to a life-size cardboard cutout of Attila and spoken in the first person as if he himself were the Whiskey Robber, announcing the release of his autobiography, *I, the Whiskey Robber,* the book based on the material Attila had written during his time in the Gyorskocsi Street jail. Rewritten by *Mai Nap*'s Judit P. Gál, the mass-market paperback — part pulp-style confessional, part how-to robbery manual — sold seventeen thousand copies in its first week, breaking Hungarian sales records.

Keszthelyi, like Magyar, had also resorted to measures that, if they'd been performed in public, may have appeared no less absurd. He was so anxious, he sometimes deployed inexplicably large forces at the slightest suggestion of Attila's presence. One night after a supposed Whiskey Robber sighting was phoned in, Keszthelyi sent a commando team in full riot gear through the windows of a farmhouse about 3:00 A.M. only to find a petrified elderly couple and their two grown children inside, one of whom bore a resemblance to Attila. Keszthelyi also had a pet project that seemed to have worse odds of catching Attila than Attila's turning himself in. Aware of the robber's affinity for exotic seaside locations, Keszthelyi had requested and received funding and personnel to open a fake travel agency in downtown Budapest catering to high-end clients. He had rented the office space and was finalizing plans for the advertising campaign. The Blue Dolphin Travel Agency would be a unique full-service operation — the only travel agency in town staffed exclusively by undercover police officers.

Meanwhile, some small but real breaks in the case were starting to develop. An informant, most likely the hooker Attila called to János's apartment in the first week after his escape, had come forward to report that Attila had been staying with a János Kovács. János, who was no stranger to the Budapest police (he had a list of petty Planet of the Zorg–type offenses to his credit), was hauled in and questioned. After several interrogation rounds, he admitted having put up the Whiskey Robber for a few days but claimed not to know where the thief had gone after leaving his apartment. Keszthelyi didn't believe him, and he placed János under surveillance.

Also, Károly "Karcsi" Antal was finally in police custody, having been arrested while trying to come over the Hungarian border from Romania on the Csíkszereda hockey team bus. Karcsi, too, claimed to have no information about Attila's current whereabouts, but Keszthelyi wanted to see what he would say after sitting in Gyorskocsi for a few months.

INTERPOL was also making some progress. There had been no sightings of Attila in Csíkszereda, the agency reported back to Keszthelyi. But according to its sources, László Veres was indeed hiding in the small village of Fitód. INTERPOL had also found and interviewed

Attila's former girlfriend Betty, in her hometown in Székelyföld, who claimed she had not seen Attila since they broke up in 1998. (She said she'd moved back to Transylvania after her more recent boyfriend threatened that if she didn't start coming home on time he would "sell" her.)

Lastly, Valter Fülöp had finally received the phone company records from Attila's Villányi Street apartment and was tracing down every number that had been dialed from the apartment since a line had been installed there in the mid-nineties. They were slowly closing the circle on Attila. It was just a matter of time.

On October 6 Attila spent his thirty-second birthday alone in Domonkos's apartment. Needless to say, it had been quite a year. Only ten months earlier, his name had been little known outside ice hockey circles of the Carpathian basin. Now, though he didn't know it, he was being hailed around the world as a folk hero. He knew only his reputation inside Hungary, where he was a bestselling author, and the subject of a rap by Gangsta Zoli ("The Whiskey Robber Is the King") that was in regular rotation on Hungarian radio. How's that for gray nobody? But he didn't feel much like celebrating. He was living like a caged animal, once again too afraid to consider leaving the confines of Domonkos's flat because of what he perceived as a slight but discernible increase in the frequency of the statements from police sources that the Whiskey Robber was out of the country by now. Attila saw the scattered assertions as a delicate and deliberate ploy to draw him into the open.

He wasn't going to fall for it. And yet he couldn't keep living the way he was much longer. In order to quell his anxiety, he was drinking so much that his face was swollen. His stomach was constantly upset. His only wish on his birthday was that he'd live to see another. If he could survive, he would go back to selling Parker pens. Anything but this.

Within a few days he'd made a decision. It was going to have to be all or nothing. The odds wouldn't be good, but he needed to go for one big score. It was time to place his bet and accept his fate, whatever it would be.

He settled on one bank, memorable for its distinctive sloped all-glass ceiling, that he'd cased and recorded in his now-destroyed encyclopedia. It was a huge institution, set in the shadow of a maudlin high-rise apartment building, on Üllői Street, one of the main arteries heading southeast out of town. It was about four minutes without traffic from the nearest police precinct station. Though Attila preferred banks with five or fewer employees, this one had approximately thirty and potentially as many customers — a clear 5 in his rating system. Plus the OTP had recently made a well-publicized investment of a billion forints ($4.3 million) in bank security systems. There would definitely be cameras, an armed guard, and a time-coded safe. But if locating a large supply of money was the only factor that mattered, it was a good choice. Attila figured there would be at least 40 million forints ($172,000) on hand, enough to enable him to set up a life far away that he could possibly even enjoy, and as a bonus, strike a final crushing blow to the police department.

He asked Domonkos to spot him some cash and to go buy him a new pair of dress shoes and a sports jacket. As usual, Attila would do the job as near to closing time as possible.

Three times the weather forecast an autumn rain and Attila began drinking early to steel himself. But each time the sky cleared by lunchtime and he aborted the plan. Finally one dreary October morning, he pushed a bullet clip into his Glock 9mm gun, packed a can of pepper spray to throw the dogs off his scent, and got dressed in the outfit Domonkos had bought him.

Unwilling to risk public transportation, he pulled his baseball hat down low and hailed a taxi. He'd drunk so much that on the ride over his head was spinning. When he got out of the car near the bank and tried to make it inside, he realized he also had a bigger problem. It was his new loafers. They were killing him. By the time he made it to the bank, their stiff backs were slicing into his ankles. He sat down in the waiting area to decide if he could go through with it, but there was no way. He could barely walk. If he was going to have a chance to pull off this job, the one thing he had to be able to do was run fast and far. He got up and limped out.

It was a week before his blisters healed enough for him to function normally in shoes again. He chose another pair of shoes and Monday, October 18, as the day — rain, shine, or shoe trouble.

Again, Attila went by taxi, sloshed. The security camera captured him entering the bank at 5:50, wearing a plaid English cap, black shoes with a buckle, dark wool pants, a black sports jacket, and glasses. The change from the cool outside air to the temperature-controlled atmosphere of the bank made him nauseous. He took a number and sat down on a couch in the waiting area, sweating whiskey.

The interior of the building was huge, almost the size of a hockey rink. About fifteen customers were scattered around the premises, changing notes and depositing and withdrawing cash. After a few minutes Zsolt Kemecsei, a teller, came out from behind the counter with a key ring in his hand. He walked past Attila toward the front door, which was separated from the main area by a small hallway and shielded by a black glass partition from the inside of the bank. When Kemecsei reached the hallway, he felt a gun at his back and heard a voice say, "Don't do anything stupid. Lock the door and then give me the key."

Attila clutched Kemecsei close enough that the employee could smell the liquor on the Whiskey Robber's breath. Attila took the key and put it in his jacket pocket. Still shielded by the black glass, Attila asked Kemecsei to walk with him back into the atrium and over to the haggard-looking guard. János Májor was completely surprised by what the well-dressed customer in front of him had to say. "Throw down your gun, or I'll shoot," Attila commanded, pointing his gun at Májor's chest. Májor complied without a word.

A few of the customers nearby saw what was happening and screamed. Attila wheeled around and began to yell. "Bank robbery! Bank robbery! Everyone on the ground!"

He couldn't even see all the way to the other end of the room, but it appeared that the number of people inside had multiplied while he was at the front door. Including customers and employees, about forty people were inside the bank. "Bank robbery! Bank robbery!" Attila shouted again, running up and down the length of the cavernous space. He took an earpiece out of his pocket and put it in his ear, mumbling into it every few seconds so as to appear to be working as part of a team.

When it seemed that everyone was quiet and on the floor, he went first to the two currency exchange booths on the side of the main hall for the foreign money. He took a plastic bag out of his duffel, leaving the bigger bag on the counter. Inside the duffel was one of Attila's regular

CLOSED FOR TECHNICAL REASONS signs that he'd made for the occasion but had forgotten to hang when he went to the door with the teller.

Attila started digging into the foreign-exchange desk's loot. The drawers were full of piles of Italian lira and U.S. dollars and German marks, which he stuffed into the plastic bag. Afterward he ran to the main strip of tellers, yelling, "Money, money, money!"

Though he was too drunk to realize it (and had no accomplice to warn him), he was working far more slowly than usual. The robbery was already thirteen minutes old. Sirens began sounding in the distance, but Attila knew that none of what he was doing mattered if he didn't come away with at least 20 million forints ($86,000). Booth by booth he went, emptying the drawers, as the sound of sirens got louder.

When Attila finally reached the front door, ready to run, sixteen minutes had gone by since he'd started the robbery. The police would have been inside the building already were it not for the fact that the first two cars responding to the call had gotten into separate accidents along the way, one of them flipping over as it turned the corner onto Üllői Street.

Attila stood confusedly pulling at the handle on the front door, having forgotten the key was in his jacket pocket. Dozens of police units were careening down the street toward him. *Hoppá,* he kept saying. *Hoppá! Uh-oh!* As a forest of blue lights sprung up outside, Attila took out his gun and aimed it at the lock. He'd also forgotten about the back exit.

"You are surrounded," said a voice over a megaphone on top of one of the police cars. "Come out with your hands up."

Attila ignored the warning and began shooting at the lock on the door. The cops in front of the building responded by opening fire. At about the same time, Keszthelyi was pulling up at the scene half a block down the street. Hearing the gun battle, the robbery chief nervously tried to coax a group of onlookers back from what sounded like a gruesome firefight. He knew Attila had nothing to lose.

Dazed, Attila saw his own blood dripping onto the carpet and turned away from the door, his gun empty. He walked back into the bank, which now seemed to resemble a morgue. Dozens of still, quiet bodies were sprawled out on the floor like a human shag rug.

Half a mile away, Colonel Zsolt Bérdi was driving down Üllői Street on his way home from a soccer game with friends when he saw the blue glow looming ahead of him. He turned and headed down the street's back alley to see what was happening.

From what Attila could tell, he was only bleeding from bits of broken glass that had sliced his ear and hand. He was able to run, and he did. His hat and glasses flew off his head as he raced toward the bank's back door that had escaped his mind earlier. It, too, was locked. He called out for the security guard but no one answered, so he went and sought out the old man, who was lying on the ground near his post. "Do you know who I am?" Attila asked him.

"Of course," Májor said.

"Then unlock the back door for me now," Attila said.

They went to the back and Attila crashed through the exit into the alley. Outside, a voice on his right yelled, "Stop, or I'll shoot!" Attila took off the other way.

As Attila ran down the alley, Keszthelyi and two dozen cops stormed into the bank from the front. Attila's blood was all over the entrance floor. When the cops got inside the bank's main atrium, forty sets of arms pointed up from the floor toward the back. Keszthelyi ran to the rear door, which was hanging open, just in time to see two of his guys dashing down the alley. He also saw Zsolt Bérdi's Volkswagen.

Keszthelyi assumed from the little pools of blood on the bank floor that Attila had been seriously wounded and wouldn't get far. But he had to be sure, and with one call to the Death Star, Budapest was sealed shut again, along with the country's borders.

With the police on his trail, Attila sprinted through a parking lot and then across a busy boulevard, where an oncoming city bus swerved to avoid him. Then he turned down a side street and ducked underneath a parked car as several police units sped past. When he climbed back out, he saw that he was in front of a house. Not wanting to stay on the street, he headed for the backyard, which was separated by a tall chain-link fence. In his haste to get out of sight, he fell headfirst over the fence, breaking two of his fingers and knocking himself unconscious when he landed on the other side.

All night, the police searched the streets but found no sign of Attila, who was passed out in a thicket of rosebushes three hundred yards from the bank.

If there had ever been a worse morning at the Death Star, no one could remember it. The rookie cop who'd yelled for Attila to freeze at the bank's back door and then didn't fire a shot at him when Attila ran was publicly excoriated and demoted to a desk job. Keszthelyi was so enraged and incredulous that Attila could have gotten away without someone's help that he told members of his team that he'd seen Bérdi's car at the scene, insinuating that the investigative chief of the Gyorskocsi Street jail was in cahoots with the Whiskey Robber. When Bérdi got wind of Keszthelyi's slight, he was so incensed that he decided to resign from the force. (THE WATERLOO OF THE POLICE, read the headline of the story about the fallout in *Mai Nap* two days later.)

About noon, most of the city's media outlets crammed into George Magyar's law office for a hastily called press conference in which the Whiskey Robber's lawyer announced that his client was responsible for the latest heist. And to prove it, he produced Attila's homemade T-shirt, reading aloud the message Attila had written for the police — "Corrupt cops will never catch me" — which quickly became the newest slogan to be emblazoned upon Whiskey Robber T-shirts and websites.

Keszthelyi was no longer sure about anything but this: he was in a race against time. Attila had taken a record 51 million forints ($220,000) from yesterday's robbery. Wherever he was now, he wouldn't be there for long.

Attila didn't have a chance to enjoy his latest publicity coup. After awakening in the rosebushes the night of the robbery, he stayed put until well after midnight, then picked his way through the neighborhood, unwittingly shedding banknotes along the way. He made it to Budapest's national sports stadium, not far from the Keleti train station, where he slept for about an hour inside the shell of the stadium's generator. When dawn arrived and he could see people out on the street, he wiped his bloodied face with saliva, shed his wrinkled sports jacket, and hurried to a nearby bus stop, where he caught a ride back to Domonkos's apartment.

Hungover and battered, he was having trouble seeing straight when he got home, so he lay down on the floor in what remained of his filthy disguise and didn't wake up for twenty-four hours. The following afternoon, a Wednesday, two days after the robbery, he hobbled downstairs to the public phone on the ground floor to call Domonkos. Attila needed his Székely friend to go to Transylvania immediately to get him the best fake passport and identification papers money could buy.

Funny, he couldn't find his phone card.

*   *   *

It took Keszthelyi's team two days to trace the calls from Attila's phone card, which they'd found in the Üllői Street bank, inside the bag of extra clothes Attila had forgotten on the foreign-exchange counter.

There were three calls on the card, all made on the day of the robbery. Two of them were to 107, the police emergency line. The first was made at 4:45 P.M., reporting a bomb threat to a building on the opposite side of town. Then at 4:49 P.M. there was another call, saying there was a drug deal taking place in a shopping mall parking lot, also across town from the Üllői Street bank. And earlier in the day one call was made to a mobile phone belonging to a Domonkos Kovács.

Nine days later, on October 27, Domonkos returned from Transylvania. He was to meet Attila at the apartment at 6:00 P.M. It had turned out that he couldn't get the documents on the spot, but they were being prepared. At 5:10 P.M. Domonkos was sitting in traffic near downtown Budapest when suddenly he found his homey Honda surrounded by police.

Domonkos was arrested and put into a car headed for the Death Star. On the way there, he promised himself that no matter what the police did to him or how much they beat him, he wasn't going to talk. But once he was set down in interrogation room 736, all Detective Keszthelyi wanted to know was how many ways there were to get into Domonkos's apartment and how many guns Attila was keeping there. Upon realizing that the police already knew not only where he lived but that Attila was hiding there, the hulking Székely collapsed on the floor and began weeping.

Back at the apartment, Attila was cooking Domonkos a thank-you dinner (beef tenderloin with paprika) and listening to Prime Minister Orbán on the radio, defending his Interior Minister Sándor Pintér against charges of involvement in the mafia-related oil frauds. As Attila turned toward the sink to wash a pot, he noticed something strange. The whole neighborhood had gone silent. There were no cars honking or trams squeaking, nothing but his own increasingly labored breathing.

He crept to the window and looked out from behind the curtain. On the roof across the street, he could see the outline of several men. They were holding rifles trained at the apartment.

The doorbell rang.

"Coming," Attila called, walking slowly back to the foyer. It had been a good run. But he wasn't going to make it out of the country. The game was over. He pulled the door open to a hallway filled with black helmets and assault rifles sticking out from behind curved white police shields. Wearing only a pair of shorts, Attila raised his hands in the air for the first and last time.

ONE LESS SMALL FISH, read the headline in *Népszava*.

Thirty-two

Attila's trial did not get under way until eight months later, in June 2000. Until then he made only one public appearance, on December 1, 1999, before a military tribunal. He was called to testify in the government's case against jail guards Károly Benkő, János Vajda, and Krisztián Faragó, all accused of aiding Attila's flight from the Gyorskocsi Street jail. When he took the stand, Attila told the court, "These guards had nothing to do with my escape. . . . The jail was total chaos. Once I was able to observe this, I realized it was the easiest thing in the world to walk out of that place."

Vajda and Faragó were found not guilty. But Károly Benkő, who was not carrying the required alarm stick that morning — never mind his explanation that not enough of them existed to go around — was sentenced to five months in jail for negligence and was forced to forfeit his job, pension, and benefits.

The newspapers and television networks were sated with Whiskey Robber stories provided exclusively by the police and corrections departments, detailing Attila's meal schedule and living conditions at the Gyorskocsi Street jail. But little of what was published and broadcast was true. Attila was not even at Gyorskocsi. He was being held across the river in a government building near the Metropolitan Court, in a special all-glass cage built five years earlier for the country's most notorious serial killer, Magda Marinkó, a convicted butcher of four. In order to reach Attila's new residence, one had to pass like Maxwell Smart through thirteen steel doors, none of which would open until the previous one was sealed.

Despite his hermetically sealed existence, Attila's first couple of months of captivity were somewhat of a relief. He was mentally exhausted from his 109 days on the lam. But slowly his severe new environment became oppressive. He could not see out of his cell; the glass on all sides was a one-way mirror. A video camera and bright light shone on him twenty-four hours a day. He showered and ate all of his meals in the cell and was only occasionally permitted up to an hour of exercise in a small interior corridor. He passed the time by starting to write another book, picking up his story from his escape and detailing his three subsequent robberies, for which he had signed confessions. Often he had no idea what time or day it was.

News of his capture had made headlines from Berlin to Perth and publications such as *Time* and *Foreign Policy*. But the only time Attila himself appeared in the media — even inside Hungary — was during an interview with the Hungarian television network TV2, which paid George Magyar an undisclosed sum for exclusive access. Seated in an unidentifiable white room in handcuffs and wearing a black shirt and silver tie (sent to him by Éva), Attila appeared at turns resigned, pensive, and angry. Asked about the conditions of his confinement, he said that he had almost suffocated to death recently when his cell filled with steam because the guards wouldn't turn off his hot water after a shower. After the TV2 piece aired, the national prison commander banned all further media access to Attila, citing security reasons.

In Attila's absence, Magyar began making media appearances on his client's behalf, with questionable benefit. Attila's lawyer was already under investigation by the Budapest Chamber of Lawyers, the local bar association, for possible ethics violations stemming from his hand-delivering Attila's homemade T-shirt to the police while Attila was still at large. And worse for Attila, Magyar's new round of declarations that Attila's confession was illegally extracted undermined his client's most dearly held and publicly resonant virtue, his honesty.

Attila, who had a small television in his cell and Éva and Zsuzsa working as his personal newspaper-delivery service, cringed every time he saw Magyar's melodramatic promise to appeal any conviction "straight to Strasbourg." He thought about firing Magyar but didn't know where else he would turn with his court date looming. Meanwhile, the media slowly began to turn against Attila, asserting that his story was pure myth concocted by a greedy, opportunistic lawyer who represented a new breed of unscrupulous American-style "star attorneys," or *sztar ugyved*. Some Hungarians began blaming the Whiskey Robber's undue popularity on an amoral media, prompting several soul-searching articles in the newspapers. There was a clear sense of shame emerging that, however it had happened, the country had participated in making a criminal out to be one of the first modern international symbols of its culture.

Sealed up inside the serial killer's cell, Attila came to believe that his support had disappeared entirely, which was certainly not the case. For months after his arrest, a small shrine of whiskey bottles and roses sat on the sidewalk in front of Domonkos's apartment building, the street-level wall of which bore the spray-painted sign: VISZKIS: 29; BM: 2, as if it were a final score for the ages. At the Vidám Theater downtown, yet another production featuring the Whiskey Robber opened, titled *Everyone Must Resign*. It starred Zsuzsa Csala, the most prominent of Attila's supporters, playing the part of a bank teller dreaming of being robbed by "you superprince, Whiskey Robber." Throughout the show's sold-out run, from the fall of 1999 through the winter of 2000, Csala did not make it through a performance without having to pause during her big musical number to let the applause subside. And when a popular pro soccer coach was fired from the Budapest-based ZTE team, supporters gathered at the team's offices to protest, at one point reflexively breaking into a chant of "Attila Ambrus! Attila Ambrus!" In the hearts of many of his countrymen, the Whiskey Robber was alive and well.

The prosecution ultimately charged Attila with sixty-five different counts of robbery (several of which were for taking guns from guards); "several" counts of attempted murder, for the occurrences at Heltai Square, as well as at the final OTP robbery in which Attila had tried to shoot his way out the front door; and "thirty to forty" counts of "violations of personal freedom," for holding people against their will. The total tab of the stolen money was 196 million forints, or approximately $840,000.

To Magyar's growing frustration, Attila refused to recant, or even repudiate, his confession. There would be no argument over the charges for the twenty-nine actual incidents of robbery Attila committed, nor the single failed attempt.

For the purposes of the trial, the prosecutor's office had combined Attila's case with those against Gabi, János, Domonkos, and Karcsi. The only member of the band not represented at the prodigious Hapsburg-era Budapest Metropolitan Courthouse was Attila's cousin and first accomplice, László Veres, who had successfully remained hidden inside his small home in remote Fitód.

The proceedings began in the first week of June 2000 and continued every Tuesday and Thursday beginning at 8:00 A.M. and followed the same routine: The four lesser known bandits were led in through a door on the right of the cavernous frescoed chamber and lined up shoulder to shoulder in the proscenium facing the long, dark oak bench. George Magyar and a gaggle of defense lawyers in long black robes streamed into a box on the right, while across the way in the opposite set of benches, prosecutor Ferenc Hoffer sauntered in, followed by an assistant carrying an overstuffed carton of papers. Then came Judge Magdolna Németh, the unflappable blond-haired, bespectacled woman who would decide the fate of the accused. When everyone was settled into place, a member of the Hungarian National Guard posted at the right-side door relayed word through a mouthpiece to a squadron of police, who sealed the small street outside that was lined with government office buildings. A few minutes later the oversize wooden door creaked open and in they came — one, two, three, four, five commandos preceding the Whiskey Robber into the room, two of them wearing earpieces and one leading Attila by a thick nylon leash that was latched to a metal belt around his waist.

Attila dressed in fashionable dark silk shirts, ties, and vests sent to him by Éva. But his famously handsome face was almost totally obscured by a dark, tufty Rasputinesque beard that he'd begun to grow in the spring to the consternation of the police who worried that it was part of another elaborate escape plot.

On most days the public balcony — set high above the action like an opera-house mezzanine — did not fill up. Éva, Zsuzsa, and a collection of hair-sprayed ex-romantic acquaintances eyeing one another made regular appearances, as did Gabi's mother and father.

Though not a jury trial, the proceedings gave the impression at times that the lawyers thought it was. Both Magyar and the prosecutor delivered countless grandstanding soliloquies invoking everyone from Bertolt Brecht (Magyar: "What is the founding of a bank compared to a bank robbery?") to Napoleon to Shakespeare. The defendants watched the action unfold under their noses from their seats in a long row of antique tall-backed chairs spread out across the front of the room. Only Attila and Gabi were handcuffed. Often, to the alarm of the two guards who shadowed his every move, Attila leapt from his seat to quibble with even the most irrelevant of details. On June 14 a doctor took the stand and testified that tests showed that Attila's liver was enlarged by "three fingers," a sure sign, the doctor said, that Attila was an alcoholic. Perhaps oversensitive to the charge because of his father, Attila hopped to his feet and shouted, "I would like to categorically deny that I'm an alcoholic. If I was an alcoholic, how would I have been able to play in the first division professional hockey league?" Another time Attila argued over a discrepancy of a few thousand forints at one robbery, saying he knew exactly how much he took each time and was not going to be responsible for the employees who used the opportunity to pinch something for themselves.

In contrast, when Gabi took the stand, he could just as easily have been sitting on a barstool. "The whole situation was ridiculous," he told the court at one point. "Sometimes during a robbery we just looked at each other and almost started laughing."

A couple of months into the trial, the prosecutor stopped calling bank employees to the stand. At least seven women from various banks testified in support of Attila's versions of events. On June 14 the chief teller at the Fehérvári Street OTP — the target of Attila and Gabi's first job together — had firmly rebuffed the prosecutor's suggestion that Attila behaved violently. "He did not commit any violence," she stated. "He didn't push anyone into any closet. I walked in, but he did not push me."

The prosecutor also had had a feisty exchange with a woman from the Kemenes Street post office robbery, where Attila had brought the roses. After she stated that Attila had not been aggressive with the employees, the prosecutor responded: "But he stepped on your shoulder."

"It must have been an accident," she replied.

Only two women said they suffered any injuries, though minor. One of them, from Attila's only unsuccessful robbery, at Nyugati train station in 1993, dubiously claimed she had to undergo plastic surgery after Attila pulled her by the hair when she started screaming. When she stated her version of events, the guards had to restrain Attila as he bolted out of his chair, shouting in his defense.

All of that was insignificant, however, compared to the question of the attempted murder charges. Those that stemmed from Attila's final robbery at the huge Üllői Street OTP Bank seemed unlikely to stick, as a police investigator confirmed to the court that all ten shots fired from inside the OTP had hit the lock on the bank's front door. The charges related to the Heltai Square robbery, however, took several weeks to present. Eight shots were fired from Attila's gun, according to a ballistics expert who testified, and they landed all over the place. One of the shots, the expert said, ricocheted off a car and went through a window of a second-floor apartment off the street, potentially wounding inhabitants there. Attila, not surprisingly, took issue with the expert's logic, declaring to the court, "I don't question that [the ballistics expert] learned his trade from the books, but if a bullet ricochets, it has a completely different effect if it goes off a Swedish car than if it goes off a socialist-made car."

In the end, much of the debate would come down to the testimony of officer Ferenc Laczik, the prosecution's ace in the hole, who had given a deposition to Bérdi before Attila's escape, saying that the perpetrator of the Heltai Square robbery had fired a targeted shot at him as he ran from the scene of the crime. But Ferenc, who had earlier fingered both Szűcs brothers as the primary perpetrators of the March 1998 robbery, would not deliver for the prosecution. After Laczik listened on the witness stand to a reading of Attila's version of the chase, he testified, "Actually, it's true what the perpetrator said. It was not a targeted shot because he did not stop and aim toward me. He was trying to run away. I never said he was trying to shoot me."

On December 14, after six months of testimony and seventy-one witnesses, all that was left was the verdict and the sentencing, which would be delivered together.

The occasion, nearly eight years after Attila's first robbery, brought the media back out in full force. Cameras were planted on the corners of the balcony gallery, and reporters with their notebooks hogged the front rows. Even if Attila's popularity was not what it had been at its peak, his story had remained, more than a year after his recapture, a heavily politicized issue, frequently cited as a symbol of the injustice and hypocrisy plaguing modern Hungary. Two weeks before the sentencing hearing, an independent-party member of Parliament, Lukács Szabó, addressed the prime minister in a televised, open session, demanding, "By what law was the Whiskey Robber put in a prison while another bank robber is sitting here in Parliament? . . . Mr. Prime Minister, is it true that you have made a pact with certain circles that, whatever happens, [Interior Minister] Sándor Pintér will stay?"

At 8:30 A.M. Judge Németh entered the chamber, where Éva, Zsuzsa, the figure skater Virág, and Gabi's parents were all anxiously waiting, as were József Keszthelyi and Valter Fülöp. After rearresting Attila the previous October, they had both received well-publicized promotions, along with seventy other members of the police department (some of them secretaries), from Interior Minister Pintér.

The judge began the proceedings by asking each of the defendants if he had any final words to say. Neither Domonkos nor János had anything to add. Attila's former teammate and accomplice, Karcsi, stood and offered a brief statement: "I regret what I've done," he said. "I believe I'll never do this again. Thank you."

Gabi also wanted to speak. "Honorable Court," he said. "I have committed crimes. I feel guilty. I think that during the two years I have spent in a high-security-type initial imprisonment, I have regretted what I have done. I'm only asking for the consideration of one fact: that nobody was ever harmed."

When it was Attila's turn, he and his two bodyguards stood. A week earlier, in his closing argument, Magyar had done his best to portray Attila as a little guy who became a victim of an unfair system. "Attila left his homeland because he saw no chance to realize his dreams," Magyar had said. "But in Hungary he had to face that the only thing that counts is how much money one has." It was a sympathetic argument, but Attila wanted to say his own piece. For the next thirty minutes, standing and facing the judge, hands cuffed in front of his waist, he spoke from memory.

"Honorable Court," he began as cameras began to click and flash at his back. "I'm in a very difficult position. I have tried to bring up reasons that ease my situation, but frankly speaking, it's very difficult. For a guy who has so many crimes on his account, it's futile to say anything. But everyone has had his chance to tell his stories. I would like to mention one of mine.

"Two and a half thousand years ago, a man called Socrates was put on trial. According to the legend — or at least as I understand the legend — the charge was only that his teachings did not correspond to the expectations of Athens at that time. Thus, he was defying the gods of Athens.

"The court was about to ask the death sentence for him, according to the political practice of the era. However, if Socrates would accept that he was a sinner, he would have a chance to ask for exile instead. Socrates declined that option and instead chose a glass of poison rather than giving up anything from his ideology or his principles.

"It has occurred to me that one doesn't have to be a Socrates to be faithful to his own principles and his own sense of justice," Attila continued. "I'd like to emphasize that I do not question that I'm a sinner and I have confessed many things. I can only blame myself for being here. And I must say that I understand those people who think about me in the way that they do. Because it's not a pleasant feeling to be unloved somewhere, to lie alone on the ground. So I apologize to the extreme to those whom I put in embarrassing and uncomfortable situations, because I know how one feels when one has to face a gun."

Other than Attila's voice, not a sound was audible in the courtroom.

"And I truly regret one more thing," he continued, speaking to the judge. "You probably remember that during the summer, I had an argument with two ladies here and I really feel ashamed because they were right. I believe that they did rightly what they had to do.

"But the prosecutor says he's the servant of law," he continued, without looking to his left, where the government's lawyer was fixed in an imperious glare. "I would translate it rather that he's a mercenary of power. I have not received any human approach from the prosecution. They kept kicking me. Maybe that is the fashion at their place, I don't know. I've taken so many hits in the last year, I now know the difference between punishment and revenge.

"I'm sorry about extending my speech for this, but my point is that I don't believe I'm going to receive any fair treatment from the prosecutor and I cannot expect it in the future. . . .

"Other people who have taken billions — I'm afraid that they don't deal with those guys," he said, in an obvious reference to Márta Tocsik and the billionaire Postabank embezzler Gábor Princz, neither of whom had been convicted of committing any crime. "They just catch the little mouse, like myself. We can be nailed down. . . .

"Excuse me for saying this, but Mr. Prosecutor has chosen the wrong profession. Someone who is so close to Shakespeare and loves his words so much would certainly be welcome in any theater group. But it's a bit regretful he's wasting his words here on fairy tales. I'm not blaming him for being multitalented. I can only give grandiosely appreciative remarks about his performance. So if the honorable court would allow me, I would like to surprise Mr. Prosecutor with a gift because I believe at some point, he's going to get promoted, too. Last February I received a bottle of whiskey from Lázsló Juszt," Attila continued as the courtroom began to titter at the recollection of the famous *Kriminális* moment, "and I believe that Mr. Prosecutor will not mind having it when his promotion ceremony takes place."

The room burst into laughter.

"And," Attila continued over the din, "I'd like to request that the OTP not make claims on this bottle because this was not purchased with the robbed money."

Even the judge seemed to be forcing herself not to smile as she gazed down upon the defendant through gold-rimmed reading glasses perched near the tip of her nose. Attila went on. "It sounds commonplace, but the people presented here are the victims of conditions," he said, nodding to the row of defendants to his left. "If anyone could be blamed in this whole circus show, it's only me. I have brought them into the forest. They did what they did because of my influence. This is the least I should say for them, because I'm deeply convinced if they never met me, they wouldn't be sitting here now. I was the reason for everything. And I'm asking you to please take this into consideration in your judgment. These people are not really criminals.

"Plus I'd like to ask the honorable court, regarding suspects four and five [János and Domonkos] because they have families, please be lenient with them. Because I truly believe that they only intended to help a man who was in trouble.

"I don't know how long I'll live," he continued. "I know nothing. I don't really want to deal with the future. But I know one thing: if

I receive a lenient sentence, I will do everything I can to return to society in some way. I'd like to say that I have retired my business card. I've had enough of the circus."

Attila paused. "And last but not least, I would like to apologize for my terrorist-like appearance," he said, calling attention to his long beard. "I am treated like a terrorist, so I don't want to disillusion my captors. Thank you very much for the chance to speak and for listening to me."

Attila sat back down. For several seconds the room was silent. The judge cleared her throat and called for a one-hour recess, after which she would hand down the verdicts.

When the assemblage gathered again, Judge Németh began to deliver her findings.

Károly "Karcsi" Antal: "Guilty of robbery of an especially large amount, armed, and as an accomplice." Sentenced to two and a half years.

Domokos Kovács: "Guilty of aiding and abetting." Sentenced to ten months of "light imprisonment" and two years' probation.

János Kovács: "Guilty of aiding and abetting." Sentenced to ten months of "light imprisonment" and three years' probation.

Gábor Orbán: "Guilty of thirteen serious armed robberies." Sentenced to eight years in a medium-security prison.

Then Judge Németh turned to the primary defendant. "Regarding Attila Ambrus, many things were taken into account," she said. Because of what she called "contradictory evidence," she was discarding the attempted murder charges. But her verdict, she said, was based in part on the fact that Attila was responsible for an increase in bank robberies "that has swept this country in these times." Calling his robberies "one continuous act based on a single decision," she sentenced Attila to "fifteen years in a maximum-security prison."

The cameramen spun around to get the courtroom reaction. Zsuzsa Hamer pierced the silence first with a loud gasp followed by violent sobs. A few people clapped; others blew their noses into tissues. Éva sat silently in her third-row seat, shaking her head. She didn't know if Attila would be able to tolerate such a long incarceration. Up in the last row, Keszthelyi and Fülöp stood smirking. Though murderers in Hungary were often sentenced to less than fifteen years, Keszthelyi complained to the press after the hearing that Attila's sentence was too short.

Attila stood and was led out of the courtroom. As he exited, several reporters shouted questions at him — *Was it worth it?* one asked — but he did not look up at the gallery.

Epilogue

The village of Sátoraljaújhely is three and a half hours northeast of Budapest by train, on Hungary's border with Slovakia and Ukraine. It sits on a small plain in a quiet, hilly region of the country, next to Tokaj, where the famous Hungarian sweet wines are produced. From the colorful narrow streets and flowery storefronts, it appears pleasant, even placid. But the view from inside the hulking yellow former underwear factory, beside a barbershop and an Italian restaurant on Main Street, is decidedly different. In a letter he wrote to Éva soon after arriving at Hungary's highest-security prison, Attila described his new home as being "at the end of the earth, where even the birds don't fly."

For the first year and a half of his incarceration in Sátoraljaújhely, Attila was kept in a cell with four heavy smokers and, because he was considered a flight risk, was not allowed out of the cell unless the rest of the prison population was locked down. While most of the other inmates had work privileges, Attila did not. Isolated inside his smoke-filled, cement-floored living quarters, he tried to block out his surroundings by reading history books delivered from the prison library and teaching himself English, only to give up in frustration over the fact that he had no one to practice with. "I don't mean it as a claim," he said, "but the people here aren't exactly graduates of the Hungarian Science Academy."

He was allowed only one five-minute phone call a week and one hour-long visit a month — which became a rotation of Éva, Zsuzsa, the figure skater Virág, and his newest friend, Domonkos, who was released from custody after the final court hearing because he had already served more than his ten-month sentence. The prison commander had extended the Hungarian media ban on Attila, and in what was viewed both in the prison and around the country as an audacious act of defiance, Attila filed a lawsuit against the government for violating his rights to free expression. In the fall of 2001 a Hungarian court ruled in Attila's favor, not only ending the ban but also ordering the prison commander to apologize to Attila.

The legal victory provided Attila some vindication and enabled him to do a string of new getting-to-know-you interviews, during one of which he proclaimed that he was "a criminal in every bone of my body." But Attila's legal win also led to a backlash. The guards regularly shortchanged his visiting time, and Attila complained that they also began tampering with his meal schedule and exercise and shower privileges. He became so antagonistic toward his captors that he couldn't even make it down a hallway without challenging someone — once buttonholing the prison's food deliveryman to complain that the skin on the salami was too thin to remain fresh in the room-temperature refrigerators. In 2001, Attila was informed that his father had died of cancer. Deadened to the world, Attila felt "nothing." Soon thereafter, during a visit from Domonkos, Attila gave instructions about the small funeral he wanted, implying that he intended to kill himself. Éva was afraid she'd been right: Attila wasn't going to make it out of prison alive.

But Attila's original robbery case had been taken up by the Hungarian Supreme Court, and he decided to wait to make any decision about his future until he got the new ruling. In Hungary both the prosecution and the defense have the right to challenge a lower court verdict, and in this case both did. Attila's lawyer, George Magyar, argued that his client's sentence was too long for someone found guilty of nonviolent robbery, a case Attila would make cogently during one interview, saying the fact that most murderers received lesser sentences than his showed that in Hungary, "human life is worth less than money." On the other hand, the prosecutor in Attila's case appealed to the Supreme Court on the grounds that despite the earlier finding to the contrary, the evidence against Attila was sufficient to prove attempted murder, and thus, Attila's fifteen-year sentence was too light.

The case languished for more than a year until finally, in September 2002, Attila was driven to Budapest in an armored car to be present for what would be the final court hearing in his almost-decade-old saga. Before leaving the prison, Attila rejected suggestions from observers that he shave his sinister-looking beard to make a better impression on the judge, saying, "I'm tired of being a showman."

After brief arguments by Magyar, the prosecutor, and, of course, Attila, the chief justice read the ruling on behalf of the three-judge panel. Once again the attempted murder charges were dismissed as inconclusive, leaving as the only substantive charges against Attila the ones to which he had pleaded guilty in the first place. The Supreme Court, however, ordered that Attila's sentence not be reduced but extended by two years, to seventeen. "He is not Robin Hood," the ruling explained. Attila would have to pay for his popularity.

The circus was now officially over. Attila was moved to a new higher-security cell (shared by one other prisoner) and given thick gray wool pants and a blue-and-gray-patterned long-sleeve shirt — the prison garb that he had not been required to wear while his case was still proceeding through the legal system. Éva, Zsuzsa, and Domonkos agonized that they would soon receive a call informing them that Attila had taken his life. But instead, as the months passed, Attila seemed more and more at peace with himself, an evolution that happened perhaps not coincidentally at the same time as his reconnection to his mother. In the summer of 2003 Klára Ambrus, née Csibi, traveled nearly a day by train from Transylvania to see Attila for the first time in more than twenty years. She spent most of their glass-partitioned reunion in tears but managed to get across what she'd come to say: it was her fault that Attila was sitting behind bars.

Attila told his mother he didn't blame her for the course his life had taken, but he was glad she came. He'd never known until then that the reason she had left the family was not something he'd done but that his father had beaten her, too.

Since then, Attila has been consumed with using his idle time to educate himself properly. He spends much of his days reading, though he complains that the prison library is so thin that he's read his copy of *I, Claudius* four times. He has also begun taking basic mathematics, science, and history classes in order to get a high school degree. On a recent history exam in which he received the equivalent of an A-, he appealed, and was granted, a perfect score after pointing out an error in the test. He hopes — even though it is unprecedented for a prisoner in Hungary — to later be allowed to apply to a Hungarian university as a correspondence student.

When he's not studying or doing his exercises in the prison court-yard — where he's calculated that 104 laps around the square equals 3.1 miles — he is obsessed with following the news of the world. He has subscriptions to six publications, ranging from daily newspapers to the Hungarian edition of *Playboy*, and can eloquently hold forth on topics from Yasir Arafat's formative years to the disgrace of the *New York Times* reporter Jayson Blair. When the hall warden allows television privileges, Attila practices his English by watching CNN on a fourteen-inch color set mounted in the corner of his cell.

What Attila sees on the screen is a far different world from the one in which he came to prominence. Once a fledgling democracy, Hungary is now a full member of NATO and the European Union. Corruption is still rampant, but violent street crime has abated and the economy, though tepid, is relatively stable. Meanwhile, the U.S. economy that Hungary had tried so hard to emulate deflated like a balloon in the spring of 2000. And the attacks of September 11, 2001, brought an emphatic end to the twelve-year period when the world order was defined by the fall of communism.

The reverberations within Hungary have been obvious. The coun-try's national elections in the spring of 2002 were arguably the most contentious in its history, becoming in many ways a referendum on the tumultuous postcommunist era. At the geographic center of a unified new Europe, Hungarians faced a choice between the government of the incumbent prime minister Viktor Orbán, of the Alliance of Young Democrats, and that of a former communist and secret intelligence agent, Péter Medgyessy, who had become the leader of the left-leaning Socialist Party. The Orbán government tried to frame the election as being about patriotism, a case made clumsily a few weeks before the election by one of Orbán's top party deputies, who declared, "Whoever is not for us should get a rope, a hammer, and a nail and hang them-selves."

Among those who cast their ballots on election day was Attila Ambrus, who still had the right of suffrage because his case had not yet been finalized by the Supreme Court. Attila had never voted before in his life, and his heavily guarded journey to the Sátoraljaújhely voting station at the town hall was covered by a herd of photographers and camera crews. After deliberating for weeks, he decided to pull the lever for the Socialists, whom he still calls "the commies" — those former representatives of the political system he had spent the first twenty years of his life running from. Indeed, they won an unexpected victory over the Young Democrats.

More than a decade after he first began making news by stealing 548,000 forints ($5,900) from his neighborhood post office, there is rarely a week that goes by in which Attila does not appear on television or in the newspapers. When a bank in the town of Mor was robbed after a bloody gun battle that left eight dead, Attila was interviewed by several Hungarian news outlets as an expert crime analyst. Sometimes, even Don the dog makes the front pages of the tabloids, as he did recently when an anonymous tip led police to dig up the yard in which he is living, to search vainly for a buried stash of loot.

Though popular opinion in Hungary is now divided as to whether Attila is a positive or negative figure, the overwhelming majority of lower- and middle-class Hungarians commonly refer to him as the "Sándor Rózsa of our days" and "the modern Robin Hood." In Transylvania his image remains almost uniformly heroic.

But regardless of his legacy, it is Attila's past that remains so stunningly emblematic of the world in which he lived. He is a living relic of a bygone era, trapped inside the postcommunist snow globe he penetrated when he rode into Hungary beneath a train in 1988, just before the whole scene was shaken up. It is all but certain that he could not have carried out his seven-year, twenty-nine-robbery streak the way that he did — nor become the sensation that he did — at any other time, or possibly any other place in history. Hungary's police force today may not be the world's strongest, but it employs more than double the number of officers it did in 1993, who have access to contemporary vehicles, carry working weapons, and are linked to a central crime computer system. (They also remain closely allied with the United States; in August 2003 Hungary agreed to the U.S. request to become a primary training center for the new Iraqi police force.) And like the American Depression-era times that produced folk hero John Dillinger, it would take a special set of social circumstances to create another Whiskey Robber. Even now, much of the media that fed Attila's legend and that had exploded onto the scene when press freedom arrived — including László Juszt's hit show, *Kriminális* — no longer exist.

Whether that makes Attila one of the luckiest or unluckiest people in the world is debatable. He worries whether he will have any chance to get a job or have a family when he is released in 2016 at age forty-nine. (It is possible, but unlikely, that he could be paroled as many as five years earlier for good behavior.) Yet like his country and his people, all Attila ever really wanted was to be respected and to belong somewhere he could call home. And though that may not have transpired the way he envisioned, it has indeed come to pass. On the floor of Attila's cell, among his growing collection of history books is a large encyclopedia of Hungarian history, *Magyarok Kronikája*. Sometimes when he can't sleep at night he opens it to page 816. There, next to the entry about the Balkan War, the chronological reference book tells the story of the Transylvanian hockey goalie who became known as the Whiskey Robber, "a national fairy tale hero." On good days, Attila can convince himself it was worth it.

Postscripts

LAJOS VARJÚ, FORMER ROBBERY CHIEF, BUDAPEST POLICE
While discussing the Whiskey Robber case recently, Lajos's new girl-friend interrupted the conversation, first to remind him that "the whole country was laughing at you" and then to ask, "He [Attila] did *two* in one day? I'd sleep with him!" Lajos currently works as head of security for the Hungarian Post Office.

LÁSZLÓ JUSZT, FORMER HOST OF *KRIMINÁLIS*
After being thrown off Hungarian television when he was arrested and charged with "revealing state secrets" for his reporting on the "Hungarian Watergate" scandal, he now hosts a political talk show on an independent cable channel. He is suing the Hungarian government for several hundred million forints (a couple of million dollars), one of the largest lawsuits in the country's history.

ÉVA FODOR, ATTILA'S FORMER GIRLFRIEND
Every few months, she drives four hours each way to visit Attila in prison and speaks to him regularly by phone. When he called on December 5, 2001, she had just been told that her boyfriend had been killed in a car accident, but wanting to remain strong for Attila, she did not mention it.

BETTY GERGELY, ATTILA'S LAST GIRLFRIEND
Last seen by Attila on the prison cable television system, where she appeared as a dancer in an erotic film.

BUBU, ATTILA'S FORMER TEAMMATE AND FRIEND
Still an "unemployed hockey player," as his business card states. Recently lost a front tooth in a fight outside a Csíkszereda bar.

KARCSI ANTAL, ATTILA'S UTE TEAMMATE AND SECOND ACCOMPLICE
Recently rearrested for violating parole by entering Hungary on the Csíkszereda hockey bus.

UTE HOCKEY TEAM
Ordered a Whiskey Robber flag reading HARJRÁ VISZKIS! (*Tallyho, Whiskey Robber!*) that will fly over the stadium. Still broke and championshipless.

SÁNDOR PINTÉR, FORMER NATIONAL POLICE CHIEF AND INTERIOR MINISTER
Leading up to the 2002 elections, opposition party posters depicted his face next to a time bomb and the words WHO'S PROTECTING WHOM? Was replaced as interior minister when the new prime minister was sworn in and, after a stint as a security consultant for the OTP Bank, is now self-employed.

FBI
No longer counts Sándor Pintér as its primary liaison in Central Europe.

MÁRTA TOCSIK, LINCHPIN OF HUNGARY'S SCANDAL OF THE CENTURY
After five separate trials, has never served a day of jail time nor been found guilty of anything.

JÓZSEF KESZTHELYI, CURRENT CHIEF OF BUDAPEST'S ROBBERY DIVISION
Claims that "the Whiskey Robber case was not so big. We have bigger cases every day." Hanging on the wall behind his desk is a plaque inlaid with two color photos, one of his capture of Attila at the Romanian border in January 1999, the other of his recapture of Attila in Budapest in October 1999. No other plaques or awards adorn his office.

ZSOLT BÉRDI, FORMER CHIEF OF THE GYORSKOCSI STREET JAIL INVESTIGATIVE UNIT

Resigned from the police department, primarily because of the Whiskey Robber case, which he calls the "vet's horse," because through it, one can see everything that is wrong with Hungary. Now practicing as a lawyer in a Budapest firm.

VALTER FÜLÖP, BÉRDI'S SUCCESSOR AS CHIEF INVESTIGATOR

Recently investigated several criminals who kept Attila's book, *I, the Whiskey Robber,* on their night tables as if it were the Bible. Intermittently seeks updates on Attila's physical condition, as he is convinced Attila will attempt another escape.

LÁSZLÓ VERES, ATTILA'S COUSIN AND FIRST ACCOMPLICE

Still living in Fitód with a wife and two young daughters. He is the only culprit in the Whiskey Robber case who was never caught — and he never will be. The statute of limitations on his crimes has expired.

DON, THE DOG

Still makes the news a couple of times a month. Eats like a canine king thanks to Attila, who often spends his entire five-minute weekly phone allowance specifying to Zsuzsa the type of food Don should be served. Virtually no chance he will ever see Attila again.

KLÁRA ORBÁN, GABI'S MOTHER

Believes, erroneously, that in Hungary, a prison sentence will be reduced if you pay down the financial damages from the case. Has started playing the lottery.

GABI ORBÁN

Serving his time at the Márianosztra medium-security prison two hours south of Budapest, where he plays on a soccer team and is not required to wear handcuffs outside his cell. When his mother began crying during a recent visit, he told her, "Stop whining and behave like a gangster's mother." His own book, *The Whiskey Robber's Partner,* remains unpublished.

ATTILA AMBRUS

Asked if he would consider attempting to escape again, he said, "Regarding this, I couldn't say. I wouldn't be sincere."

Notes on Sources

This book is the culmination of more than three years of work, including eight months spent on the ground in Hungary and Transylvania and a couple of weeks in Berlin and Prague. I interviewed more than a hundred people over the course of my reporting, many of them several times. Almost all my interviews were done in person, most of them through an interpreter. I was careful to discuss each interview with my interpreters so as to ensure accuracy not just of the language but also in style and nuance. I assume responsibility for any errors of translation.

The scenes and dialogue that I depict come primarily from my direct interviews with the subjects involved but are often augmented by other sources. I was able to gain access to numerous official documents, including the forms Attila filled out at the immigration office when arriving in Hungary, as well as his passport applications and visa requests. These were particularly helpful for the scene in the immigration office as well as the details of Attila's escape from Romania.

I spent five weeks at the Supreme Court building in Budapest poring through all the police and court files from the case. These documents greatly enhanced my ability to portray many of the robbery scenes as well as specific meetings and measures taken by the police (most of whom consented to my numerous interview requests). I was present at the final Metropolitan Court hearing in the case on December 14, 2000. I spent several days viewing videotape at the Hungarian Television (MTV) archive, which provided much of the basis for the scenes involving *Kriminális*. In addition, I had literally hundreds of Hungarian newspaper stories translated, many of which are specifically cited in the text.

Attila's first girlfriend in Transylvania, Katalin, whom I could not locate, appears under a pseudonym. His first girlfriend in Budapest, Judit, did not wish to be interviewed for this project, and she too appears under a pseudonym. Information about them comes from my interviews with Attila, Attila's aunt and uncle, as well as, in the case of Judit, a section of Attila's first book *Én a Whiskys,* written with Judit P. Gál (IPM Konyv, 1999).

The prison in Sátoraljaújhely, where Attila is held, and the lesser-security pen in Márianosztra, where Gabi is held, were strict, but for the most part fair, and allowed me long days with my subjects. Over a span of three years, I spent twelve full days with Attila and three with Gabi. Most of my other sources with whom I spent significant time are thanked in the Acknowledgments.

For money conversions, I used an average of the official exchange rates on the first and last day of each year. For 1988, it was 50 forints: U.S. dollar. For 1989, it was 58; 1990: 62; 1991: 69; 1992: 80; 1993: 93; 1994: 107; 1995: 125; 1996: 153; 1997: 183; 1998: 212; 1999: 233; 2000: 267.

Below is a citation list of sources I used for specific information that did not come from my own reporting. I have not listed sources for information about widely known events. I also do not repeat the sources for information when the citation is already specified in the text.

p. 7: The "century's most persistent" quote comes from a story in *Magyar Hírlap* that appeared on January 18, 1999.

p. 13: The "nest of Robin Hoods" quote comes from a story in *Hargita Népe* by Zoltán Szondy, July 24, 2002.

p. 17: John Whitehead talking about the "gray, monstrous snake" from an Associated Press story by Frieder Reimold, October 12, 1988.

p. 43: Both of Antall's quotes come from a story in the *Los Angeles Times* by Carol J. Williams, October 9, 1990.

p. 44: The story about Wayne Gretzky appeared in Hungary's *Népsport,* August 2, 1990.

p. 55: Some of the information about Attila's father is augmented by interviews he gave to *Erdély Napló* in the summer and fall of 1999 and to *Nők Lapja* on August 4, 1999.

p. 59: The detail about more than a thousand cops being arrested comes from a story in the *Guardian* by Carol Williams, October 13, 1990.

p. 64: The scene with Uncle Béla comes from my interviews with Attila (who once accompanied Béla on a hunt) and László and with villagers living near Béla.

p. 68: The detail about the IKEA billboards comes from interviews as well as a story by the Inter-Press Service by Ken Kasriel, June 9, 1992.

p. 85: The detail about the Warsaw protesters comes from an article in the *Chicago Tribune* by Linnet Myers, December 20, 1995. The details about the town meeting regarding the Jewish Quarter comes from an article in the *New York Times* by Jane Perlez, August 18, 1993.

p. 88: Information about the Budapest police chief's being disciplined came from MTI Econews, October 13, 1992.

p. 100: The excerpt is from a police robbery department file, dated September 14, 1993.

p. 119: The press release is from a police robbery department fax dated July 22, 1994.

p. 120: The detail about the largest military operation comes from a speech by President Clinton cited in the *New York Times* story by Alison Mitchell on January 14, 1996. FBI "trained some 27,000 officers, including one Hungarian," from MTI Econews, March 2, 1995. The quote from Louis Freeh comes from a story in the *Chicago Tribune* by Linnet Myers on December 20, 1995.

p. 131: The information about thirty-seven illicit shipments comes from a story in the *New York Times* by David Johnston on April 17, 1995. The story in *Blikk* appeared on January 14, 1995.

p. 132: The figure of 1,200 openings in Hungary for police comes from a story in the *Los Angeles Times* by Dean Murphy on February 28, 1995.

p. 137: The statistic about crime committed every sixty-three seconds comes from MTI Econews, November 12, 1996. The statistic about thirty-seven daily car thefts comes from MTI Econews, July 17, 1996.

p. 139: The detail about the waiting list for telephone lines comes from a story in *USA Today* by James Cox on November 7, 1994. The information about the automobile accidents and destruction of property cases comes from MTI Econews, September 26, 1996. The tourism minister's quote comes from a story in the *Virginian Pilot* by Greg Raver-Lampman, October 29, 1995. The information about the sewerage museum comes from the *Budapest Business Journal,* January 27, 1995.

p. 147: The detail about the International Bodyguard and Secret Service Association comes from a story in Agencie France-Presse, September 9, 1995. Much of the information from the *Kriminális* scene comes from the program that aired on Hungarian Television (MTV) on April 4, 1996.

p. 149: The *Blikk* story headlined BANK ROBBERY WITH A BOUQUET OF FLOWERS ran on March 26, 1996. The *Kurír* story headlined YEAR OF THE ROBBERS appeared on March 27, 1996.

p. 151: The *Reform* article with the police sketches and comment about "Budapest's own private robber" appeared on April 9, 1996.

p. 158: The comment about Attila having taken on "a servant" comes from a story in *Népszava,* September 5, 1996.

p. 159: The information from *Kriminális* aired on August 29, 1996, Hungarian Television (MTV). The comment about the Whiskey Robber making life for the police "an absolute misery" comes from a story in *Blikk* on August 30, 1996. The *Népszava* story that suggests the Whiskey Robber is giving his money to the poor was published on September 5, 1996.

p. 167: The black market estimates come from a BBC story from June 26, 1996. The detail about the Hungarian Olympic team comes from an Associated Press story on September 23, 1996. The details about Juszt's Mitsubishi being a stolen car comes from *Kurír,* November 15, 1996. The information about the 230 cop convictions comes from a story in the BBC, July 22, 1997 (which cited Hungarian Radio as its source). The details about the Kennedy Center gala are from a story in the *Washington Post* by Roxanne Roberts on November 13, 1996.

p. 168: The police report by Lajos Seres (Dance Instructor) is dated November 21, 1996.

p. 170: The *Kriminális* program aired on Hungarian Television (MTV) on January 21, 1997.

p. 182: I was not able to interview Klányi, Kis, Stuttering József, or Klányi's ex-wife, but all the quotations from them are taken from the police reports as well as my interviews with police.

p. 193: The detail about the number of casinos in Budapest compared with other cities comes from a story in MTI Econews dated June 6, 1997.

p. 201: The information about the police department budget comes from MTI Econews on February 19, 1998.

p. 212: The information about Al Gore, Sandór Pintér, and the crime conference comes from MTI Econews, February 24, 1999; the BBC, February 25, 1999; and a *Washington Post* story by Nora Boustany from February 26, 1999. The story headlined POLICE CHIEF RESIGNS appeared in *Mai Nap*, June 5, 1998.

p. 215: The detail of Clinton and Orbán's discussions at the White House on October 7 (the same day as Attila's party, which had to be held the day after his birthday) is from MTI Econews, October 9, 1999.

p. 228: Bóta's quote comes from a story in *Magyar Hírlap* published on January 18, 1999. The quote from Kercső Árpád and from Lajos Varjú both appeared in *Mai Nap* on January 17, 1999.

p. 231: The story in *Magyar Hírlap* appeared on January 18, 1999. The *Népszabadság* story referring to Atilla as "the master" appeared on February 20, 1999. The exact quote from Zsuzsa Csala here comes from my interview with her, though it is similar to sentiments she expressed in the Hungarian media.

p. 233: The information about the man accused of stealing toilet paper comes from a story in the *New York Times* credited to Agence France-Presse on November 19, 2000.

p. 238: Gabi's interview with *Népszabadság* appeared on February 2, 1999.

p. 241: Some of the scene between Attila and Lajos was augmented by the account in the book *Én, a Whiskys,* by Attila Ambrus and Judit P. Gál. The part about Lajos's asking Attila if he had figured out how to escape comes from my interviews with both men.

p. 249: The quotations from Prime Minister Orbán's speech at the graduation ceremony comes from MTI Econews, July 3, 1999.

p. 255: A TV opinion poll of 20,000 callers cited by *Magyar Hírlap* on July 29, 1999, showed 79 percent of people supporting Attila. An Internet poll on July 14, 1999, of 1,008 respondents showed 91 percent support for Attila. The "would you have climbed down from the window on a shoelace?" poll in *Mai Nap* appeared on July 13, 1999. The "Hungarian Butch Cassidy" reference appeared in *HVG,* July 17, 1999.

p. 258: Pintér's comments appeared in *Magyar Nemzet,* July 22, 1999.

p. 264: A series of stories about Attila, headlined BIG CITY COWBOY, ran in *Hargita Népe* in March 1999.

p. 265: The story in *Magyar Szó* appeared on July 22, 1999.

p. 266: The story headlined THE INTELLIGENCE OF THE HUNGARIAN CRIME SQUADS COULD NOT BE LOWER is from *Népszabadság*, August 4, 1999. The *Christian Science Monitor* story appeared on August 10, 1999. The London *Independent* story appeared on July 31, 1999. The story in *Le Figaro* appeared on July 20, 1999. The story in *Sports Illustrated* appeared on August 16, 1999.

p. 267: The story in the police magazine, *Zsaru*, appeared on August 3, 1999.

p. 269: The "Monica Lewinsky story of Hungary" comment was made on the program *Deep Water*, aired on Hungarian Television (MTV) on August 13, 1999. The television reports about Attila's past were cited in a *Christian Science Monitor* story by Michael J. Jordan, August 10, 1999.

p. 281: An account of Prime Minister Orbán's radio appearance was published by the BBC on October 29, 1999.

p. 282: The story headlined ONE LESS SMALL FISH ran in *Népszava* on November 8, 1999.

p. 284: The investigation of Magyar was made public in *Népszabadság*, October 22, 1999.

p. 289: The comment by Hungarian member of Parliament Lukács Szabó is from the BBC summary of the Hungarian TV2 satellite service broadcast on November 28, 2000.

p. 295: The interview in which Attila said he was a "criminal in every bone in my body" appeared in the Hungarian edition of *FHM* magazine, October 2001. Attila's comment that "human life is worth less than money" appeared in *Magyar Nemzet*, December 15, 2000.

Bibliography

Ambrus, Attila, and Judit P. Gál. *Én, a Whiskys*. Budapest: IPM Konyv, 1999.

Ash, Timothy Garton. *The Magic Lantern: The Revolution of '89 Witnessed in Warsaw, Budapest, Berlin and Prague*. New York: Random House, 1990.

————. *History of the Present: Essays, Sketches and Dispatches from Europe in the 1990s*. New York: Random House, 2000.

Braun, Aurel, and Zoltan Barany. *Dilemmas of Transition: The Hungarian Experience*. Lanham, Md.: Rowman & Littlefield, 1999.

Brzezinski, Matthew. *Casino Moscow*. New York: Free Press, 2001.

Friedman, Robert I. *Red Mafiya: How the Russian Mob Has Invaded America*. Boston: Little, Brown and Company, 2000.

Gerõ, András. *Modern Hungarian Society in the Making: The Unfinished Experience*. Budapest: Central European University Press, 1995.

Gyuricza, Péter, and Ernõ Kardos. *A Whisky Szokesben*. Budapest: Arabesk, 2000.

Kádár, András, ed. *Police in Transition: Essays on the Police Forces in Transition Countries*. Budapest: Central European University Press, 2001.

Kaplan, Robert D. *Balkan Ghosts: A Journey Through History*. New York: St. Martin's Press, 1993.

Konrád, George. *The Melancholy of Rebirth: Essays from Post-Communist Central Europe*. San Diego: Harcourt Brace, 1996.

Köpeczi, Béla. *History of Transylvania*. Budapest: Akadémia Kiadó, 1994.

Kürti, László. *The Remote Borderland: Transylvania in the Hungarian Imagination*. Albany: State University of New York Press, 2001.

Lukacs, John. *Budapest 1900: A Historical Portrait of a City and Its Culture*. New York: Weidenfeld & Nicholson, 1988.

Molnár, Miklós. *A Concise History of Hungary*. Cambridge: Cambridge University Press, 2001.

Murphy, Dervla. *Transylvania and Beyond*. New York: Viking, 1993.

Phillips, Arthur. *Prague: A Novel*. New York: Random House, 2002.

Ramet, Sabrina Petra. *Social Currents in Eastern Europe: The Sources and Consequences of the Great Transition*. Durham, N.C.: Duke University Press, 1995.

Remnick, David. *Lenin's Tomb: The Last Days of the Soviet Empire*. New York: Random House, 1993.

———. *Resurrection*. New York: Random House, 1997.

Romsics, Ignc. *Hungary in the Twentieth Century*. Budapest: Corvina Books, 1999.

Rosenberg, Tina. *The Haunted Land: Facing Europe's Ghosts After Communism*. New York: Random House, 1995.

Sugar, Peter F., ed. *A History of Hungary*. Bloomington: Indiana University Press, 1990.

Török, András. *Budapest*. London: Pallas Athene Publishers, 2000.

Appendix

LIST OF ATTILA AMBRUS'S ROBBERIES

LOCATION	DATE	ACCOMPLICE	HAUL (IN FORINTS)
1. Villányi Street post office	January 22, 1993		548,000 ($5,900)
2. Hűvösvölgyi Street post office	March 12, 1993		667,000 ($7,200)
3. Budapest Tours travel agency (Árpád Street)	May 3, 1993		1,166,000 ($12,500)
4. Nagykáta and Vidéke savings bank	June 18, 1993	László Veres	2,912,000 ($31,300)
5. Pilisvörösvár Bank (Ágoston Street)	August 3, 1993	László Veres	398,000 ($4,300)
6. Orczy Square post office	August 27, 1993	Károly "Karcsi" Antal	3,351,000 ($36,000)
* Budapest Tours travel agency (Nyugati train station)	November 3, 1993		

LOCATION	DATE	ACCOMPLICE	HAUL (IN FORINTS)
7. Colibri Travel Agency	December 27, 1993		407,000 ($4,400)
8. Mór and Vidéke Savings and Loan	February 2, 1994		1,380,000 ($12,900)
9. Bakonyvidéke Savings and Loan	March 21, 1994		4,562,000 ($42,600)
10. Eurotours International travel agency	July 21, 1994		955,000 ($8,900)
11. Bakonyvidéke Savings and Loan	January 12, 1995		2,797,000 ($22,400)
12. Pilisvörösvár Bank (Lajos Street)	July 24, 1995		2,467,000 ($19,700)
13. Kemenes Street post office	March 25, 1996		9,536,000 ($62,300)
14. Fehérvári Street post office	August 29, 1996	Gabi Orbán	5,267,000 ($34,400)
15. Grassalkovich Street OTP Bank	September 24, 1996	Gabi Orbán	7,546,000 ($49,300)
16. Budakeszi OTP Bank	November 21, 1996	Gabi Orbán	13,598,000 ($88,900)
17. Budakeszi OTP Bank	January 15, 1997	Gabi Orbán	7,909,000 ($43,200)
18. Heltai Square OTP Bank	March 10, 1997	Gabi Orbán	9,635,000 ($52,500)
19. Etele Square post office	March 10, 1997	Gabi Orbán	3,965,000 ($22,000)
20. Vasút Street OTP Bank	April 24, 1997	Gabi Orbán	1,500,000 ($8,200)
21. Grassalkovich Street OTP Bank	May 28, 1997	Gabi Orbán	25,302,000** ($138,300)
22. Grassalkovich Street OTP Bank	December 16, 1997	Gabi Orbán	8,002,000 ($43,700)

LOCATION	DATE	ACCOMPLICE	HAUL (IN FORINTS)
23. Irinyi Street OTP Bank	February 5, 1998	Gabi Orbán	5,705,000 ($26,900)
24. Heltai Square OTP Bank	March 11, 1998	Gabi Orbán	5,051,000 ($23,600)
25. Újhegyi Street OTP Bank	January 5, 1999	Gabi Orbán	297,000 ($1,250)
26. Frankel Leó Boulevard OTP Bank	January 15, 1999	Gabi Orbán	18,394,000 ($78,900)
27. Grassalkovich Street OTP Bank	July 29, 1999		1,507,000 ($6,500)
28. Vecsés OTP Bank	September 28, 1999		224,000 ($960)
29. Üllői Street OTP Bank	October 18, 1999		50,738,000** ($217,800)
Total haul (in forints)			195,745,000
In dollars (using 1999 exchange rate)			840,000

* failed robbery attempt

** Some of this sum was in foreign currency.

Note: The year-by-year conversion rates are cited in the Notes on Sources.

Acknowledgments

The process of reporting this book often felt like running an international business, and my first thank-you has to go to Vera Rónai, my indefatigable interpreter, who found me an apartment in Budapest, held down the fort while I was in New York, and helped coordinate countless interviews and, most important, successfully negotiate a path through the Hungarian police, court, and prison systems.

Several other interpreters and translators were also enlisted over the course of the project, including Villő Korányi, Drew Leifheit, Katalin Tóth, and David Simon in Budapest; the Romanian- and Hungarian-speaking Adél Hodor in Transylvania; Anna Szalai, Norbert Puskás, and Mária Mazei stateside. During the five weeks I spent examining court files and police reports at the Supreme Court building in Budapest, I was flanked by both Vera and another patient interpreter, Anna Hives.

From the first day I met Attila Ambrus at the Budapest Metropolitan Courthouse in December 2000, he was incredibly forthcoming. He opened up his life to me and responded to every inquiry and cross-examination with what (upon further investigation) always proved to be earnestness and honesty. Over the twelve full days I spent with him in the prison, he earned my respect and my sincerest hope that he can make it out and get another chance to use his many talents for good ends. Plus, I'd love to have a drink with him.

Lajos Varjú also spent significant time with me despite his busy schedule and the fact that this story is not exactly his favorite topic. He is a fine person who never let me leave his home sober and who, despite the way his story played out in Hungary, was (like Attila) a decent man doing his best under trying circumstances.

Literally dozens of others graciously accepted me into their lives and often their homes during my reporting. Those who deserve special thanks include Jenő "Bubu" Salamon (who personally showed me around Csíkszereda), Gabi Orbán, George Orbán, Klára Orbán, Zsuzsa Hamer, Péter Bárándy, János Egri, and the lovely Éva Fodor. At UTE, George Pék, Gustáv Bóta, Zsolt Baróti, Kriztián Nádor, and Attila Tolnai were always helpful. In Csíkszereda, László and Margit Szabó and László Veres overcame their fear and trusted me. From the police, Valter Fülöp and Zsolt Bérdi were generous with their time, and even József Keszthelyi usually put up with me. Many others I would like to mention asked that their names not be used, but I want them to know how appreciated their contributions to this work are.

I was lucky to have my understanding of Central Europe in general, and Hungary in particular, augmented by a number of excellent Hungarian journalists and writers, including József Jónás, László Bartus, Gergely Fahidi, János Elek, Balázs Weyer (whom I still owe dinner), Endre Aczél, Ernő Kardos, Tivadar Farkasházy, and László Neményi. In Transylvania, Robbie Szűszer, Zoltán Szondy, and László Kürti. Ferenc Kőszeg of the Helsinki Foundation, Sándor Orbán of the Center for Independent Journalism, and the excellent essayist and novelist George Konrád were generous with their time and contacts. Marian Perkin offered warmth and hospitality in Budapest.

Back in New York, I am blessed to have the best collection of friends and supporters around, without whom I couldn't have completed this book. I should start with Virginia Heffernan, then at *Talk* magazine, who was the first person to believe in this strange story. Phoebe Eaton, then at *Details*, ultimately sent me to Hungary and, along with Dan Peres, saw the magazine piece through to publication. David Mizner helped persuade me not to pass up the chance to do this as a book. Vanessa Mobley, Alex Sherwin, and Jack Wright were also early believers.

The following talented people offered help and/or insightful comments on the manuscript: Nina Siegal, Elizabeth Kadetsky, Dale

Maharidge, Edward Lewine, Francesco Fiondella, Donnell Alexander, Jack Murnigan, Jesse Upton, Nick Fowler, Lisa Pollard, Boris Fishman, Pete Wells, Jeff Howe, Hillary Rosner, Jenn Leitzes, Maya Nadkarni, Jozsi Litkei, David Davis, and Kostya Kennedy. All of my compatriots at the New Real (particularly Celia Farber and Steve Kettmann) were, as always, important and inspiring advisers.

At Little, Brown, my excellent editor, Geoff Shandler, saw and understood the potential of this story from the outset; his skillful pencil and calming demeanor not only made the text better but made the whole experience better. Liz Nagle also offered helpful suggestions to the manuscript and quick-response answers to any question or need I had. Sándor Szatmári, the Hungarian legend, was a wise and spirited lunch date. Steve Lamont was there when I really needed him. And Michael Pietsch's support and encouragement were invaluable.

I am also grateful to the Dick Goldensohn Fund for offering me a grant that helped ease the financial burden of reporting an overseas story. And I would like to thank the New York City Public Library, where some of this book was written.

I couldn't have done this without the support of my parents, who encouraged me to take on the project even though it took me far away from home for chunks of time while my father was ill. And lastly, the biggest thank-you goes to the smartest and best literary agent around, Lisa Hyman, my wife, whose commitment, support, and superb editing is evident on virtually every page.

About the Author

Julian Rubinstein's work has appeared in such publications as the *New York Times Magazine, Rolling Stone, Sports Illustrated, Details, Outside,* the *Washington Post,* and *Salon* and has won several awards, including selection by *Best American Crime Writing* and two citations from *Best American Sports Writing.* Raised in Denver, he lives in New York. This is his first book. For more information, please visit www.julianrubinstein.com.